SEEKING THE PAST

SEEKING THE BEST

SEEKING THE PAST

WRITINGS FROM 1832 – 1905
RELATING TO THE
*History of the
Town of Riverhead*

Suffolk County
New York

EDITED BY
TOM TWOMEY

NEWMARKET PRESS NEW YORK

FIRST EDITION
ISBN 1-55704-617-4
1   3   5   7   9   10   8   6   4   2

Library of Congress Cataloging-in-Publication Data is available upon request.

QUANTITY PURCHASES
Companies, professional groups, clubs, and other organizations may
qualify for special terms when ordering quantities of this title. For information,
write Special Sales Department, Newmarket Press, 18 East 48th Street,
New York, NY 10017; call (212) 832-3575; fax (212) 832-3629;
or email mailbox@newmarketpress.com

www.newmarketpress.com

Manufactured in the United States of America

Contents

THE PUBLICATION OF THIS BOOK
WAS MADE POSSIBLE THROUGH MAJOR UNDERWRITING BY

TWOMEY, LATHAM, SHEA & KELLEY
Attorneys at Law

AND

SUFFOLK COUNTY NATIONAL BANK

WITH SIGNIFICANT FUNDING FROM

RIVERHEAD BUILDING SUPPLY

FRIENDS OF THE RIVERHEAD FREE LIBRARY

THE RIVERHEAD FREE LIBRARY MEMORIAL DONATION FUND

As a result of this wonderful generosity,
one hundred percent of the proceeds from the sale of this book
will be dedicated to enhancing, preserving, and building the
Long Island Collection at the Riverhead Free Library.

Dedication

This book is dedicated to the Friends of the Riverhead Free Library.

Founded in 1958 with the generous gift of their Court Street home from sisters Clara and Alice Perkins, the mission of the Friends of the Riverhead Free Library has been to support the library and its programs and to help promote the library in the community—in fact the contribution from the Perkins sisters inspired the library trustees to plan for a new building, which opened on the Court Street location in 1964. Only the carriage house, or Yellow Barn, as it has come to be called, remains—lovingly restored as an important part of the library's history.

Countless hours of volunteer work by its members and fundraising events such as their annual Piano Plus Concert Series, popular used book sales in the Yellow Barn, spring luncheons and winter galas, support the Friends organization and provide the many gifts—from computers to children's puzzles and games to this book—that help the library and its staff improve service to the community.

It is our pleasure to dedicate this book to such a worthy cause and a way to say to The Friends—Thanks.

Board of Trustees
The Riverhead Free Library

CHARTER MEMBERS
OF
FRIENDS OF THE RIVERHEAD FREE LIBRARY

Organized Thursday, April 24, 1958

OFFICERS

President:	Mrs. William Hannah
Vice President:	Mr. Irving Zeitz
Treasurer:	Mrs. Halsey Reeve
Secretary:	Mrs. Columbus Terry

Members ($1.00 dues)

Mrs. John Atwood	Mrs. Harold Taylor	Mr. & Mrs. Paul Gerard
Miss Joan Kimball	Mr. & Mrs. Howard Hovey	Mrs. Charles Brennan
Mrs. Columbus Terry	Miss Marion Petraske	Mr. & Mrs. William Harrup
Mr. & Mrs. Alfred Demarest	Miss Eva Terry	Miss Rose Terry
Miss Mary Aldrich	Mr. & Mrs. George Batchelder	Mr. Irving Zeitz
Mrs. William Hannah	Mr. Nathanial Talmage	Mrs. Edward Connors
Mrs. Reginald Young	Mrs. Muriel Reeve	Miss Betty Blue

As reported in the *Riverhead News-Review*, May 15, 1958

FRIENDS
OF THE
RIVERHEAD FREE LIBRARY
EXECUTIVE BOARD
2003-2004

Barbara Hellering, Co-President

Laurel Sisson, Co-President

Dorothy Pennell, Corresponding Secretary

Wini Titterton, Treasurer

John & Muriel Groneman, Membership Chairs

Helen Drielak, Book Sales Chair

Elizabeth Richard, Art Gallery/ Display Cases

Gerry Heggner, Memory Book

Thelma Booker, Photography Show Chair

Ronnie Kaplan, Piano Plus Sales

MEMBERS AT LARGE

Rita Hutchinson

Mary Lundberg

Dee Mulcahy

PAST PRESIDENTS

Helen Hannah

Francis & Hywel White

Dr. Albert Sunshine

Peter Danowski

Helen Easter

Michon Griffing

Eileen Grover

Lois Reeve

Carol Talmage

Mary Fairley

Mary Lou Dreeben Fisher

Barbara Hellering

Dorothy Pennell

Laurel Sisson

LETTER FROM THE FRIENDS OF
THE RIVERHEAD FREE LIBRARY

New residents to the area are often interested in learning more about their new home, trying to develop a sense of place. There have been many, many changes to our town since Benjamin Franklin surveyed distances and placed mileage markers along what is now Sound Avenue. Riverhead (which was still part of Southold at that time) has progressed from forested wilderness, laced with streams, to its current status as a busy, crowded commercial center. Although, we can't relive its history, reading about it helps us understand and appreciate how the changes happened.

For over 100 years, the Riverhead Free Library has been a source of information about the town. Sometimes the wealth of resources held in the Long Island Collection can be overwhelming, especially to youngsters working on school assignments. Church histories, genealogies, ancient newspapers and pamphlets, printed to celebrate special events are housed here. How much easier it will be to access the information they contain now that it has been gathered and distilled in this one source.

How appropriate that the library's Board of Trustees and the Friends of the Library should be involved in the production of this resource. We will all use it, with gratitude, I am sure. As Friends of the Riverhead Free Library, we are pleased to have contributed to the process.

Remember, it's not a chore to read first-hand records of history, it's fun. Have fun with this book.

Laurel Sisson
Barbara Hellering
Co-Presidents
Friends of the Riverhead Free Library, Inc.
Former Assistant Director
Riverhead Free Library

Gratitude

———∽∾∿———

This first collection of some of the historical accounts of River-head's past was made possible through the tireless efforts of a number of individuals who, without their help, this historical account would not have been possible.

First and foremost, we would like to thank the Authors whose writings appear in this book; Tom Twomey for selecting and editing these writings, for supplying a good portion of the photographs, and for his constant help in directing this project; Janice Olsen for her transcribing all of the information in this book into its present form; Stacey Schweitzer for indexing the book; and Keith Hollaman and Esther Margolis of Newmarket Press for the production of this book.

We would also like to thank the staff of The Riverhead Free Library for their support and for providing material, author biographies, and proof reading.

Finally, we would like to thank Tom Lennon, Steve Patterson, and Renee Roberts-Osborne, three current Trustees of the Riverhead Free Library, who procured the funding necessary to make this project possible.

Board of Trustees
The Riverhead Free Library
November 2003

Foreword

O n behalf of the Riverhead Free Library, the Trustees would like to welcome you as you read through the historical accounts presented in this book and would like to thank you for your support of the Riverhead Free Library through the purchase of this book.

As you will see while reading through the various accounts herein, different people in different times offer different perspectives of our past. It is important that all of these accounts be considered when we truly try to understand our past, with the knowledge that these are historical accounts given from varying individuals' views. Within that framework, this book is more of a passing on of information rather than a pure historical account of the town's past. We hope that you will enjoy these excerpts as much as we have and pass them on for generations to come in the hopes of preserving our town's history and in a sense—keeping the past alive. A knowledge of the past provides an understanding of the present. It is our hope that reading the rich accumulation of the Town's colorful history will stir the reader's imagination.

Today's Riverhead has changed quite a bit from the Riverhead of the 1800's as described in the various accounts herein. Although Riverhead still has its downtown riverfront area, remains the County Seat, contains a plethora of farmland, has sandy beaches, and remains the center of Eastern Long Island's commercial activity, it bustles with tourism and continued growth not seen in the past. We now have family-geared tourist attractions, world class vineyards, numerous golf courses, large shopping centers, and is a center for culture and arts on the Eastern End of Long Island. For young and old, Riverhead is a great place to live, attend school, work, or retire. The sandy beaches, breathtaking views of the Long Island Sound, scenic vistas of farmland and vineyards, seasonal fairs and festivals celebrating the area, all contribute to making Riverhead a special place.

The Riverhead Free Library has become a key part of Riverhead and it's year-round population of approximately 27,000. The Library currently serves over 1,000 patrons each day with programs for children and adults, access to computers for all ages, training classes ranging from computer use to tax preparation to driving classes, and other special functions such as a newly created lecture series by local authors. And, of course, the library still provides good old-fashioned books to check out. The Riverhead Free Library has become a cultural center as well as a source for information, education, and entertainment for the Riverhead community.

We would like to once again thank you for your interest in this book and support of the Riverhead Free Library. Please enjoy the historical excerpts that follow.

Board of Trustees
The Riverhead Free Library
November 2003

THE RIVERHEAD FREE LIBRARY

The Riverhead Free Library was organized on April 4, 1896. The word "Free" in the library title had special significance. It meant that all community residents could borrow books without charge. Prior to this, there had been a library in Riverhead, but it had been a subscription library. The membership fee was $2.00 annually.

The location of the library has changed through the years. Its first site was the Reading room of the Riverhead Savings Bank. It was then relocated to rooms over a Main Street store and then to rooms in the Roanoke Avenue School. It was finally relocated to Court Street on January 27, 1964.

The original 9,000 square feet has been expanded twice since 1964. A 1981 expansion increased the building to 19,000 square feet and the most recent addition, to 30,400 square feet, was completed in July of 2000.

The library is governed and guided by an elected Board of Trustees composed of nine community members. The trustees serve as the liaison between the library and the public, establishing policies that are responsive to the community's needs.

The Riverhead Free Library is an association library chartered by the New York State Department of Education. It serves the residents and property owners of the Riverhead Central School district in the Towns of Riverhead, Southampton and Brookhaven, an area of 83 square miles.

The mission of the Riverhead Free Library is to strive to inform, enrich and empower every person in our community by promoting easy access to a vast array of ideas and information and by supporting an informed citizenry, lifelong learning and a love of reading, to recognize changes that occur in society and to adapt these changes to the delivery of people-oriented library services.

Introduction

Tom Twomey

"Tell ye your children of it, and let your children tell their children and their children and other generations."
Joel, I: 3.

THE IMPORTANCE OF LOCAL HISTORY

We all need to know how we have become who we are in order to conduct our own lives successfully. Communities require the same self understanding in order to function satisfactorily. For individuals and communities alike, experience produces a self-image and a basis for deciding how to behave, manage problems, and plan ahead. Without memory, individuals and communities would be forced to start fresh in analyzing each situation and deciding how to respond. Life would become extremely complicated. Even minor decisions would take much time and effort. The ability to observe and recall what has taken place in the nearby world constitutes an essential aspect of human intelligence and well being. History serves the community as memory serves the individual and has the same values and flaws.

And a community is more than a physical location with boundary lines on a map. A community can be a few people, a small neighborhood, or a whole Town. It is a place where we feel welcome—where we have participated. A place where we have invested part of ourselves. Where we have given to others, not just taken. Historian Arthur Link has said, "The single most important attribute that enabled man to emerge from his primitive savage state was memory. Collective memory, preserved for long ages at first by oral tradition, enabled primitive man to maintain the practices and customs and to develop the institutions necessary to an ongoing social life."

Historian Donald Parker said "someone has compared a community which does not know its own history to a man who has lost his memory."

THE SHAPING OF A LOCAL COMMUNITY

At the time the speeches and articles in this book were written, the United States was still an infant in the world of nations. Regionalism had set in dividing the north from the south. The west was being opened at a rapid pace. Change was occurring at an exponential rate— railroads and telegraphs were shrinking distances and blurring community boundaries. After the Civil War, the nation needed time to heal. Communities needed time to think about the terrible tragedy that had occurred and why communities were so different one from the other.

Perhaps, these writers understood that their mission was to trace the past and tell stories, which were little known or understood in Riverhead. To help their neighbors understand who they were and from where they had come. To build their confidence. To instill some pride that they were living in a unique community on the East End.

Whether we were born on the East End or we chose this community as a place to live, much of what makes the East End a special place to live is its sense of community flowing from a connection to a history that began more than 350 years ago.

THE PURPOSE OF THIS BOOK

One purpose of this book is to bring together in one volume virtually all of the important early histories about Riverhead. Written between 1832 and 1905, these histories are not widely known or available to the general public. However, they are vital to fully appreciate Riverhead today.

This is the first time these local histories have been printed in one book with a common detailed index for easy access. In fact, most of the original writings did not have an index at all making them time consuming to use for research purposes.

Another purpose is to help preserve the Riverhead community for future generations. As we all know, Riverhead is changing. It is vitally important that its residents, new and old alike understand its past. For that, the community needs access to it. That is the motivation behind this book: to get Riverhead history into the hands of as many of its residents as possible; otherwise, eventually the Town's collective sense of itself and self-worth will become muddled. Its identity will become confused. Change will submerge its self-image, cutting off the present from its roots. Riverhead will be absorbed into a generic suburbanization, which has already intellectually gutted so many small towns in America. Riverhead's heritage will be lost and with it, the reason so many Riverhead residents choose to live here to begin with.

One should not infer from the inclusion of these histories in this book that all of the facts presented by the authors are now known to be true and accurate. To the contrary, no fact checking or editing to correct erroneous or contradictory information has been made. Nevertheless, the chronological presentation will help provide a better understanding of the way in which the written history (and myths) of Riverhead evolved during the 19th century. Each history presents a snapshot of the culture and times in which the history was written. For that reason, each history itself becomes an interesting historical document of greater interest as time passes and cultural change continues.

THE EAST END AND THE WORLD ECONOMY

The East End was the product of truly global forces at work in the region. It was not simply a few utopian men and women deciding for religious reasons to settle in the woods of eastern Long Island.

What global forces? The men and women who settled here in the seventeenth century were, for the most part, from the upper middle class in England. They owned businesses and property in England before they left. To finance the purchase of boats and supplies for the journey and for the early years of living in the new England, they were able to borrow the necessary funds from London bankers. Property owned in England was used as collateral with interest rates of 8% or higher. Upon arrival in New England, with gold and silver lacking, timber, fish, and furs were sent back to London to pay back the loans. Each colony appointed an agent in London to assist with the transactions.

For 15 years or so after the English arrived on the Mayflower in 1620, the English settlers found plenty of natural resources to send back to London to reduce their loans. Timber, fish and even furs were plentiful. Eventually, these natural resources became relatively scarce. Ships bringing more settlers would also bring cheap blankets, pots, pans, and tools to trade for furs from the Indians. The fur most sought by London merchants was beaver skin since it would hold its shape and remain waterproof when converted into top hats for the London upper-class. Beaver skin was sought then much the way mink is sought today. At first, beavers were plentiful along the southern New England shore where the colonists first settled. But once a family of beavers was caught, others did not replace them since beavers are not roaming animals. They generally stay fixed in a particular area all of their lives. As the beavers became more and more scarce along the coast, the English settlers looked desperately to other ways of securing this valuable fur to repay their loans.

Let's keep following the money. Indians in Canada and northern New England, for many years before the English arrived, began using wampum in religious ceremonies and for just plain old-fashioned courtship—much the way diamonds, rubies, and other gems are used in our society. Wampum was a small, cylindrical white or purple bead made by our own local Indians from a certain shell found in the Peconic Bay. Because of the uniqueness of the shell and our local Indians' ability to handcraft these special beads, the Dutch shortly after they arrived in what is now New York, referred to the East End of Long Island as the "mine of the New World".

So how does all this fit together? A young engineer, soldier, and pioneer named Lion Gardiner was hired by Lord Saye and Lord Brook to build a fort at the mouth of the Connecticut River to serve as a trading post and a new settlement. This was done shortly after an expedition to Long Island in 1633 by the English in Massachusetts, which confirmed the large quantity of wampum being made on the East End. The fort was placed in a strategic location to keep the Dutch in New York from spreading their trading empire east. Lion Gardiner was commander of this fort at the time of the Pequot War in 1637, which destroyed the ferocious Pequot Tribe in southern Connecticut.

For many years, the Pequots had collected a tax—or a tribute, as it was called back then—from the East End Indians. This tax was willingly paid by the Montauketts for the same reasons we pay taxes today. Indians throughout the East Coast had organized themselves into tribes or what we call today "municipalities". The Pequots and Montauketts were part of the Algonquian nation and, therefore, it was appropriate for the Pequots to collect a tax from the East End Indians for, what I suppose we would call today, "national defense". Since the Indians had no currency, the Pequots collected 10% of the special little bead called "wampum" produced on the East End as the tribute. The Pequots used this bead to barter with northern Indians for goods.

Lion Gardiner, having direct contact with the Pequot Indians, became aware of this tax and also became aware of how valuable this bead was to the Indians from Canada and northern New England.

After the decimation of the Pequot tribe in 1637, Gardiner was contacted by Wyandanch, the chief of the Montaukett Indians. Gardiner discovered that the Montaukett Indians were very willing to pay the English settlers the tax that Wyandanch had been paying the defeated Pequots. In return, Wyandanch wanted protection against the Indian enemies of the Montauketts and a treaty for direct trade with the English. (Such trading rights are still being negotiated today when undeveloped countries seek most-favored-nation status with the United States.) To Wyandanch, this was a terrific deal since it cost him nothing more than what his tribe was previously paying the Pequots, and it now included direct trading rights with the English. To Lion Gardiner, this was a great deal since the English settlers could secure for free the valuable wampum bead directly from the Montauketts and use it, in turn, to trade for the beaver skins. By securing a free source of wampum, the English settlers no longer needed to bring from England wool blankets, pots, pans and tools to trade for the beaver skin sought by the London merchants. By nurturing his relationship with Wyandanch, Lion Gardiner guaranteed peace with the Montaukett Indians, eliminating them as a threat to future settlers of the East End. Best of all, the alliance between Gardiner and Wyandanch produced a free and plentiful source of wampum which, in turn, created fortunes for Gardiner and his allies in New England.

But Gardiner needed to move quickly to consolidate the East End under English control. The Dutch in New York City and Albany had become aware of the value of wampum and its origin on the East End. Lion Gardiner was the first to move to the island right in the middle of Peconic Bay in the middle of the wampum mine.

And so the settlement of the East End, with Riverhead ultimately as its capital, stemmed from the international trade between our early settlers and England in the mid-seventeenth century. The East End was born from the business strategy of Lion Gardiner and his partners to secure a monopoly on a precious natural resource that was as valuable as gold or diamonds are today—wampum.

RIVERHEAD AND THE WORLD AROUND IT

As was customary for writers of local history during the last two centuries, very little was included in local historical writings connecting a town or region to the world around it. The interplay between what occurred in Riverhead Town and the global forces at work in Europe—or even New England—were not considered within the proper scope of a local history. This was an understandable approach to local history since reconstructing what occurred in the town itself a few hundred years earlier was a large enough task for most local historians.

In recent years academically trained historians, prefer a broader view of local history than what was written in the past. These professional historians spend a great deal of time tying a local occurrence or individual life to what was happening in the world at large. It is a wonderful and fascinating methodology to provide the reader with a better view—a better context—of what may have caused a certain historical event.

However, few readers of any of Riverhead's early history are provided information regarding political events, which were occurring in Europe and the Far East during this period, which had such a profound impact on the attitudes and actions in Riverhead itself. The political in fighting in England had a significant effect on immigration to the East End. The vicious political battles and trade wars and subsequent treaties between England and the Netherlands controlled much of Riverhead's early economic development. The power of Charles I and James II of England and their relationships to Parliament had an enormous impact on the early political struggles of the area.

How many realize in 1614 when Dutch settlers arrived in Manhattan, Michelangelo was still painting his masterpieces? Or that Shakespeare died a few years thereafter?

Who realizes that in 1633, when Peconic Bay was considered the "mine of the New World", containing the source of wampum so vitally important to the economic well-being of Riverhead, Galileo was tried by the Inquisition in Rome and forced to recant his belief that the earth revolves around the sun?

Who would have thought that in 1639, when Lion Gardiner received his grant from the Earl of Sterling for Gardiner's Island, Peter Paul Reuben was painting his masterpieces?

Or how about the fact that a year after Southampton and Southold were founded and became part of Connecticut, Descartes wrote "Discourse on Method and Meditations (Cogito Ergo Sum)"?

And in the few years before and after 1640 when Southold was founded, Charles I surrendered to the Puritans, the divine rights of king was destroyed, Frans Hals painted "Portrait of a Young Man," Rembrandt painted "Man with the Golden Helmet," King Charles was beheaded, and Oliver Cromwell became the leader of England.

About 1653, the Taj Mahal was built, red corpuscles were discovered and Moliere was writing his plays.

In 1664, when the Duke of York (who ultimately became King James II of England) annexed the East End to New York over the wild objections of its citizens, 100,000 people perished in London from the

Great Plague and, shortly thereafter, the Great Fire of London nearly destroyed the entire city.

In 1682, about the time the New York Colonial Legislature was founded, the Palace of Versailles was built and the microscope was invented by Dutch scientist Anton van Leeuwenhoek.

About 1685, when the Dongan Patent was signed governing much of the property rights on the East End, Newton set forth his law of universal gravitation in his book, *Principia Mathematica*.

And a few years later, when eastern Long Island became known as Suffolk County, John Locke wrote his essay concerning human understanding and also his classical *Statement of Political Theory and Social Contract of Government*.

And in 1717, Daniel Defoe wrote *Robinson Crusoe* and, a few years later, Jonathan Swift wrote *Gulliver's Travels*.

A GOOD BEGINNING

As I said at the outset, to preserve this community for future generations, we need to know our past. To accomplish this, the historical writings in this book are a good beginning.

So, sit back and enjoy yourself. Reading this book should be thought provoking, invigorating, and even fun. The most important thing you can do after you read a few articles is talk to your neighbors and friends about what you have learned. Think about what makes Riverhead so unique. Share something you found interesting. Pass along our heritage. In doing so, you will be making Riverhead a better community—a better place to live; now and throughout future generations.

SEEKING THE PAST

CHAPTER I

EXCERPT FROM HISTORICAL COLLECTIONS OF THE STATE OF NEW YORK CONTAINING A GENERAL COLLECTION OF THE MOST INTERESTING FACTS, TRADITIONS, BIOGRAPHICAL SKETCHES, ANECDOTES, &C. RELATING TO THE HISTORY AND ANTIQUITIES WITH GEOGRAPHICAL DESCRIPTIONS OF EVERY TOWNSHIP IN THE STATE

Written by John W. Barber in 1832

Born in Connecticut in 1798, John Warner Barber became an apprentice engraver at the age of 16. By the time he was 25, he was operating his own engraving business in New Haven. His primary interest was in writing history and religious works for which he engraved illustrations. At the age of 30, he began publishing a new book every few years until he was about 50 years old. Many of his works were "Historical Collections" of various states and communities from New Jersey through Maine. He published "The Historical Collections of New York" in 1841, from which this excerpt regarding Riverhead was taken. He died in 1885 in New Haven, not far from his birthplace.

1

R IVERHEAD, the shire town, was taken from Southold in 1792. Only a comparatively small portion of the town is under improvement; much of its territory is covered with wood, which has for a long period been a staple article for transportation.

The following is a southern view of the central part of the village of Riverhead, as seen from the residence of Mr. J.P. Terry, about 50 rods S. from the courthouse. The village is situated upon Peconic creek or river, a mill stream, about 2 miles above Peconic bay, about 90 miles from New York, 24 from Sagg Harbor, and 23 from Greenport. The village contains about 70 dwellings, a large proportion of which are one story in height, 1 Methodist, 1 Congregational, and 1 Swedenbourg or New Jerusalem church, an academy, and about 500 inhabitants. The courthouse, seen in the central part of the engraving with a small spire, has stood more than a century. James Port is a recent village E. of Riverhead. Old Aquabogue, Upper Aquabogue, Fresh Pond, Baiting Hollow, and Wading River, are small villages.

CHAPTER II

EXCERPT FROM THE HISTORY OF LONG ISLAND FROM ITS DISCOVERY AND SETTLEMENT TO THE PRESENT TIME. WITH MANY IMPORTANT AND INTERESTING MATTERS; INCLUDING NOTICES OF NUMEROUS INDIVIDUALS AND FAMILIES; ALSO A PARTICULAR ACCOUNT OF THE DIFFERENT CHURCHES AND MINISTERS

Written by Benjamin F. Thompson,
Counsellor At Law, in 1843

Born in 1894, Benjamin Thompson was educated at Yale College where he studied medicine with Dr. Ebenezer Sage of Sag Harbor. He practiced medicine for about ten years, after which he became a lawyer. At the age of twenty-nine, he was elected to the New York State Assembly representing his home district in Brookhaven for two terms. At the age of fifty-five, he published a history of Long Island in one volume. A second edition, greatly enlarged and improved, was published in 1843 comprising two volumes. It is from this edition that the below chapter on the Town of Riverhead is taken. Still later, Thompson began preparations for a third edition which was not published until 1913—some sixty-four years after his death. His volumes on Long Island history were per-

3

*haps the first comprehensive, thorough writing on the sub-
ject—all three editions being invaluable classical histories of
Long Island to this date.*

TOWN OF RIVERHEAD

FORMERLY, a component part of Southold was organized as a separate town, by the act for dividing Southold into two towns, passed
March 13, 1792. It is bounded S. by the middle of Peconic river, dividing
it from Southampton, W. by Brookhaven, N. by the Sound, and E. by
Southold. The name of the town was derived from that of the principal
village, so called, because of its location at the head of boat navigation
on Peconic river.

At the first town meeting, April 3, 1792, the following persons were
chosen town officers:—Daniel Wells, supervisor; Josiah Reeve, clerk;
John C. Terry, Joseph Wells and Benjamin Petty, assessors; Jeremiah
Wells and Spencer Dayton, commissioners of highways; Deacon Daniel
Terry, Zachariah Hallock, and Daniel Edwards, overseers of the poor;
Nathan Youngs, Eleazer Luce, Rufus Youngs, John Corwin, Zophar Mills,
Peter Reeve and Merritt Howell, overseers of highways; Sylvanus
Brown, collector; and David Brown, Abel Corwin, and Benjamin Hor-
ton, constables.

Of the lands in this town, scarcely one-third part is under improvement—most of the remainder, from its natural sterility, being considered incapable of any profitable cultivation. A large portion of the
territory is covered with forest, and fuel has long been a staple article
for transportation, of which a vast deal has been shipped to New York
and other places. On the southern part of the town, the surface is level,
the soil light and sandy, and the timber chiefly pine, interspersed only
occasionally with oak, while on the north the surface is rough, the soil
a sandy loam, and upon which oak timber more generally prevails. The
hills near the Sound, are a continuation of the ridge or spine of the island, and the cliffs adjoining the shore are high and precipitous.

There are two considerable streams in the town:—1st, the Wading
river, called by the Indians *Pauquacumsuck*, being on its western border. This commences on the southerly side of the town, and discharges
itself into a creek, setting up from the Sound, 2d, the Peconic river,
which has its origin in the town of Brookhaven, and after running easterly for about twelve miles, terminates in Peconic Bay, at the village of
Riverhead. Upon this stream are several mills and manufactories, which
have been in operation many years, and the quantity of water is doubt-

less quite sufficient to propel double the machinery yet erected. Many plans have been in agitation to improve its navigation; and among other measures for the accomplishment of that object, a company was incorporated the 10th of March, 1835, with a capital of ten thousand dollars, for the purpose of making a sloop channel from the head of navigation in Peconic river, to the damn or bridge at the village of Riverhead; which plan, if carried into effect, as is confidently expected, the value of property in the neighborhood will be greatly enhanced population increased, and business of every description experience fresh inspiration.

Capital and enterprise only are required, in connection with the many advantages afforded by nature, to make this place the theatre of a variety of useful manufacturing establishments.

The recent improvements that have taken place here, are satisfactory indications of what industry and enterprise can accomplish, in a very limited period.

The first settlement in this village, now the seat of justice for the county, was commenced by John Griffing and his associates in 1690, and five years thereafter a grist-mill was erected, but the growth of the place was so slow, that at the end of 100 years it contained only four or five houses.

During the last thirty years, the improvements have gradually progressed, till the village now contains more than seventy dwellings, and nearly 500 inhabitants. Besides the court house and jail, there are several handsome private residences, a commodious female academy, erected in 1835, a new congregational church, dedicated Dec. 1, 1841, a methodist meeting house, and another devoted to the religious principles of Emanuel Swedenborg.

The surrogate's office is now kept here, as is also the office of the town clerk.

The county hall stands in the midst, like a faithful sentinel watching over the welfare of the people, while the cross-barred windows of the jail frown indignantly upon all violations of the laws.

The following observations in relation to this part of the country, are contained in President Dwight's journal of his travels through Long Island in 1804:—

"Riverhead (says he) is the shire town of this county. The court house, a poor decayed building, and a miserable hamlet, containing about ten or twelve houses, stand near the efflux of the river. From this account of the court house, it will naturally be expected that the business of lawyers and sheriffs is not here in very great demand, nor in very high reputation. The suspicion is certainly well founded. The county court, or court of common pleas, sits here twice a year; assembles on Tuesday, and, after having finished its whole business, adjourns almost always on the succeeding day. No lawyer, if I am not misinformed, has hitherto been able to get a living in the county of Suffolk. I entertain a very respectful opinion of the gentlemen of the bar, but all will agree with me in saying, that this exemption from litigation, while it is a peculiar, is also a very honorable characteristic of this county. Not far from this hamlet is a spot of ground, about three miles in diameter, which, as I was informed by good authority, is covered with shrub oaks and pines not more than five or six feet in height. In the whole tract, there is not a single tree of the usual size, although it is surrounded by a forest of such trees. The cause of this phenomenon, in a place where the soil is substantially the same with that of the neighboring country, is not easy to assign."

Were the venerable president now alive, and to travel over the same ground, he would experience the disappointment, as well as satisfaction of seeing a decent looking court house, something more than a miserable hamlet, and a very respectable population of intelligent and industrious citizens. He would find, too, that even in the county of Suffolk the annual crop of litigation is considerable; that there are about a dozen lawyers in it, (two of whom are located in this village,) and all of them getting a tolerable living by their profession alone. But it may be said that times are materially changed in the course of forty years, and improvement is now the order of the day.[i]

The village of Riverhead is distant from Oyster Pond Point about 30 miles, from Greenport 23, from Sag Harbor 26, and from New York city 90 miles.

The other settlements in the town are Upper Aquabogue, Lower Aquabogue, Northville, Fresh-ponds, Baiting Hollow, Wading River and James Port, in most of which churches and school houses have been erected, the particulars of which we have not been able to satisfactorily ascertain.

James Port is situated near the head of sloop navigation, five miles and a half below Riverhead, it possesses several dwellings, a wharf and other conveniences for trade and commerce. There are now owned here two or three whaling ships, besides a number of coasting vessels.

A church was built at Upper Aquabogue early in the eighteenth century, of which the Rev. Timothy Symmes was for some years pastor. He was a descendant of the Rev. Zachariah Symmes, who arrived at Charlestown, from England in 1634, where he was the second minister, and successor of the Rev. Mr. Wilson. He died in Feb. 1671. His grandson of the same name died at Rehoboth in 1709. He was the father of Timothy, who was born in 1690, graduated at Harvard 1715, and came to this town about the year 1738, where he remained till 1750, when he removed to, and died at Ipswich, Mass. in 1753. His wife was Mary, daughter of Capt. John Cleves of Southold, who after the decease of her husband returned again to her native place, and died in 1784, aged 89. Her father had been an officer in the Pequot war and came here from the province of New Hampshire.

His father George Cleves, was the person sent by Charles II. to investigate the conduct of Gov. Winthrop in 1637. Rev. Timothy Symmes left two sons, John Cleves and Timothy Symmes.[ii]

In the course of the last war with Great Britain, several vessels owned here were captured by the enemy in the Sound, and either wantonly destroyed or allowed to be redeemed upon very exorbitant conditions. This of course roused the indignation of the inhabitants, and they resolved to retaliate upon the lawless plunderers of their property, should an opportunity at any time present itself.

In the summer of 1814, an occurrence took place which reflects credit upon those engaged in it, the facts of which were communicated by letter from Capt. Wells to Lieut. Colonel Moore. A copy of which is here given.

> "Riverhead, June 1, 1814. Sir,—I have the honor to inform you that a battle was fought here yesterday, about eleven o'clock in the forenoon, between a few of the militia of your regiment and double their number of the enemy, which terminated in the total defeat of the latter. About ten o'clock in the forenoon, an alarm was given that two large barges were standing for our shore from the British squadron, then lying six or seven miles out in the Sound. About thirty militia of Captain Terry's, Reeve's, and my company, collected before they reached the shore. The enemy advanced with two large barges, containing about twenty-five or thirty men each, within musket-shot of the shore, when they saluted us with their cannon and a volley of musketry, and then gave three cheers and proceeded to the sloop Nancy, lying on the beach. As they were on the eve of boarding her, we opened a destructive and well-directed fire upon both the barges, which silenced their fire, and stopped their oars in an instant. They were so slow in wearing the barges and rowing off, that we had several fires into them before they could get out of musket-shot. I am happy to say that the men fought well, without a symptom of fear,

neither was a man wounded among us. But from what we saw, we have reason to believe that many of the enemy were killed and wounded. We made immediate preparations for another engagement, thinking they might send a large reinforcement, which we should have been happy to have met, as *we* received a reinforcement shortly after the engagement, who found they were too late to take part in the affair. The officers present were Captain John Terry, myself, Usher H. Moore, and ensign James Fanning.

Yours respectfully,

"To Lieutenant Colonel Jeremiah Moore.   JOHN WELLS, Captain."

Rev. Benjamin Goldsmith, was formerly pastor of the union churches of Aquabogue and Mattetuck. He was the son of John Goldsmith, a farmer of Southold, and born there Nov. 5, 1736. He graduated at Yale 1760, and was settled over these churches June 28, 1764, in which he officiated alternately till his decease Nov. 10, 1810, a period of forty-six years. His intellectual endowments were respectable, of plain and unaffected manners, cheerful in temper, and highly useful as a christian minister. His first wife was Sarah Conkling, by whom he had two sons, Benjamin and Joseph, and two daughters, Amelia, who married James Hallock, and Lydia, who married Moses L. Case. By his second wife, Hannah, widow of Thomas Conkling, he had only a son, now the Rev. John Goldsmith of Newtown.[iii]

CHAPTER III

EXCERPT FROM A HISTORY OF LONG ISLAND, FROM ITS FIRST SETTLEMENT BY EUROPEANS TO THE YEAR 1845, WITH SPECIAL REFERENCE TO ITS ECCLESIASTICAL CONCERNS

Written by Nathaniel S. Prime in 1845

Nathaniel Scudder Prime was born on April 21, 1785 in Huntington, Long Island, where he was ordained to the ministry and worked most of his life. He was a colleague of Lyman Beecher, and for a five-month period, was the minister in Cutchogue. In the autumn of 1806, he was appointed minister of the Church at Sag Harbor. Within six months, one hundred persons joined the congregation. Two years later, at the age of 23, he married Julia Jermain, daughter of Major John Jermain of Sag Harbor. He became the minister in Huntington in 1809. In his sixtieth year, he wrote "The History of Long Island From its Settlement by Europeans to the Year 1845" in two parts: I. Its physical features and civil affairs; and II. Anals of the Several Towns Relating Chiefly to Ecclesiastical Matters. The following is taken from this book. Rev. Prime continued his ministry in upstate New York and Massachusetts until he died in 1856 at the age of 71.

Number of acres improved————————————12,302
"　　　"　　　" unimproved————————24,198
Ratio of population to the acre, 1 to 15.

THIS is the County town of Suffolk, bounded on the north by the Sound—on the east by Southold—on the south by Peconick Bay

9

and River, and on the west by Brookhaven. The Court House is situated at the head of the Bay, near the south line of the town; and, till within a few years, was encircled by one continuous forest, with only a small cluster of houses in sight. It was one of the most cheerless landscapes that could meet the eye; having not a single bright point, except the stream of water flowing through the sand; nor any avenue to a fairer prospect, except a small opening in the woods produced by the head of the Bay.

The whole township is one of the most sterile in the county—only one third of its territory being capable of repaying the labor of cultivation. For 150 years it constituted a part of Southold, and was made a separate town by an Act of the Legislature, dated March 13th, 1792.

A settlement was commenced here, as early as 1690, by John Griffin and others, who erected a grist-mill, on the mouth of the River; but the increase of the inhabitants was very small for more than a century. In 1804, after this spot had been the seat of justice for the County almost 80 years, Dr. Dwight describes it as "a miserable hamlet containing about 10 or 12 houses," and "the Court House, a poor, decayed building."

The days of modern improvement have wrought a considerable change here, as elsewhere. The village has been laid out into streets, and a large accession to the buildings, both public and private, has been made; till it presents quite an imposing appearance. Besides the Court House, three Churches and an Academy, there are about 70 private dwellings, and the village contains nearly 400 inhabitants.

This village being of very recent origin, no public buildings, except the Court House, were erected here, till within a few years. When this County was first formed, the Courts were held at Southampton and Southold.

In 1725 a Court House and Jail were erected here; and from that time, this has been the shire-town. It was formerly a sorry looking building, of contracted dimensions. The Court and Jury rooms, and the cells for prisoners, were under the same roof. Within a few years, the Court House was remodeled and repaired; and a prison separate from the Hall of Justice erected.

No house appropriated to religious worship, nor even a church organization existed here till some 12 years ago. Previously to that time, occasional preaching by ministers of diffferent denominations, was held in the Court Room.

In 1830, the Methodists commenced regular preaching here, and in 1833, a society of 9 members was constituted. A house of worship,

34 by 42 feet, was erected in 1834, and dedicated in the following year. The number of members is now about 100.

A Congregational Church was organised in Oct. 1834, consisting of 39 members, who formed part of a secession from the church of Upper Aquebogue, which will be more particularly noticed hereafter. They were first supplied by the Rev. Mr. Moser, until the spring of 1836. A Female Seminary, erected in 1835, afforded a convenient place of worship, which they occupied for several years. From May 1836, Mr. Gilbert supplied this church for one year, when he was succeeded by the Rev. Charles I. Knowles; who removed in 1844, and was succeeded in the spring of 1845, by the Rev. Mr. Brooks, who is now labouring here. This congregation is feeble and has been aided several years, by the Home Missionary Society.

In 1831, Elijah Terry, a respectable resident of this village, embraced the doctrine of Emmanuel Swedenborg and united himself with the New Jerusalem Church at Baiting Hollow. On the 12th of May 1839, a church of this order, consisting of 10 members, was organised in this village. Their place of meeting is a comfortable building, which they have erected for the twofold purpose of public worship and a select school; both of which receive a very limited patronage. Until the past year, they have never enjoyed the stated labours of a minister; but since Nov. 1844, a Mr. Carll has divided his services between this place and Baiting Hollow. Their present number of members is 9.

In regard to the morals of the village, there has been a very manifest improvement, within a few years, especially in regard to temperance, and the sanctification of the sabbath. There are few places in the land, in which the efforts of the friends of temperance have been crowned with more triumphant success. Most of the Hotels or Taverns are conducted on temperance principles.

From the Annual Report of the Temperance Society of this village, it appears that the quantity of liquor sold in the first year of its existence, was reduced from 3,600 to 900 gallons; and in the next year, down to 600. Can a more favourable account be given of any other shire-town in the state?

Upper Aquebogue.—This is a continuous settlement, the centre of which is about three miles north-easterly, as you proceed from the Court House, down the northern branch of the island. It forms the largest parish in the town; and although its religious history is comprized within the last one hundred years, its commencement is veiled in great obscurity.

The present Congregational Church was organised, March 26th, 1758, by the Rev. Elisha Paine, pastor of the Separate Church of Bridgehampton; and consisted of 16 members. A house of worship, in dimensions 24 by 33 feet, had been previously erected, on the burying ground, nearly opposite the present church. The first interment in that ground was made in 1755, and it is supposed that the church had been previously erected.

From an old record, still extant, though deficient in dates and other particulars, it seems probable, that a church had previously existed here, to which a Mr. Lee had ministered, and that it was under Presbyterian organization. It is also said that the Rev. Timothy Symmes supplied it for some years, preceding the middle of the last century. But when he came, and how long he remained, are equally unknown. He must have left the island, as early as 1746, as he was the pastor of Connecticut Farms and New Providence, N.J., from that year to 1750. During that period, his name appears in the records of the Synod, as a member of the Presbytery of New York.

The church organised in 1758, evidently grew out of the separation produced by Mr. Davenport's operations, in these eastern towns. In no part of the island, was that spirit more rife, or attended with more permanent consequences. The lower parish had been much agitated and divided by the new meaasures introduced among them. In April, 1749, "the difficulties that for sometime past had subsisted among the people of Aquebogue," say the Presbytery of Suffolk, "were laid before that body." And after hearing the case set forth "by each party" a letter was sent to the congregation "containing a Christian reprehension of what had been contrary to the order of the gospel; and an exhortation to labour after a forgiving and peaceable spirit, one towards another."

Here it is easy to discover the origin of the subsequent separation, and new organization, which took place a few years afterwards.

The old church edifice at Upper Aquebogue remained till within the recollection of not a few, who are still living. In 1797, a new church 30 by 42 feet, was erected, on the opposite side of the street. It had full galleries, and would accommodate a large assembly. In 1833, it was remodeled, and, excepting the frame, entirely rebuilt, with the addition of a steeple, which is furnished with a bell. It is now universally known throughout the town and vicinity as the "Steeple Church."

Since the above was written, a respected correspondent, to whom the writer is indebted for many facts in the history of this town, says, in relation to the previous organization, "I have since learned that it was a Presbyterian church, and that Mr. Lee was the minister." It is probable that Mr. Symmes preceded this individual.

MINISTERS.

The Rev. Timothy Wells was the first pastor of this church. He was ordained Oct. 25th, 1759, by Mr. Paine of Bridgehampton, and Mr. Marshall of Canterbury, Conn. He died at Cutchogue, Jan. 15th, 1783, aged 62. "He was an uneducated man, but one of considerable talent, and of deep and ardent piety."

The Rev. Daniel Youngs was called March 28th, 1782, and was ordained in the following year, by the Strict Con. Convention of Conn. He and Mr. Wells, his predecessor, were both natives of the parish, and were trained up in the exercise of their gifts, in their naative church. Mr. Youngs had been preaching, for several years preceding his call to this charge. He was a man of considerable powers and influence. "He was at the head of his own denomination on the island. Considering his limited advantages for preparatory studies, he eminently excelled. His reasoning powers were strong. His language, though not always in accordance with the niceties of grammatical precision, was, nevertheless, forcible and often sublime. His eloquence was sometimes bold and awful." He died in 1814 at the age of 70 years.

The Rev. Moses Sweezy succeeded Mr. Youngs, in 1815. He was a native of Brookhaven, but had spent his early life in the parish, and first united with this church. In 1808, he was ordained by the L.I. Convention, pastor of a church in New Jersey. He died January 28th, 1826, aged 55 years.

From September, 1826 to 1827, the church was supplied by the Rev. Thomas Edwards, from England, and from 1728 to 1831, by the Rev. Evan Evans, from Wales. Both of these gentlemen held their ecclesiastical connexion with the New York Association. From 1831 to '34 this church was supplied by the Rev. Parshall Terry, from '34 to '37 by the Rev. John Gibbs, from '37 to '40, by the Rev. William Lyall, and from 1840 by the Rev. Thomas Harris, who is still employed.

The history of this church records more than a dozen special seasons of revival, since the year 1783. The present number of communicants is 275. The church having withdrawn from the Long Island Convention now occupies strictly independent ground.

Lower Aquebogue.—The first church edifice, within the present limits of this town, was doubtless erected in this parish, about 6 miles north east of the Court hosue. It was built in 1731. A church had probably been organised a short time before this; of which the Rev. Nathaniel Mather is supposed to have been the first pastor. From the private record previously referred to, Mr. Mather's ordination is said to have taken place May 22d, 1728. No place is mentioned, but as he afterwards appears to have been the pastor of this church, at the organization of the Presbytery of Suffolk, and his name occurs in connexion with no other congregation, it may be inferred, that he was originally settled here. He died March 20th, 1748.

In April 1749, the Presbytery having licensed Mr. John Darbee, appointed him to preach in this congregation, and at Mattituck, which he continued to do for two years. In the course of this first year, however, a complaint was brought by certain disaffected individuals, against "Mr. Darbee's preaching and private conversation," which, after a careful investigation by the Presbytery, was judged to be without foundation. Mr. D. subsequently laboured in other congregations, and was ordainted as an evangelist, Nov. 10th, 1757, at Oysterponds, at the time of Mr. Barber's ordination.

It has been previously stated, in the history of Mattituck, that at the ordination of Mr. Parks, June 10th, 1752, the two churches were united, and continued under his charge till February 11th, 1756; and for a number of years after, under the Rev. Nehemiah Barker. He afterwards restricted his labours to Mattituck, and the congregation of Aquebogue was left to its own resources.

The Rev. Benjamin Goldsmith was ordained pastor of this church June 27th, 1764. After thirteen years devoted exclusively to this congregation, a re-union with Mattituck was formed, and he continued in charge of both, till his death, Nov. 19th, 1810, in the 75th year of his age.

At the time of his settlement, it would seem, that the church was exceedingly reduced. At the first church meeting, after his installation, only 4 members attended, and only 17 at the first communion. There sere several seasons of refreshing, during his ministry, particularly in 1801-2 and 1808-9. The whole number added to the church was 94— baptised 771, marriages 380, and he attended 386 funerals.

The writer had but a partial acquaintance with Mr. Goldsmith, and he gives the following notice of him furnished by one of his successors.

"He was a man of sound mind, solid acquirements, plain and unostentatious in his manners and habits—exceedingly diffident of his own powers, "given to hospitality," and of unfeigned piety. His theological views were of the New England stamp. His favourite authors, Edwards, Bellamy and Hopkins. Henry's Commentary was his daily companion. His sermons were unusually well conceived, plain, scriptural, instructive; and his manner solemn and affectionate. He was eminently happy in the influence he exerted, to preserve the peace and unity of the church, and the edification of the body of Christ. Christians were of one mind, and more intelligent and devout than now. The old-fashioned "conference-meeting" was well sustained, during Mr. Goldsmith's ministry. The members assembled once a week, usually at the pastor's house, to discuss, in a familiar manner, some passage of scripture previously assigned. Some gave their views orally; others in writing. This meeting was a school of Theology. The members being familiar with the best standard works, would refer to, and quote them with the utmost readiness and accuracy. They became, to use one of the common words of that day, soundly "indoctrinated." And they were the Aarons and Hurs, to uphold and aid their minister, in every good word and work. Would that the school might be revived, and that love of the truth might once more take the place of a desire to hear or tell some new thing. In those days, the children in the common schools were accustomed to recite the Shorter Catechism, on Saturday of each week; and Mr. Goldsmith usually attended to the recitation, accompanying it with suitable counsels, exhortation and prayer. It was a pastoral visitation, regarded with favour by all. The teacher desired it—the children were gratified with it—public sentiment not merely approved, but required it. How changed the times!"

The Rev. Benjamin Bailey succeeded, as the next regular pastor of this church. He was ordained by the Presbytery of Long Island, Nov. 6th, 1811, and dismissed May 18th, 1816. After his dismission he removed and settled in the western part of the state, where he is still living without charge.

The Rev. Nathaniel Reeve was employed here from 1817, to 1823.

Since that time, excepting one year occupied by the Rev. Jonathan Huntting, and two years by Mr. Gilbert, as stated in the annals of Mattituck, the Rev. Abraham Luce has been and still continues the stated supply of these two congregations under the name of UNION PARISH.

Jamesport is a small settlement of recent origin, a short mile south of the last mentioned parish, and 6 miles below Riverhead. It owes its origin to the speculation-fever of 1835-6, in the bosom of a single individual, who reuined himself by the operation. In 1833, there was not a single human habitation here, now some 40. The object of erecting the village was for the purposes of navigation, and a whaling ship or two are sent out from the port; but being situated at the extreme point of ship navigation on the Peconick Bay, the harbour difficult of access, and the channel constantly diminishing in depth, there is no reason to anticipate any great enlargement. It has made no advance of late years.

A Methodist society has been formed here, which consists of 45 members. They worship in a building erected at the commencement of the settlement for a school-house, or place of worship, as need might require.

Northville, is a small settlement, on the north side of the island, about 2 miles from Upper Aquebogue. The church here owes its origin to a secession from the church of Upper Aquebogue in 1829; on account of dissatisfaction with the minister employed by the majority, and the adoption of "a revised Confession of Faith and Covenant." Sixty members, adhering to the Confession and Covenant of 1758, withdrew, and set up separte worship, claiming to be the "First Strict Congregational Church of Riverhead." In 1831, they erected a church edifice, 32 by 42 feet, which was located about a mile south west of the former, and within 2 miles of the Court House. From the time of their separation to 1834, they were supplied successively by the Rev. Christopher Youngs, Mr. Fuller, the Rev. Nehemiah B. Cook, and the Rev. Mr. Moser, the last two being connected with the L.I. Presbytery. In the fall of 1831, the church was favoured with a refreshing season, and more than 20 were added to its communion.

In 1834, under the conviction, that the interests of religion required some special exertions to rear a church at Riverhead, this society agreed to divide, and form two congregations—the one at Northville, and the other at the village of Riverhead. The church was removed to Northville, that portion of the congregation paying a stipulated sum to the other, for the purpose of erecting a house of worship near the Court House.

In the winter of 1834-5, the Northville church was supplied by the Rev. Jonathan Huntting, and from 1835 to '39, by the Rev. Abraham Luce, both of whom were members of the Presbytery.

The Rev. William Hodge supplied them from 1839 to 1841. He united with the L.I. Convention in April, 1840, having previously been a baptist minister. He died Jan. 17th 1843. Mr. James Smith, a Presbyterian licentiate succeeded Mr. Hedge until the spring of 1845.

This congregation is small, consisting of about 40 families, and the church numbers 130 communicants. It is strictly independent, having no connection with Presbytery, Assocation or Convention.

Bating-Hollow [sic] is a small parish about 6 miles west of Northville on the same north road. The settlement was commenced as early as 1719, but no house of worship was erected till 1803. At that time, a building, 26 by 30 feet, was reared.

A church, consisting of 7 or 8 members was organised here in 1792, under the style of the "Third Strict Congregational Church of Riverhead." In Aug. 1793, the L.I. Convention ordained the Rev. Manley Wells pastor, who died May 8th, 1802, in the 55th year of age. The Rev. Nathan Dickinson succeeded, but at what date and how long he remained is not ascertained. In Aug. 1820 the Rev. David Benjamin was ordained here, by the Convention, and is still living. This parish is small, including only about 30 families.

In 1813 or '14, a member of this church by the name of Horton, imbibed the doctrines of Emmanuel Swedenborg; and in 1815, set up a separte place of worship. In 1831, a New Jerusalem Church was organized, consisting of 13 members. In 1839 a house of worship, 24 by 36 feet, was erected; but until quite recently Mr. Horton has been the principal conductor of their services. Since Nov. 1844, the Rev. M.M. Carll has been employed here, a part of the time. From 15 to 20 families attend, and the present number of members is 24.

Wading River is situated at the northwest corner of the town of Riverhead, directly on the line, so that about one half of the settlement is within the limits of Brookhaven. The church is only a few yards east of the line.

It is not known definitely, at what time the first house of worship was erected; but it is supposed to have been about the middle of the last century. About that time, at the request of the people, the Presbytery of Suffolk repeatedly appointed supplies at this place, and it is confidently asserted, by some, that the first church organised here, was Presbyterian.

The first building was nearly square, being 26 by 28 feet. It stood till 1837, when a new and very neat edifice 33 by 42 feet, was erected, with a steeple and bell.

The parish consists of about 60 families, and what is remarkable, they are all, without exception, of one denomination.

A church of 8 or 9 members was organised here, in 1785, by the Rev. Daniel Youngs, with the style of the "Second Strict Cong. Church of Riverhead," and its delegate was present and took part in the formation of the L.I. Convention in 1791.

The Rev. Jacob Corwin, who had preached here a number of years, was ordained as their pastor, by the Convention, in Nov. 1787. He was dismissed in 1800, and died Sept. 20th, 1833, in the 88th year of his age.

He was succeeded by his nephew, the Rev. David Wells. He had been licensed by the Convention in 1802, and was ordained at this place, in 1809. He died Sept. 12th, 1821, in his 46th year.

"After the death of Mr. Wells, the church were only occasionally supplied with preaching from the ministers of the L.I. Convention, until Nov. 11th, 1831, when the Rev. Parshall Terry was employed for one half the time, or every other sabbath. Mr. Terry closed his labours with them, May 1832, and was succeeded by the Rev. Elizur W. Griswold, 1832, a member of the convention, who continued his labours for one half of the time, until May 1834." Mr. Griswold had been received by the Convention from the "Methodist Society," and afterwards united with the "Protestant Methodists."

The Rev. Christopher Youngs commenced labouring here in the spring of 1835, and continued till 1841.

The Rev. John H. Thomas, supplied this people for 18 months, from 1842.

Since his removal they have had only occasional supplies for a few months, and are at present entirely vacant. They have had no settled pastor since the death of Mr. Wells in 1821.

In the early settlement of this place, through the benevolence of some individuals, though the history of the transaction appears to be well nigh lost, this congregation became possessed of a large tract of land, which it is said, would now be worth $20,000. In former days, however, it was considered of small value, and was therefore disposed of with little discretion, till it is now reduced to the value of about $3,000. It may be a matter of surprise that a congregation thus endowed, and united in their religious views, should be willing to live with such an irregular supply of the means of grace.

Summary. In this town, there are 10 distinct religious organizations, and as many houses of worship, viz., 1 Presbyterian, 5 Congregational or Independent, 2 Methodist, and 2 Swedenborgians.

The territory included in this town, being formerly a part of Southold was a principal seat of those churches, which were organised in affinity with the Separate Churches of New-England. Both there and here, they remained for many years, in a strictly independent form. But, in process of time, those churches in Connecticut, with their ministers, formed an ecclesiastical organization under the style of the "Strict Congregational Convention of Connecticut"; and in 1781, they published a "Confession of Faith and Form of Government," which was republished on Long Island in 1823. In connexion with this, they gave a "brief history of their separtion from the Standing Order," and an account of the organization of their first church, and the ordination of its first minister. In the same pamphlet they set forth the reasons of their separation, and "some of the errors that attended" that event.

On the 26th of August, 1791, a similar organization was formed at Upper Aquebogue, in this town, under the style of "The Strict Congregational Convention of Long Island." The original members were the Rev. Messrs. Daniel Youngs—Jacob Corwin and Noah Hallock, (all of whom had been ordained by the Connecticut Convention;) with delegates from the churches of Aquebogue and Wading River. This body has received or ordained between 20 and 30 ministers, and have formed a number of additional churches, in various towns in Suffolk County, and in the northern parts of the state of New Jersey. The Connecticut Convention, it is believed, has been extinct for many years, as the L.I. Convention was called upon, in 1817, to ordain a pastor for the church at Lyme, Ct., who held his connexion with this body, till his death. This Convention has continued its existence till the present year, though at the time of the organization of the L.I. Association, it was reduced to a single ministerial member.

These churches have always been the friends of evangelical religion, and have been favoured with many interesting and powerful revivals of religion.

Asperities of feeling, naturally engendered by circumstances that have been hinted at, kept these ministers and churches and those of the Presbyterian order, aloof from each other for a considerable length of time. But contiguity of situation and occasional intercourse in the social and religious relations of life, gradually allayed these feelings, and ultimately led to the suggestion of something like an interchange of ministerial labour. Accordingly April 10th, 1793, the Presbytery of Long Island "approved of those ministers being invited to preach occasionally, by any of the ministers of their body who should think it expedient." Two ministers and their elders, from the western part of the island, protested against this vote.

In the review of this record in 1794, the Synod of New-York, in their vote of approval, made an exception to "the determination of that Presbytery to invite certain gentlemen to preach in their pulpits, with respect to whom there was no evidence that they had been introduced into the ministry, in such a way as ought to be approved." And "the Synod recommended to the Presbytery of Long Island to reconsider their detemrination on this subject." In the following year, the Presbytery reported, that "they had proceeded according to the recommendtion of the Synod, to reconsider their resolutions, as to the admission of certain men occasionally to preach in their pulpits; and having spent some time in deliberating upon it, could not find sufficient reason to reverse their judgment upon this subject, at present."

This interchange of ministerial labour was kept up, with mutual satisfaction, for a number of years; till in 1807, it was interrupted, by the reception into the Convention, of a member of the Presbytery, who had fled from discipline; but in 1812, suitable satisfaction having been given, harmony was restored, and has remained uninterrupted to the present time.

It may be added that the Long Island Convention, at its meeting in April last was, by consent of the members, dissolved, and each left to seek such ecclesiastical connexion as he might choose. At that time, it consisted of six ministers and four churches.

CHAPTER IV

EXCERPT FROM GAZETTEER OF THE STATE OF NEW YORK EMBRACING A COMPREHENSIVE VIEW OF THE GEOGRAPHY, GEOLOGY, AND GENERAL HISTORY OF THE STATE, AND A COMPLETE HISTORY AND DESCRIPTION OF EVERY COUNTY, CITY, TOWN, VILLAGE AND LOCALITY

Written by J.H. French in 1860

Born in 1824, John Homer French oversaw the publication in 1860 of "The Gazetteer of the State of New York". This was a monumental work which included publishing surveys of every county as well as collecting the information as contained in "The Gazetteer". Mr. French served as General Superintendent for this privately funded effort. In the preface to "The Gazetteer", he points out "the time spent in surveys, collection of materials, writing, engraving, proof-reading, etc. has been equaled to the time of one person 125 years. It is believed that no similar enterprise of equal extent and involving the outlay of so large a capital has ever been undertaken at private expense in this or any other country." In the "Dictionary of North American Authors", John French is described as an "educationist". He had an L.L.D. degree in law, he was a member of the American Association for the Advancement of Science, and a member of the New York Historical Society. He died in 1888.

RIVERHEAD—was formed from Southold, March 13, 1792. It lies upon the s. side of the island, between Brookhaven and Southold, and has 16-1/2 mi. of coast upon Long Island Sound. Peconic River and Great Peconic Bay form the s. boundary, and Wading River[iv] a part of the w. The surface in the s. part is level, but in the N. it is hilly. The shore is lined with high and precipitous bluffs of clay and hardpan. The soil is light and sandy, and in most parts but moderately fertile. The poor-house is located on a farm of 45 acres. RIVERHEAD, (p.v.,) an important station on the L.I.R.R., is situated on Peconic River at the head of boat navigation. It is the county seat, and contains the co. buildings, 3 churches, a seminary,[v] and several manufactories.[vi] Pop. 813,—723 in Riverhead and 90 in Southampton. From Riverhead E. to the line of Southold, a distance of about 6 mi. upon the "South Road," is a continuous settlement, which has received at different places the names Upper Aquebogue, (p.o.,) Old Aquebogue, (Jamesport p.o.,) and Franklinville, (West Suffolk p.o.) Old Aquebogue and Franklinville are stations on the L.I.R.R. Jamesport[vii] is situated about one-half mi. s. of Old Aquebogue, on Great Peconic Bay, and contains 1 church; pop. 148. Northville, (Success p.o.,) in the N.E. part, contains 1 church and 35 houses; Baiting Hollow, (p.o.,) in the N. part, in a scattered settlement, has 2 churches; and Wading River, (p.v.,) on stream of same name, 1 church and 25 houses. Settlement began at Riverhead, in 1690, by John Griffing and others. There are 10 churches in town.[viii]

CHAPTER V

HISTORY OF THE TOWN OF RIVERHEAD, SUFFOLK COUNTY, N.Y.

Written by Hon. George Miller in 1876

George Miller was born at Miller's Place on March 16, 1799 and, as a child, attended Clinton Academy in East Hampton. He established a law practice in 1825 in Riverhead where he resided for 57 years. In 1836, he married Eliza Leonard of Massachusetts who, for many years, was a teacher in the Riverhead Academy, which her husband had founded. He served as Suffolk County Surrogate in the 1840's, represented Suffolk County in the New York State Assembly in 1854, and was county judge in 1857, but subsequently resigned to serve as County District Attorney. He died in 1883 at the age of 84 years.

THE Town of Riverhead embraces all that part of the Town of Southold, as constituted by statute, bounded northerly by the Sound, easterly by the east line of the Albertson farm, so called, extending from the Sound to the bay, and chiefly belonging to the late Israel Fanning; southerly by Peconic Bay and Peconic River, and westerly by the town of Brookhaven. The original east line of that town extended from a pepperidge tree standing "at the head of a small brook that runneth into the creek called Panquacunsuck," (which is Wading River creek,) north to the Sound and south to the ocean. That tree stood nearly opposite the house late of Gabriel Mills, deceased, now of Robert H. Corbett, and has ever been regarded as the bound between the towns. The territory west of the said north line and east of the Wading River creek belonged to Brookhaven, but that town ceded it to Riverhead, on condition that the latter town should support a pauper that lived there.

The patent of the town of Southold was bounded on the south line by a line running from the head of Red Creek to the head of the said brook at Wading River. It crosses Peconic River at Riverhead in the neighborhood of the present waste gate, and from thence westward. It has always been a known line, and a landmark between the divisions of land lying north and south of it.

The land on the south was granted by the Colonial Governor to Chief Justice Smith by a patent bounded on the west by the Brookhaven line; on the northeast by this Manor line to Red Creek; thence southeasterly by a line extending from Red Creek to the head of Seatuck. It is believed that the portion of this patent lying between the Manor line and Peconic River was joined to the town of Southold by the earliest legislative division of the towns, and that people of Southold purchased of Judge Smith the land north of Peconic River and allotted it.

There is nothing in the records of the town of Southold to show that the proprietors under the patent of that town ever made a recorded allotment of their lands now within the town of Riverhead. But most of the proprietors took the land severally allotted to them without entering the same on record.

It appears that in 1659 the proprietors granted to John Tooker and Joshua Horton the privilege of building a saw mill on Peconic River, with a little land. Tooker in 1711 conveyed 400 acres of land to John Parker, bounded east by Parker's land, south of Peconic River, west by widow Cooper's land, and north by the Sound. Parker owned the land on the south side of the river.

In 1726, by deed of gift, John Parker conveyed to Joseph Wickham and Abigail Wickham, his daughter, all his land north of Peconic River, to the said Joseph for life and then to his daughter and her heirs. Her husband died in 1749. His widow died in 1780, and her oldest son, Parker, inherited her estate, which was confiscated after the war and purchased by Gen. Floyd, who sold the property to Mr. Jagger.

In 1753 Thomas Fanning sold the hotel property, 130 acres, with the dam as far as the saw mill, to John Griffing, for £1,000. In 1775 John Griffing conveyed his land south of the highway, with the grist mill and his part of the stream, to Nathaniel Griffing, his son, for £500. John Griffing was a patriotic Whig and went to Connecticut with his family when the war came on, and died there in 1780, intestate, and all his estate descended to his eldest son, John, who occupied the property until he sold it to Benjamin Brewster about the beginning of the century. He, within ten years, conveyed it to Bartlett Griffing, the youngest son of John Griffing the elder, and he within a year conveyed it to his brother, William Griffing, in whose family it ever after remained until it was conveyed to John P. Terry, the present proprietor, in 1864. The main building of this hotel was erected by the Messrs. Griffing in 1844.

The village of Riverhead for nearly 30 years after the Revolution remained stationary, with but four houses, viz: The Griffing Hotel, Joseph Osborn's house, on Terry & Wells' corner, David Jagger's house, and the mill house, built by William Albertson, the owner of the grist mill. David Horton lived in the Court house and kept the jail. Stephen Griffing occupied the place late of Dr. Thomas Osborn.

In 1815 Nathaniel Griffing, Jr., built the house now occupied by Mr. Miller, on premises his father had purchased 40 years before. The same year Hubbard and Wells Griffing built the sloop McDonough, the first vessel built in Riverhead after the war. They ran her until 1825 and then sold her and built the sloop Pacific. Afterwards Capt. James Horton bought the McDonough, rebuilt her and ran her many years and sold her. She is now in Connecticut and was seen in New York last summer in quite good condition.

Benjamin Brewster bought the grist mill of William Albertson and ran it some years after the war of 1812. During this time it was burnt. Mr. Brewster got his insurance and rebuilt the mill, setting it on an elbow of the dam, which he carried a considerable distance northeast from the former site. When he sold his hotel, about 1808, he built the house late of Hubbard Griffing, deceased, which he occupied until he sold the mill to Ezra Hallock. In 1824 the grist mill was overhauled, and greatly improved with new water wheels. In that summer the water was drawn off the mill pond, causing, as was supposed, considerable sickness and some deaths.

In 1825 the village had considerably advanced and increased. Moses C. Cleveland had set up a shoe shop, and Jedediah Conklin a blacksmith's shop, both of whom were active business men. There were three stores, kept by Elijah Terry, William Jagger and William Griffing, Jr. Since then business and population have greatly increased. There are now some 20 stores, three drug shops, four dentists, four butcher's shops, five physicians, six lawyers, five churches and a large Union School.

The Long Island House still occupies a part of the original hotel owned by the Griffings 128 years ago, and owned by some of the family nearly ever since until it was purchased by John P. Terry, the present landlord.

Henry L. Griffing owns a large hotel near the railroad, or part of the Griffing farm, built in 1862.

The Suffolk Hotel, kept by John Corwin, was built on a part of the same property in the year 1825, first as a dwelling, afterwards greatly enlarged, and kept as a hotel since 1834.

The large brick store on Bridge street was built in 1854 by David F. Vail. John Downs built his brick block on the corner of Main street and Griffing ave. in 1871-2. The Messrs. Hill built their three story double brick store on Main street in 1874.

Dr. Thomas Osborn was the first physician in the village and the only one for thirty years. He commenced practice very early in this century and died in 1849. Dr. Joseph Doane practiced in this village 12 years and died in 1847. Dr. _____ Conklin was the first physician in the town. He lived and practiced at Lower Aquebogue.

Riverhead has two Engine Companies. The first, Red Bird, was organized in 1833. It has now two hand engines and 40 members; Gilbert H. Ketcham foreman. The second, Washington, was organized in 1862. It has one hand engine, and a new steamer purchased in 1875; members 36; Oliver A. Terry foreman.

The Riverhead Savings Bank was organized in 1872—Richard H. Benjamin then and still President, with twenty Trustees whose services are gratuitous. It has averaged more than one new depositor for every day since, has paid $113,000 to its depositors, and has now invested over $200,000. Its influence has been very beneficent.

An early individual enterprise was performed by the late Isaac Swezey, Sr., by which in 1848 he dug a canal over 80 rods long and moved his grist mill from the dam on Little River to the village at the verge of the Great River.

Charles Hallett has contributed much to the growth and material prosperity of the village. In 1856 he started a planing mill, using to some extent both steam and water power, which finally passed into other hands. In 1866 he built a steam planing mill on the north side of the river, which did a large business— the first year to the amount of $22,000, and in the years 1873 and 1874 the business amounted to $125,000 a year, and his pay roll was $32,000 in 1873 and $34,000 in 1874. He has now rented out the steam mill, which is run by Weeks & Millard, we believe prosperously for the times.

In 1870 Mr. Hallett started a paper mill for making board paper of straw. In 1872 he started a flouring mill, which he has now fitted for making flour by the new process, and is running the mill with much success, commanding patronage, by the railroad, from Queens county. His paper mill has been much improved by new inventions, adapted to the pressure of the times, so as to make a very superior board that can be sold at a profit.

The village of Riverhead has received great benefit from the improvement of the channel of the river. Congress has made three appropriations, amounting in the aggregate to $25,000, and the State has appropriated $5,000, all of which has been carefully expended in deepening the channel with a steam excavator. The result has been not only very favorable to navigation, but it has caused the water to run off at low tide nearly a foot lower, while it very unexpectedly prevents as high a rise of water as formerly with an east wind, rendering great advantages to the mill stream and making the adjoining lots and gardens, cellars and wharves more comfortable and valuable. Further appropriations are necessary to make the work more complete. It is believed that $20,000 would effect all that could be desired.

At the close of the Revolution agriculture was at a low ebb as well as business of every other kind. The cultivated lands had been worked down and become poor, and the people were without fertilizers. Manuring with fish was then unknown and the people of this branch of the Island went to Coram and Middle Island with their horse carts to buy rye to live on. People were deeply in debt according to their means to payment. As an illustration of this, it appears from the records that more than 100 writs were returnable to the Court of Common Pleas of this county during the first year after the war. Before or soon after the beginning of this century bunker fishing for manure was begun by the farmers. This soon improved their circumstances, enabled them to raise good crops, and produce manure from other sources so as to make their land permanently good, and the condition of the people very much improved. Buying fertilizers from abroad was not then practiced. Judge John Woodhull was the first man in the town to buy ashes for manure, and it enabled him to make hay superior to that of his neighbors. Fifty years ago he owned the only steel spring carriage in the town, and about that time it was thought quite an improvement for the hotel at Riverhead to have a sulky with wooden springs and thorough-braces.

The Long Island Railroad commenced running the last day of July, 1844. The passenger train run three times a week and so continued through the ensuing winter and probably longer. Fifty years ago we had the mail at Riverhead once a week by a one horse wagon, and if we went to New York by stage we must cross over to Quogue and reach the city by the mail stage towards night of the second day. After a few years we came to have a mail stage through on the middle country road. Passengers would start from Riverhead at noon, stay at Thomas

Hallock's at the Branch the first night, and arrive at Brooklyn towards evening the next day. After some years we came to have two mails a week, but the change is very great now. We have the mail to and from New York twice a day, and three trains a day in the summer.

No part of the town of Riverhead has increased so much and so rapidly in agricultural wealth as Northville. That village and the whole extent of the north road to Wading River, prove that the early historians of the town misconceived the character of a large part of the lands in the town not then brought under cultivation. They are in fact valuable for that purpose and have been much improved within a few years.

Wading River more than 50 years ago had a good deal of enterprise in the coasting business, and built some valuable vessels for that trade and launched them into the Sound. The railroad, which has done so much for the prosperity of other parts of the town, has rather tended to retard the growth of this place.

The village of Jamesport has come into being within the last half of our Centennial period. It is built on Miamogue Point. The wharf was built in 1833 and the hotel in 1836. It has grown to be a considerable village and is very pleasantly situated for a summer resort enjoying great advantages for the navigation of the bay.

At about 1797 Jeremiah Petty built a Forge for making bar iron, on Peconic River at the Forge Pond, where he did business until his death, after which, in 1799, the property was purchased by Solomon Townsend of New York, who did business there for a while, and after his death and in 1818 the property was sold by his administrators to Bartholomew Collins, since which time but little business has been done with the large water power of the mill pond except as a reservoir for the mills below, and since 1870 the water has been drawn off during the summer for the purpose of cultivating cranberries on the bed of the pond. The same use is now being made of the pond above on the same stream by draining it and yet using the water of the river above by means of a canal.

The Upper Mills, so called, one mile above Riverhead village, on Peconic river, was the site of a grist mill, fulling mill and saw mill, all owned by Richard Albertson, the father and then the son, and built late in the past century.

In 1828 John Perkins became a proprietor in the water power and established a woollen factory, which has been continued ever since. It was ever regarded as very valuable to the people on both sides of the Island, and facilitates the transition from spinning and weaving cloth at home to carrying wool to the factory and taking manufactured cloth in return. The factory was run during the life of Mr. Perkins, who died in

1866, and since his death by his sons, who are merchants in Riverhead. The present woollen factory was built by Mr. Perkins in 1845.

LAW.

The first Court-house was built in Riverhead in 1728. The Court was first held on the last Tuesday in September, 1728.

An order was entered that all process should be returnable at the County Hall, and that is what it was called. Before that the Courts appear to have been held alternately in the towns of Southold and Southampton. The first term of the Common Pleas was held after the war on the last Tuesday of March, 1784. Ezra L'Hommedieu and Abraham Skinner were both then admitted to practice as attorneys and there appears on the records no other lawyer. Mr. L'Hommedieu was Clerk of the County, which office he held 26 years, during which time he was for one term a Member of Congress and many years a State Senator, besides having a very large practice as attorney, having over 80 writs returnable in the Common Pleas in one year.

Daniel Osborn, the father of the late Hull Osborn and of Dr. Thomas Osborn, was a member of the bar and a Member of Assembly in 1787; he died in 1801. Hull Osborn was a practicing lawyer in Riverhead for many years until 1817, and was for one year Clerk of the county in 1810. He died in 1834, very highly respected as a man and a lawyer.

The other practicing lawyers in early times were George Smith of Smithtown—he moved to Connecticut—Jos Strong of Orange county, who moved into this county and practiced law a number of years, and Silas Wood of Huntington. Eliphalet Wicks of Jamaica, a man of high standing, practiced law in the county many years. These are all the members of the bar who had ceased to practice in the county before 1825. The following are the lawyers that were practicing in Suffolk county when the writer came to the bar in 1825; Abraham Skinner, Chas. A. Floyd, Selah B. Strong, William P. Buffett, Abraham T. Rose, Hugh Halsey and Daniel Robert. All these, together with every officer who then attended Court, have passed away except Mr. Robert, who is still living in New Utrecht. His office was in New York, but he attended all our courts and was one of the reading advocates until 1831.

The first Judges were Selah Strong, the elder, Abraham Woodhull, Thomas S. Strong, Joshua Smith, Jonathan Conklin, Hugh Halsey, William P. Buffett, J. Lawrence Smith, George Miller, Henry P. Hedges and John R. Reid. The last four are still living.

The following persons have been Members of Assembly from this town: Capt. John Wells, Usher H. Moore, who was also a member of the Constitutional Convention in 1821; Capt. Noah Youngs, John Terry, David Warner, George Howell, John C. Davis, James H. Tuthill, John S. Marcy and Nathan D. Petty. The three last have been members for two sessions each.

The first Clerk's office was built in 1846. The new Court-house was built in 1856. In 1875 the first Clerk's office was sold and a new building erected for Clerk's and Surrogate's offices.

RELIGION.

At the time of the Revolution it is believed that the only places of worship in the town were at Lower Aquebogue, Upper Aquebogue and Wading River, the first Presbyterian and the other two Congregational. At Baiting Hollow a Congregational house of worship was erected in 1802 and built anew about 1839. In 1815 separate worship was set up by Swedenborgians and in 1839 a house of worship was erected by them. In Wading River the first house was built about 1750 and a new house was erected in 1837. In Lower Aquebogue the first house was built in 1734; it was repaired in 1830 and rebuilt in 1859. The church some years ago became Congregational. At Upper Aquebogue a house of worship was erected in the fore part of the last century. In 1797 a new church was built. In 1834 it was remodeled and rebuilt. A new church edifice was built in 1862. This society became in a measure the mother of two other congregations. There was a separation of the congregation in 1829 and the seceders built a house two miles east of Riverhead. In 1834 this new congregation harmoniously divided, and one portion took the meeting-house and moved it to Northville; the other portion removed to Riverhead, receiving compensation for their interest in the building, and worshiped in the lower room of the Seminary building until 1841, when the present Congregational Church was built, which was enlarged in the year 1868.

The Methodist Society in Riverhead was organized in 1833 and their first meeting-house was built in 1834. Their present noble edifice was built in 1870.

The Swedenborgian Society was organized in 1839. Their house of worship was built in 1855. Before the erection of their church they occupied a comfortable room as a place of worship, which was also used as a school room.

The Episcopalians commenced stated worship in Riverhead in 1870, and in 1873 they erected a neat chapel.

The Free Methodists erected a meeting house in 1872.

The Roman Catholic Society held services for several years in the old Court-house and in a house on East street. In 1870 their present handsome church and parsonage were erected.

At Jamesport a building was erected in 1839 and has been occupied as a place of worship for the Methodist Society since and sometimes as a school house.

The village of Riverhead was in 1825 and always had been a part of the Congregational Society of Upper Aquebogue. Mr. Swezey, the minister, stately preached in the Court house every other Sunday at 5 o'-clock, or in the evening. The Methodist circuit rider stately preached in the Court house every other Friday afternoon or evening, and was entertained at Dr. Osborn's. In March, 1827, a stated weekly prayer meeting was established and ever after maintained. In June following a Sunday School with nearly 100 scholars was established in the Court-house and kept up, except that it was not held in the winter.

In 1828 or 1829 meetings were held and a sermon read in the Court-house at 11 o'clock on the Sabbath and kept up for several years. At some time afterwards meetings were held stately in the Court-house on Sunday evening, at which the Congregational and Methodist ministers preached alternately. So the two societies grew up together as the population increased. We thought then and we think still that there was much more moral and religious influence for good exercised than if only one denomination had occupied the whole ground.

EDUCATION.

There have been great advances in the cause of education since the Revolution. During that war the Island was in possession of the British, and the people were great sufferers from their troops and from marauders (plunderers they used to be called), who came from New England, so that the opportunities for schools were small; and then came up a generation during the war whose education was very limited, and no considerable public provision was made for education until long after the war. In the early part of this century there were two schools taught by native teachers that were very commendable for those times, and many young men received an education there which well fitted them for active life. We allude to the schools kept at Upper and Lower Aquebogue, the former by Josiah Reeve, afterwards Sheriff of the county, and the latter by Judge David Warner. No special efforts for extra education were made until the Franklinville Academy was erected in the year 1832. That soon became a prosperous and efficient institution and many young men were educated there. It continued to flourish for many years and constituted a new era in education in this part of the county and drew many pupils from other towns.

The standard of female education on this branch of the Island was very low up to this time. Indeed it had been so throughout most parts of the county. When Dr. Beecher preached at East Hampton his wife taught quite a class of female scholars from different parts of the county. The influence of those scholars told very favorably upon the communities where they were afterwards located. With that exception we know of no schools in the county for the special education of females.

The opportunities of girls in the two academies of East Hampton and Huntington were in those days very secondary. Indeed academies afforded inferior opportunities for thorough education. They were generally taught by young men who had little primary education, but had devoted their efforts to the classics and mathematics sufficiently to pass through college, and during their progress to a profession taught academies and high schools, imparting chiefly such learning as they had acquired. Female education had been overlooked or neglected, and thorough primary instruction nearly as much so.

In view of this state of things Dr. Joshua Fanning and the writer undertook to organize a Female Seminary, and in the year 1834 we erected the present seminary building in the village of Riverhead. In the spring of 1835 the school was begun with good success. Its object was to give thorough instruction in all the primary branches of an English education, with Latin and Mathematics. The effect of the school was almost magical upon the community. The ideas of people in regard to female education were raised more than one hundred per cent. in a short time, and the difference in the estimate of people in regard to thorough primary education soon became great and told upon the academies of the county, and the examination day at the close of the terms were for years among the proudest days of Riverhead.*

At the beginning it was supposed that young ladies must be educated in exclusive schools, but this was after a while found to be a mistake with us, and it is now generally conceded that schools of both sexes can be best governed and instructed.

This seminary and nearly all other schools in Riverhead have been superseded by the Union School, established in 1871, which has been a great success. A school of this kind acts under the sanction of the law and is amenable to the judgment and good sense of the whole com-

---

* When this was read at our Centennial our neighbors were not entirely satisfied, and requested that it should appear that Miss Leonard of Massachusetts taught the Seminary in its first years, and afterwards as Mrs. Miller taught it at different times, in all twenty-one years.

munity, and has advantages of discipline and good government which can never be enjoyed by a private school.

HEALTH.

Riverhead is believed to be remarkable for the healthfulness of its climate. There have been no prevailing climatic diseases in the village in 52 years. The make of the earth is such that there can be no stagnant water above or below ground, and water for use is drawn from pure white sand, which makes it perfect in quality, while it is as cool as persons in poor health should desire. Summer diseases, which at times prevail in almost every village, have never been prevalent here.

At the south of Riverhead there is a pitch pine barren seven miles in extent, over which the ocean breezes pass, often loaded at the start with fog and dampness, which are absorbed by the dry country over which they pass. Fogs are very common on the south side but rare at Riverhead. In the spring the aroma from the pine growth is often perceived in the southerly breeze by strangers. This dry pine country is probably little inferior to the pine barrens at the South, which are often sought by invalids. It undoubtedly has a favorable effect upon the health of the village. The same causes, we think, render Jamesport equal if not superior to any watering place on the north side of Peconic Bay.

It is easy to chronicle events but not always so easy to relate with accuracy the moral state of a people or community as it bears on past and present times. The state of things now and fifty years ago in regard to morals and good government is vastly different and the question is have we advanced? Are there proportionally more happy families, and more children trained to knowledge, virtue and industry? The truth is, that if we would have advancement in the right direction we must go still further and higher. There must be great reforms in every department of the government, and the people must hold their servants to a responsibility not thought of heretofore.

There can be no doubt that there have been great changes in some of the moral and social relations of the people. In regard to intemperance the change is great. In 1828 the liquor drank in the town was five times as much as it was two years afterwards. The first temperance meeting in Riverhead was held late in January 1829, when 17 signed the pledge. At the next meeting a fortnight later the signers were doubled and the consumption of liquor was undoubtedly lessened one half in three months. Before that liquor was almost everywhere. Every merchant and man of business kept his own bottle. On every public occasion drunkards abounded. But as soon as the principles of total abstinence was adopted a change came over the community. At the very next town meeting the people all went home before night sober. At the next launching of Capt. Henry Horton's vessel no liquor was used. Fishermen abandoned it; merchants who sold other goods quit the sale of it. The people soon saw clearly, what fifty years has proved to be true, that even the moderate use of liquor is not necessary but hurtful, and that sound morals and good government require that its habitual use should be abandoned. It would be hard to estimate the amount of temporal blessings this great reformation in principle and practice has caused to households and individuals.

O if some of our temperance friends would only get the foolish crotchet out of their heads that no man is fit for any office if he will not at once vote for total prohibition, we might soon prove by the laws we have whether we are in a condition to have laws more efficient than the Local Option Act. If they would join in one party or the other the great body of honest voters of the State in the present struggle to elevate the standard of official duty and purify the politics of the country, they will find themselves standing on a much firmer basis for further assistance from the laws. Let us be sure, if possible, that men are honest and capable whom we support for office, but never let us reject such because they are not for prohibition where such a law is not in question.

Our advantages for education and the training of children are vastly greater than they were 40 or 50 years ago, but do we improve them as we should? Are children and boys just passing to manhood restrained as they should be? The foundation and corner stone of good government is that boys should never be suffered to run at large in the streets in the night time. Laxness in this matter is preparing children for the slaughter. Above all things, if possible, make your family a happy home for your children. In no point of view have I for 35 years looked upon the young ladies educated at our Seminary with so much interest as with the hope that they would acquire knowledge and training that would the better fit them to make their homes happy, with the more skill to control children and youth under their care. We look with great hope for the good influence of our Union school in this matter.

We could not well say less in regard to moral questions which have affected us to deeply in time past and must for time to come. We enter upon the second century of our national existence under very auspicious circumstances and in nothing to much as the feeling that has arisen among thoughtful and true men of all parties that the standard of morals in politics, and in the conducting of our National and State governments, must be greatly elevated.

CHAPTER VI

RIVERHEAD

—⟳⟳⟳—

Written by R.M. Bayles in 1882

He was born in Coram, March 23, 1846, and was descended on both his father's and mother's sides from some of the earliest settlers in Brookhaven town. Mr. Bayles was educated in the common school and at Northville Academy when that institution was under Joseph N. Hallock, who later became the owner and editor of "The Christian Work." Mr. Bayles began his career by writing a historical article for the press when a lad of about 18 years. He spent several years teaching in the schools in Coram, Eastport, Center Moriches, Manorville and Middle Island from 1877 to 1893. All of his books are large and no one but a person with a genius for history or one of Mr. Bayles' patience and love of research, would or could have attempted them. Beside compiling these works, he found time to contribute articles for newspapers and periodicals and from 1886 to 1908, he wrote the Long Island articles for the Brooklyn "Eagle Almanac".

THE town of Riverhead lies on the northern side of the county and island, occupies fifteen miles in length, from east to west, and has an average width of five miles. Peconic River and Bay separate it from Brookhaven and Southampton on the south, it is washed by the sound on the north, on the east it is bounded by Southold and on the west by Brookhaven. The surface along the north side is elevated and broken, while that along the south side is level and low. The soil of the elevated portion is strong and fertile. A continuous settlement of well-to-do farmers extends through the north side the entire length of the town. There are no harbors, therefore no favorable sites for commercial villages are afforded in this section of the town. There are, however, many delightful sites for summer residences, overlooking the sound and the distant hills of Connecticut. Though but few of these have as yet been occupied doubtless many of them will ere long be improved. Many city people have found that this section has attractions for rusticating which in some respects are superior to those of the more popular resorts of the south side. Abundant crops of grain, hay and potatoes are grown in this part of the town. The north Country road runs through it, and most of the settlement is on that road. The soil along the southern side of the town is more or less mixed with sand, though farming is successfully carried on, and forms the chief occupation of the people. Small fruits, garden vegetables and root crops are raised in the eastern part of this section, and cranberries are raised to a considerable extent in marshes which abound in the western part, about the headwaters of the Peconic River.

PURCHASES AND BOUNDARIES.

The principal part of the territory of this town was purchased of the Indians by the inhabitants of Southold and included in their patent. A purchase which included this territory, which was then called Aquabouke, was made in 1649. To confirm this and other purposes a deed was obtained from the Indians December 7th 1665, in which the boundaries including the land now occupied by the town were given as "the River called in the English toung the Weading Kreek, in the Indian toung Pauquaconsuk, on the West, * * * * * and with a River or arme of the sea wch runneth up between Southampton Land and the aforesaid tract of land unto a certain Kreek which fresh water runneth into on ye South, called in English the Red Kreek, in Indian Toyonge; together with the said Kreek and meadows belonging thereto, and running on a streight line from the head of the afore-named fresh water to the head of ye Small brook that runneth into the Kreek called Pauquaconsuk; as also all necks of lands," etc. The boundaries given in Andros's patent of 1676 are substantially the same. The straight line mentioned as running from the head of Toyonge to the head of Pauquaconsuk was afterward interpreted as the line from the head of what is now known as Red Creek, in Southampton, to the head of Wading River Creek, a point but little more than a mile inland from the sound at Wading River. This line, running in a northwesterly and southeasterly direction, across what is now the southwest part of the town of Riverhead, afterward became the northeastern boundary of Colonel Smith's "St. George's manor," and it is still known in real estte descriptions as the "manor line." That part of the territory (by this boundary line given to Southold) which lay on the south of Peconic River and west of Red Creek was also claimed by the inhabitants of Southampton. After considerable litigation, in which the rights of the Indians of whom either party respectively claimed to have purchased it were diligently investigated, this controversy was finally settled by a mutual agreement made March 11th 1667, by which the land was acknowledged as within the limits of the town of Southampton, though reserves were made to individual inhabitants of Southold.

The line which separated Southold from Smith's patentship crossed Peconic River in the vicinity of Bridge street in the present village of Riverhead. At what time the present shape and dimensions were given to the western part of Southold is not definitely known. That part of it which lay southwest of the "manor line" was purchased of Colonel William Smith by the inhabitants of Southold. This was surveyed and divided among the individual owners March 10th 1742, by a commission composed of William Nicoll, Robert Hempstead, Joseph Wickham, Daniel Wells and Elijah Hutchinson. This tract was of course triangular in shape, the west end being several miles in width while the east end came to a point. The allotment was made by running lines north and south across the tract. The names of the owners of these shares (which varied in size) in their order from west to east were as follows: Caleb Horton, David Corey, Thomas Reeve, Richard Terry, Samuel Conklin, John Salmon, William Benjamin, David Horton, James Horton, James Reeve, Elijah Hutchinson, John Goldsmith, Solomon Wells, John Tuthill, John Conklin, Jonathan Horton, David and Israel Parshall, Joshua Tuthill, Zebulon Hallock, Joseph Wickham, Nathaniel Youngs, Joshua Wells, William Albertson, Joshua Wells, Noah Hallock.

By reference to the map it will be seen that the head of the brook Wading River, a point which from the earliest days was recognized as the point of separation between Southold and Brookhaven, is considerably further east than the mouth of the creek. The patent line of Brookhaven ran from that point north to the sound as well as south to the ocean. The tract of land bounded on the east by this north and south line and on the west by the brook and creek was given by the trustees of Brookhaven to the town of Southold May 3d 1709, with £4 in cash, in consideration of the latter town's assuming the care of a certain indigent person by the name of John Rogers. Thus the channel of

Wading River became through its whole length the line between these towns.

The whole section lying west of the east line of the present town of Riverhead was called Aqueboke, or Aquebouk. There seem to have been at least four divisions of land made at different times within this territory, though the records of those divisions have for the most part been lost. The first and second divisions were probably in the eastern part of the present town of Riverhead. An existing record of the third division shows that it covered a small tract extending from the head of Wading River to the sound and about a quarter of a mile in width. This was divided by lines running crosswise, and the width of the several owners' lots, in rods, was as follows, beginning at the head of the brook: Minister's lot 14, Mrs. Mary Mapes 25, Thomas Osman 14, Mr. Moore 7, widow Cooper 7, Christopher Young sen. 7, Mr. Hobart 14, Barnabas Horton 14, Theophilus Corwin 7, widow Hutchinson 7, John Swazey 28, John Conkling 21, Mr. Arnold 7, Josiah Barthol 7, Richard Clarke 7, John Young sen. 21, William Halliock 14, Mr. Budd 21, Thomas Tosteen 14, Daniel Terry 7, Stephen Bayley 7, Mr. Tooker 7, Benjamin Youngs 12, Samuel Glover 12, Mr. Edes 12, Richard Brown 12, John Harrod "to the clift." A fourth division is also spoken of, the lots in which extended from the "manor line" north to the sound. The division mentioned in the following memorandum may have been the same:

> "Southold April th 10 1733, the 50 Acres Lotts att the Waideing River was surveyed and bounded on the south End by the Mannor Line, By Jonathan Horton, John Pain, John Tuthill and Benjamin Emmons, and computed att 28 pole In wedth, and the Great Lotts upon of Mannor Loin are Said to be 76 pole wide. A true copie.
>
> "RT. HEMPSTEAD, TOWN CLERK."
>
> "April 2 1771."

SETTLEMENT AND ORGANIZATION.

Up to the time of the Revolution but few settlements had been made within the present limits of this town, and these were small. The settlements at Aquebogue were made in the early part of the last century. They were probably begun even at an earlier date. The settlement at Wading River was made about the same time. As early as 1737 the militia met at Aquebogue for drill, under the command of Captain Israel Parshall. A company of men residing at Wading River had been in the habit of joining in the training exercises at Aquebogue, but, considering the fatiguing distance they had to travel to get there, a special arrangement was made by which they remained at home, and were drilled in the military art and inspected according to law by Captain John Pain, under the direction of Colonel Henry Smith, who had command of the Suffolk militia.

The town of Riverhead was created by an act of the Legislature passed March 13th 1792, of which the following is the text:

"Whereas many of the freeholders and inhabitants of Southold, in Suffolk county, have represented to the Legislature that their town is so long that it is very inconvenient for them to attend at town meetings, and also to transact the other necessary business of the said town, and have prayed that the same may be divided into two towns; therefore,

"I. Be it enacted by the people of the State of New York, represented in Senate and Assembly, that all that part of the said town of Southold lying to the westward of a line beginning at the sound and running thence southerly to the bay separating the towns of Southampton and Southold, and which is the eastern boundary or side of a farm now in the tenure or occupation of William Albertson and is the reputed line of division between the parishes of Ocquebogue and Mattetuck, shall, from and after the first Monday in April next, be erected into a distinct and separte town, by the name of River Head; and the first town meeting of the inhabitants of the said town shall be held at the dwelling house of John Griffin, at River Head; and the said town shall enjoy all the rights, privileges and immunities which are granted to the other towns within this State by an act of the Legislature passed the 7th of March 1788, entitled 'An Act for Dividing the Counties of this State into Towns.'

"II. And be it further enacted, that the poor of the town of Southold, on the first Monday of April next, shall afterwards be divided by the town of Southold and the town of River Head, in such proportions as the supervisors of the county, at their next annual meeting, shall direct, and the contingent charges and expenses of the town of Southold that have already arisen, or shall arise before the first Monday in April next, shall be assessed, levied and paid in the same manner as if this act had not been passed."

The first town meeting of Riverhead was held at the house of Thomas Griffing, April 3d 1792. Daniel Terry was chosen moderator and David Conkling clerk. Major Benjamin Edwards and Daniel Terry jr. were chosen "to carry in the votes." The officers then elected for the town were a supervisor, a clerk, two assessors, three road commissioners, three overseers of the poor, three constables, seven overseers of highways, one collector and nine fence-viewers.

April 17th following, the poor were let out for the year to the lowest bidder at a public vendue. The following were the subjects of this dispensation of public charity, with the price per week given for the keeping of each: Mary King to John Corwin, 7s.; Abigail Terry to Ambrose Horton, 4s. 10d.; Bethiah Reeve to Henry Corwin, 2s. 9d.; a negro boy to David Osborn, 1s. 8d.; Deborah Moore to Benjamin Luce, 3s.; Richard Payne to Benjamin Luce, 1s.

EARLY ORDINANCES.

It was voted by the town in 1792 and the following year that the old acts of Southold should remain in force in the new town for those years. For several years afterward three men were elected annually to revise and establish laws for the town. At a special town meeting held May 29th 1794 laws and regulations were passed by the people. Among these it was ordered that a pound 40 feet square with fence 7 feet high should be built at Baiting Hollow, on land of John Corwin, and another of the same dimensions at Aquebogue, on land of Isaac Wells. Jeremiah Wells was engaged to build the pounds, at £5 sterling each.

At a town meeting April 7th 1795 tavern licenses were granted to Timothy Lane and Daniel Hallock at 10s. each.

Frequent regulations restricting the free range of sheep and cattle on the commons and in the highways were made. In the year 1800 the town appropriated £150 to the support of the poor.

A special town meeting held at the county hall Monday July 13th 1812, to consider the pending war with Great Britain, passed resolutions approving the belligerent measures of the government, and appointed a committee to call similar meetings thereafter if deemed advisable. This committee consisted of Josiah Reeve, Usher H. Moore, Daniel Edwards jr., Daniel Youngs jr., Abraham Luce, James Fanning and John Penney.

The plan of providing for those who were dependent upon town charity by letting them out to the bidder who would keep them for the least money was followed for many years. It evidently was not altogether satisfactory, for we find that as early as April 1st 1817 the town appointed a committee to purchase or rent a suitable place for the accommodation of the town poor. The object, however, was not accomplished at that time. When the project of a county poor-house was before the people in 1831 the town meeting (April 5th) instructed the supervisor to oppose it. In the following year the town meeting made the overseers of the poor and the supervisor a committee to purchase a poor-house and farm, and appropriated $800, to be raised the current year, toward paying for it. The house and farm were purchased during the year (at Lower Aquebogue), and at the following town meeting a committee was appointed to visit the house every month. The old house was repaired in 1862, and in November 1871, the poor having been removed to the new county-house, the property was sold.

For many years the custom prevailed in this town of letting the collection of taxes for the support of the poor to the man who would collect them for the least commission. They were frequently collected for a fee as low as three per cent., and at one time competition was so sharp that the taxes were collected for nothing.

The town meetings from nearly the first were held in the county hall or court-house in the village of Riverhead. After the new court-house was built the old one, being still used as a public hall, was continued as the place of holding town meetings. This old "stamping ground" was finally abandoned in 1872, the town meeting in 1873 being held in the new brick building of John Downs in the same village. During the years 1853-69 the custom of opening town meetings with prayer, and sometimes with Scripture reading, was observed.

ACTION IN THE CIVIL WAR.

The following paragraphs will show the action of this town during the war of 1861-65:

A special town meeting was held August 27th 1862, at which the action of the supervisor in offering a bounty of $125 to all who would enlist to the credit of this town was approved by a vote of 152 against 4.

Another special meeting was held on the 8th of the following September, at which it was voted that the town should pay to the wife or dependent parent of every volunteer $5 a month, and $1.50 a month for each child of such volunteer between the ages of two and twelve years, these payments to commence at the date of the meeting and to continue during the service of such volunteer, or during the war in case of his death before its close.

At the regular annual town meeting April 7th 1863 it was voted tht bonds to the amount of $13,100, bearing interest at five per cent., should be issued to meet the expense of bounties and family aid.

At a special meeting held February 17th 1864 the board of supervisors was requested to raise on the credit of this town such a sum of money as should be necessary to pay a bounty not exceeding $400 each for a sufficient number of men to fill the quota under the pending draft. David F. Vail, George Howell and J. Henry Perkins were appointed a committee to act with the supervisor and clerk in raising the money and securing the men. Similar resolutions were passed at another special meeting held on the 26th of the following March to provide for the call which had then been made.

June 13th 1864 a special meeting was held in anticipation of another call for men. It was voted that forty men be secured in advance, by the payment of a bounty not exceeding $400 each, and that when the expected call was made the balance of the quota should be made up. The board of supervisors was requested to authorize the raising of funds on the credit of the town, and J. Henry Perkins was appointed a committee to assist the supervisor and clerk in procuring the volunteers.

At another special meeting, August 23d 1864, the action of the supervisor and clerk in procuring substitutes for drafted men instead of volunteers was approved. It was also voted that each drafted man should pay for a substitute $125 for three years, or $60 for one year, and that the town should make up the necessary balance. A similar plan was adopted by a special meeting January 6th 1865 to provide for the quota under the call which had then been made for the final 300,000 men.

To meet the expenses incurred by this town in providing bounties and family aid, bonds were issued, and the amounts used in the reduction of this debt each year, closing with the 29th of March, were as follows: 1864, $3,000; 1865, $8,500; 1866, $6,500; 1867, $7,250; 1868, $6,500; 1869, $10,600; 1870, $6,000; 1871, $8,000; 1872, $10,000; 1873, $8,000; 1874, $6,816.49. The total amount paid for the direct expense of the war was $81,166.49.

TOWN OFFICERS.

The supervisors of this town, from its organization to the present time, have been:

Daniel Wells, 1792, 1793; Dr. David Conkling, elected at a special town meeting September 24th 1793; Josiah Reeve, 1794-1803; David Warner, 1804-10; Usher H. Moore, 1811-13, 1815; Daniel Youngs jr., 1814, 1829; Richard Skidmore, 1816; John Wells, 1817, 1818; John Woodhull, 1819, 1826-28, 1830, 1831; Luther Youngs, 1820; John Terry, 1821-25, 1834, 1835; Jonathan D. Conklin, 1832; Benjamin F. Wells, 1833; Noah Youngs, 1836-38, 1840; Herman D. Foster, 1839; Sylvester Miller, 1841-60; Daniel H. Osborn, 1861; Luther Skidmore, 1862, 1863; John C. Davis, 1864-66; Joshua L. Wells, 1867-69, 1871; Simeon S. Hawkins, 1870;

Gilbert H. Ketchum, 1872-75; Hubbard Corwin, 1876, 1877; John R. Perkins, 1878 to the present time.

During the same time the town clerks have been:

Josiah Reeve, 1792-95, 1807-10; John Woodhull, 1796-1806; John Wells, 1811-13; Elijah Terry, 1814-17, 1826, 1827; Nathaniel Griffing, 1817-22; William Griffing jr., 1823-25, 1828; George Miller, 1829-33; Henry T. Penney, 1834-40; Nathan Corwin, 1841-70; Jeremiah M. Edwards, 1871-74; Benjamin K. Payne, 1875-78; Horace H. Benjamin, 1879 to the present time.

The following persons held the office of justice of the peace during periods of longer or shorter duration between the years 1811 and 1836, inclusive: John Woodhull, Samuel Skidmore, David Warner, Daniel Edwards jr., Benjamin Edwards, James Fanning, Isaac W. Davis, Luther Youngs, David Edwards, Jonathan D. Conklin, Benjamin King, Ezra Woodhull, David Williamson and Noah Youngs. Since the latter date the following persons have held the office:

Noah Youngs, 1838-41; David Williamson, 1839-42, 1851-58; Sylvester Miller, 1840-68; Asaph Youngs, 1842-57; Jonathan D. Conklin, 1843-50; Nathan Corwin, 1845-72; Daniel Warner, 1859-62; George Buckingham, 1858-61; John R. Perkins, 1862-69, 1875-80; J. Halsey Youngs, 1863 to the present time; Benjamin K. Payne, 1870-73; Thomas Cole, 1869-75, 1880 to the present; Orville B. Ackerly, 1873, 1874; Horace H. Benjamin, 1874-744; Charles E. Wells, 1876-79; James I. Millard, 1878 to the present time; George F. Stackpole, 1881 to the present time.

The town records show that the following men were elected to the office of inspector of common schools, of which there were at first five and afterward three in the town:

David Warner, 1813-19, 1824, 1827; James Gardiner, 1813; Benjamin King, 1813-15, 1817-20, 1822, 1827, 1836, 1837; Matthias Hutchinson, 1813; Abraham Luce jr., 1813-15, 1817-19, 1821, 1833, 1834; Nathaniel Griffing jr., 1813, 1817; Moses Swezey, 1815-21; Benjamin Bailey, 1815; Zophar M. Miller, 1815-18, 1824-26; Richard Skidmore, 1816; Jonathan Horton, 1816, 1819, 1823, 1828-32; Jonathan D. Conklin, 1816; Nathaniel Warner, 1820-22, 1829, 1835; Samuel B. Nicoll, 1822; Ezekiel Aldrich, 1823, 1826; Joshua Fanning, 1824-26, 1833, 1834; Usher H. Moore jr., 1825; George Miller, 1827-32, 1841; Samuel Youngs, 1828; Eurystheus H. Wells, 1830-32; Asaph Youngs, 1833; Sidney L. Griffing, 1834-39; Elijah Wells, 1835; Elijah Terry, 1836; Jesse W. Conklin, 1837, 1838; Franklin Skidmore, 1838, 1839; Clark Wright, 1841, 1842; Joshua L. Wells, 1841-43; Herman D. Foster, 1843.

The town for many years elected annually three commissioners of common schools. They were as follows:

John Terry, 1813, 1814; Abner Reeve, 1813; Richard Skidmore, 1813-15; Thomas Youngs, 1814; David Brown, 1815; Josiah Reeve, 1815-17; Jonathan Horton, 1816-18, 1821-24, 1827, 1833-38, 1841-43; Jonathan D. Conklin, 1816-23; Zophar M. Miller, 1818, 1829, 1830, 1841; David Warner, 1819, 1826; William Penney, 1819; Isaac Swezey, 1820; Israel W. Davis, 1820; Usher H. Moore jr., 1821, 1823; Asaph Youngs, 1822, 1825, 1839, 1843; Eurystheus H. Wells, 1824, 1829, 1835; Ezekiel H. Aldrich, 1824, 1827, 1830-32, 1841; Noah Youngs, 1825; Benjamin King, 1825, 1826, 1828, 1831, 1832; George Miller, 1826, 1827; Joshua Fanning, 1827, 1830-32; Benjamin F. Wells, 1828, 1829, 1840; Samuel Youngs, 1829, 1833-40; Benjamin E. Warner, 1833; Israel Fanning, 1834, 1836; Sylvester Miller, 1837, 1838; Alden Wells, 1839, 1840; Thomas Osborn, 1842; John Griffing, 1842; James S. Skidmore, 1843.

The office of town superintendent of schools during its existence was filled by Joshua L. Wells jr., 1844-48, and James H. Tuthill, 1850-56.

VILLAGES AND NEIGHBORHOODS.

WADING RIVER.

In the extreme northwest corner of this town lies the ancient settlement of Wading River. A settlement was probably begun here by the people of Southold about the time of or soon after that made by the order of the Brookhaven town meeting in 1671. The original boundary line between the two towns was a north line from a pepperidge tree which stood at the head of the brook which was called by the Indians Pauquacunsuk, and by the English Red Creek. This tree was for a long time a recognized bound, and its site is still marked as such. It stood on the opposite side of the highway, near the residence formerly owned by Gabriel Mills and later by Robert H. Corbett. The brook below this furnishes water power for a grist-mill. The right to establish a mill here was originally granted to John Roe jr., by the town of Brookhaven, May 4th 1708. Some adjoining land accompanied the water privilege. The grant stipulated that the mill should be set up within two years, and that it should be maintained continually. The change of the town boundary from a north line from the pepperidge tree to the brook and creek to the sound, which was made in 1709, has already been explained. The village contains a population of about 300. Its growth during the last quarter century has been but little. This may be partially attributed to the decadence of the firewood business, which was once an important interest, and the greater attractions of other villages which have been stimulated by direct railroad service.

THE FIRST CHURCH EDIFICE

erected in this neighborhood was built, as is supposed, about the middle of the last century. It was in size 26 by 28 feet, and stood until it was replaced by a new one in 1837. It is claimed that this early church belonged to a society of the Presbyterian name, and that the Presbytery of Suffolk appointed supplies for it. The early records were lost, and the church declined until but a feeble remnant was left. In 1785 a church of eight or nine members was organized here under the title of the "Second Strict Congregational Church of Riverhead." This church has since occupied the field. The present church edifice was erected in 1837, and at once supplied with a steeple and a bell. Its dedication took place in January 1838. It is a noteworthy fact that the people of this village have always been singularly united in their ecclesiastical relations, the unanimous support of the people having always been given to this one society. Several tracts of land were given to this church by some of the early inhabitants. Since the organization of the present church the following ministers have been engaged by it: Jacob Corwin, from about the time of its organization till 1800; David Wells, 1802-21; Parshall Terry, November 1831 to May 1832; Elizur W. Griswold, 1832-34; Christopher Youngs, 1835-41; John H. Thomas, February 1842 to August 1843; Luther Hallock, 1849-51; Eusebius Hale, 1852, 1853; J.H. Johnson, January to November 1854; J.H. Francis, 1855-61; Harvey Newcombe, August 1861 to March 1862; L.B. Marsh, 1863-65; Charles P. Mallory, 1865-69; G.D. Blodgett, 1871-75; William H. Seely, October 1875 to the present time. A Sunday-school in connection with this church has been in operation many years, the first superintendent of which is said to have been Deacon Luther Brown. The school at present numbers about 122, and its library contains some 400 volumes.

BAITING HOLLOW.

Striking eastward from Wading River we find Baiting Hollow, a settlement of sixty or more farm houses scattered along the north Country road through a distance of three or four miles. Farming and furnishing firewood have been the chief employment of the people. The locality was once called Fresh Pond. It is supposed that settlement commenced here as early as 1719.

BAITING HOLLOW CHURCHES.

A church of seven or eight members was organized here in 1792, called the "Third Strict Congregational Church of Riverhead." In 1803 a house of worship, 26 by 30 feet in size, was erected, which stood without material alteration until 1862, when it was superseded by the present building, which had been erected mainly during the previous year and was dedicated March 13th 1862. The following ministers have been its pastors: Manly Wells, from its organization till his death, May 8th 1802; Nathan Dickinson, for an unknown period; David Benjamin, 1820-40; Azel Downs, 1840-51; Christopher Youngs, 1851-66; William A. Allen, 1866-70; G.L. Edwards, two years; Eusebius Hale, 1876 till his death, October 1880; John A. Woodhull, 1881 to the present time. The Sunday-school of this church was organized in 1826, with Christopher Youngs superintendent. Its present membership is about 75.

The Swedenborgian or New Jerusalem church here had its origin about the year 1815, its initial movements being under the leadership of Jonathan Horton, a member of the Congregational church who had become a disciple of Swedenborg. A separate place of worship was established in the year mentioned. A church was organized in 1831, with 13 members. This society in 1839 erected a house of worship 24 by 36 feet in size, which is sitll occupied. Services have been conducted by the following persons: Jonathan Horton, will 1844; Rev. M.M. Carll, a few years; Jonathan Horton again after the death of Mr. Carll; Savilian Lee; N.D. Hutchinson, to the present time. The society is said to be diminishing in numbers.

JERICHO LANDING,

on the sound shore near Baiting Hollow, is a point from which quantities of cordwood were formerly sent to market by the sloops which then frequented the sound. During the war of 1812 the sloops engaged in this business, which was then a profitable one, were harassed by the English frigates that were cruising up and down the sound. Several vessels belonging to this town were captured. An exciting skirmish took place on the shore near here on May 31st 1814. A party of men was sent from a British squadron, which lay six or seven miles from shore, to capture several sloops lying on the beach to load with wood. The attacking party was met by about thirty militia under the leadership of Captain John Wells, and a brisk engagement followed. The British, who were in two large barges, opened fire with cannon and musketry and were promptly met by the fire of the resolute yeomanry. An attempt to board the sloop "Nancy" was unsuccessful, and was directly followed by a retreat. It was supposed that some of the enemy were killed or wounded in the encounter, though no injury was sustained by the militia.

The continuation of the settlement along the north Country road two miles or more east of Baiting Hollow is called Roanoke. A post-office was established here about the year 1871, and discontinued a year or two later.

NORTHVILLE.

Northville is a settlement of thriving farmers on the same road. It occupies an extent of about four miles, reaching to the east line of the town. This village is one of the most pleasant rural settlements along the north side of the county. The location is elevated and remarkably healthful; and, while it is as retired as could be wished, the stirring scenes of life and business are within convenient reach by a half hour's drive over a pleasant road to the county seat at Riverhead. A post-office by the name of Success was established here about a quarter of a century ago, and was discontinued in 1880. An organization known as the Riverhead Town Agricultural Society was in operation in this village. It was a combination of farmers, one of its principal objects being the reduction of prices of fertilizers, seeds, implements and other articles in which reduction could be effected by the purchase of large quantities.

During the war of 1812 an American cutter in an effort to escape a pursuing British man-of-war ran ashore near this place. The militia quickly gathered to the assistance of the Americans on board the cutter, and by their united and determined efforts the British marines sent to board the cutter were driven off. Failing in this attempt the ship joined the fleet which lay in the east end of the sound, and on the following day returned to the assault, now capturing the disabled prize.

THE CONGREGATIONAL CHURCH OF NORTHVILLE

was an offshoot from the old church at Upper Aquebogue, a more particular notice of which will be found in connection with that church. The Northville church entered upon its existence as a distinct society in 1834. During the same year the church which had been built upon the road between Upper Aquebogue and Riverhead, within two miles of the latter, was moved hither. The church at that time consisted of about 130 members. In 1859 a larger building was erected on the south side of the street, nearly opposite the old church, which was now fitted for an academic school-room in the upper story and a lecture room below. The new church was in size 40 by 70 feet, with a spire 90 feet high, and cost, when furnished, upward of $5,000. It was dedicated in March 1860.This building stood until May 14th 1877, when it was fired by the hand of an incendiary and its destruction made complete. The society then returned in its worhip to the lecture room in the old church, and there continued until the completion of the present edifice early in 1881. This building, 46 by 65 feet in size, was erected during the years 1879 and 1880, at a cost of about $9,000. It occupies the site of the burned church, and in appearance and finish is one of the finest in the county. It was dedicated January 13th 1881, and at that time the entire funds to pay its cost had been subscribed. This society from its organization was independent until May 1880, when it united with the Long Island Association. It was incorporated in March 1864, under the name of the "Northville Congregational Society." The following names are those of its successive ministers: Jonathan Huntting, during the winter of 1834-5; Abraham Luce, 1835-39; William Hodge, 1839-41; James Smith, 1841-45; John O. Wells, 1845-57; Clarke Lockwood, 1857-61; Thomas Harries, 1861-65; J.A. Woodhull, 1865, 1866; Mason Moore, six months; candidates for several years; S. Farmer, July 1871 to 1873; William Thomas, 1873-77; H.N. Wright, three months in 1877; A.O. Downs, 1877 to the present time. The Sunday-school connected with this church was organized in 1835. Asaph Youngs was its first superintendent. It now has about 140 pupils. A large library belonging to the school was destroyed by fire with the church.

In the preparation of this church history, as well as in that of nearly all the others of this town, we have been assisted by Samuel Tuthill, a resident of this village and a member of this church, whose active efforts and interest in behalf of the preservation of fast fading historical facts are worthy of recognition and appreciation.

NORTHVILLE ACADEMY,

established in the old church as mentioned above, and opened in 1859, had an existence of about twelve years, during a part of which time it enjoyed a flattering degree of success.

MANORVILLE AND CALVERTON.

A part of the settlement of Manorville extends into the southwest corner of the town. This locality abounds in swamps and ponds which form the sources of Peconic River. These characteristics hold all along the south side of the town, following the course of that river as far east as the village of Riverhead. These marshes have been made exceedingly valuable in the cultivation of cranberries.

About midway between Manorville and Riverhead lies the settlement of Calverton. A grist-mill has for many years been established here on Peconic River. The locality preserves the ancient name of Conungam. Immense quantities of cordwood were formerly cut from the surrounding forests and sent to market. To facilitate this commerce a side track was laid on the railroad, and this point became a center of much activity in the cordwood business. This was at first called Hulse's Turnout, and after it had risen to the importance of a "flag station" it received the name of Baiting Hollow Station, in honor of the village which lies nearly opposite, about four miles distant. Still later the name Calverton was applied to it and a post-office by that name established. A part of the locality which lies on the middle Country road has been named Buchananville.

AQUEBOGUE.

Aquebogue, the most ancient settlement of the town, extends along the middle Country road from Riverhead eastward nearly to the farther limit of the town, though the eastern part, formerly known as Lower Aquebogue, is now called Jamesport. Upper Aquebogue is about three miles east of the county seat. Settlement is supposed to have been made here at a very early date, though the exact time is not known. The settlement however was of sufficient importance to demand the establishment of a church in the early part of the last century.

CONGREGATIONAL CHURCH AT UPPER AQUEBOGUE.

The early ecclesiastical history of this village is wrapped in obscurity. There are some evidences to support the tradition that a Presbyterian church existed here early in the last century. The fact that this settlement was an offshoot of Southold, and was settled by people who were intimately associated with the Southold people, makes it easy to believe tht the church organized here at that early period was, like its mother church, Presbyterian in form. But of this early church we have been able to gather only a few fragmentary items. It is supposed that a Mr. Lee and Rev. Timothy Symmes were at different times its pastors previous to 1746, but which of them occupied the pulpit of that old church first, or for how long a period either filled it, or by whom they were preceded or succeeded, we have no means of knowing. A house of worship 24 by 33 feet in size had been erected, as is supposed in the early part of that century. It stood on the south side of the road, and in accordance with the custom a burying ground was established about it. The first interment is said to have been made in 1755. This repository of the dead has spread itself out over the adjoining fields until its grass-grown mounds cover an area of two acres or more, which is still increasing.

Soon after the last mentioned date the history we are reviewing emerges from the darkness into the light of a better preserved record. This tells us that on the 26th of March 1758 a Congregational church was organized here with 16 members. This occupied the house of worship already noticed. This society grew until it became the largest in the town. It was called the "First Strict Congregational Church of Southold," and was organized by Rev. Elisha Payne. During the winter of 1794-5 a number of members were added, and a similar increase occurred in the winter of 1801-2. In 1809 69 members were added. Another revival occurred in the winter of 1825-6, and still another in 1838, resulting in the addition of 28 members to the church. The history of the "Long Island Convention" records the fact that three of the members of this church in its early years entered the ministry under the auspices of that body, and became worthy ministers of the gospel. These were Rev. Manly Wells, ordained at Baiting Hollow in August 1793; Rev. Daniel Youngs, ordained at Upper Aquebogue in 1783; and Rev. David Benjamin, ordained at Baiting Hollow in August 1820.

The old church stood until 1797, when a new building was erected on the north side of the street, nearly opposite. This was 30 by 42 feet in size and had full galleries. It was rebult in 1833, and a tall steeple added, which was such a conspicuous feature that it suggested the name "Steeple Church", which has ever since been applied to the building and in a measure to the locality also. This building stood until 1862, when it was replaced by a new one. This, which still occupies the site, was dedicated in February 1863, and its cost was something over $4,000. The old building was removed to Riverhead, where it is still in use for business purposes. While it was being taken down the superintendent of the work, Lewis Van Keuren, was instantly killed by the falling of a heavy piece of timber.

From its organization to the present time nearly one thousand persons have united with this church. The society was incorporated about the year 1830, and is at present connected with the Long Island Congregational Association. Its confession of faith has been twice revised, once in 1829 and again in 1841, considerable changes being made in each instance.

The following pastors have supplied this church: Timothy Wells, 1759-82; Daniel Youngs, 1782-1814; Moses Swezey, 1815-26; Thomas Edwards, 1826, 1827; Evan Evans, 1827-31; Parshall Terry, 1831-34; John Gibbs, 1834-37; William Lyall, 1837-40; Thomas Harris, 1840-48; George

Turner, 1848-51; Lewis C. Lockwood, 1851-53; Eusebius Hale, 1853-60; Richard A. Mallory, 1860-64; Archibald Sloat, 1864-67; Augustus Root, 1867, 1868; Luther Marsh, 1868-70; Thomas N. Benedict, 1870-79; R.H. Wilkinson, 1879 to the present time. A Sunday-school was organized here in May 1830. The first superintendent was Eurystheus H. Wells.

OTHER CONGREGATIONAL CHURCHES.

In consequence of the revision of the "confession of faith" of this church which was made in 1829 a considerable part of the congregation withdrew, and, holding the original articles of faith, organized a new church, and erected a house of worship about half way between here and Riverhead. This church, numbering sixty members at the outset, claimed the title of the "First Strict Congregational Church of Riverhead," reasoning that the organization from which it had seceded had by its action forfeited its right to that title. The new house of worship was erected in 1831. During the period of its distinctive existence— 1829 to 1834—this church was successively supplied by Rev. Christopher Youngs, Rev. Mr. Fuller, Rev. Nehemiah B. Cook and Rev. Mr. Moser, the last two being Presbyterian ministers. In 1834 the society agreed to a division of its membership into two churches, one to be located at Riverhead and the other at Northville. The interest of the former in the building was purchased by the latter and the church was moved to Northville, where, having done service as house of worship, lecture room and academy, it is still standing.

A REMARKABLE DISCOVERY OF INDIAN REMAINS

was made near this village in 1879. In plowing and preparing a piece of low ground for a cranberry "marsh" Nathan A. Downs found by the frequent appearance of Indian arrows and some specimens of rude pottery that he was on the site of an ancient Indian village. Investigation discovered curiosities that attracted the attention of archaeologists and the public far and near. A great number of graves were found, the bones within them being so far decayed as to fall to dust almost as soon as they were exposed to the air. The site of this Indian village was upon the bank of Meeting-House Creek, on the south side of the Country road and about one-eighth of a mile from it. This creek runs into Peconic Bay, about one and a half miles distant from this point, and its name is suggested by the fact of its head being near the meeting-house ("steeple church"). It is supposed that this creek at some time during the remote centuries of the past was the lower section of a river whose source was away to the north, among the hills which range along the sound. The site must then have been a beautiful and attractive one. Where the low swamp now lies there must have been a pretty river, the placid waters of which were richly stocked with oysters, clams and fish. Shells and refuse abound in the vicnity, and it has long been supposed that the Indian inhabitants were once numerous. In plowing, dark spots were observed in the soil. These were at first supposed to have been temporary fire-places or ovens that had been filled with ashes, broken shells, refuse and soil; but on closer examination it was discovered that they contained human bones, and that the oyster shells had been placed where they were while the oyster was intact. A refuse heap some fifty yards long contained hundreds of loads of shells, chips of flint, bones and broken implements, and must have been many years accumulating. Near the shore of the now extinct river the graves of their dead were made. The geological changes that have taken place since these graves were made suggest that possibly thousands of years may have passed since that time. The remains exhumed show a singlular phenomenon in the construction of the jaws and teeth, the molars or grinding teeth being absent and the existing teeth being fitted with interlocking points, which would give the jaws the fierce character of those of an alligator or shark.

Additional facts in reference to this interesting discovery are given in the following exstract from an article published at the time from the pen of S. Terry Hudson, whose description was the result of careful personal investigation of the subject:

"The graves, of which thirty or forty have been opened, appear to have been small pits about three feet across, into which the dead were placed in a sitting position, with knees to chin. The body was then surrounded with a liberal supply of choice oysters, clams, whelks, meat and vegetables, and in some instances a burial urn and implements, before he was abandoned to the other world. The graves are discoverable only as a dark-colored, shelly spot of soil in the native yellow sand. Numbers of them were carted into the meadow before their true character was discovered. Fragments of almost every part of the human skeleton are abundant, and indicate a power race. The teeth and jaws are those of a very low type. The pottery is composed evidently of clay mingled with burned and pounded oyster-shells, hardened by a low heat. They seem to have been made by digging a hole in the ground and plastering the sides and bottom with the prepared mortar, which in time hardened and was taken out, burned, and put to use.

"One of the finest implements, together with the largest pieces of pottery, was taken from a grave supposed to be that of a chief. It is a perforated spear or arrowhead nearly three inches on each angle, with a true hole drilled from point to base; the edges are notched regularly like saw teeth, and the sides smoothly polished.

"A broken bone from the kitchen heap was found, which bore marks of having been sawn off for some purpose by a rude and slow process; probably the tool used was the edge of a shell; various gashes were started, the cuts being on four sides, and when partly weakened by the surrounding notches the bone was impatiently broken by the operator. Bird arrows, hunting arrows and a variety of chips and flakes and stone tools have been picked up in this vicinity, but the most interesting relic of all is the square clay walls of a temple or other structure, which was found beneath three feet or more of solid soil on the further side of the creek. Away from the main village, with no shells near, and only a few arrow-heads to show its Indian origin, this is quite a mystery. What is it? It is too far from the village for a dwelling, and it would be useless to our later Indians, who, as far as we know, had no religion. Is it the sacred alter of a race who flourished before them, that had wholly disappeared beneath the shifting soil? The dimensions of this curious structure are about 9 by 10 feet, with a dividing wall across the middle. There are traces of logs at the sides and beneath the floor, which are bedded in the purest clay, that must have been brought in canoes from the abundant clay beds near the swamps where the river-bed took its rise."

LOWER AQUEBOGUE.

Proceeding eastward along the Country road a distance of about two miles brings us to the locality formerly called Lower Aquebogue, or, as it is sometimes named, Old Aquebogue, the general size and character of which are similar to those of the village last noticed. Settlement was probably begun here during the latter part of the seventeenth century. One of the most ancient landmarks is an old cemetery. The present generation has seen but little progress in the original part of the village, but that section bordering the bay, about a mile below the former, is of recent origin, and its name (Jamesport) has been given to the whole neighborhood, including the railroad station and the post-office.

The old town poor-house was located on the road leading to Northville from Old Aquebogue. The farm, with the house upon it, was purchased in 1832, and continued in the use indicated until it was sold, November 21ˢᵗ 1871, the poor having been removed to the newly completed county-house at Yaphank. The house was repaired in 1861. In 1863 the farm produced 4 tons of English hay, 500 bushels of ears of corn, 140 bushels of wheat, 50 bushels of oats, 22 bushels of potatoes,

1,400 pounds of pork, 550 pounds of beef, and butter, poultry and eggs to the value of about $80.

THE FIRST CHURCH IN THE TOWN.

Probably the first church within the present limits of this town was located here. The date of its organization is not known, but it was of the Presbyterian form, doubtless an offshoot from the old church at Southold. The first item of history we find concerning it is the ordination of Rev. Nathaniel Mather, supposed to have been the first pastor of this church and ordained as such. This took place May 22nd 1728. The church united with the Presbytery of Suffolk on the organization of that body, in 1747. The first church edifice was erected in 1731. This was repaired and enlarged in 1830. The society appears never to have been very robust. At times it was united with Mattituck in ministerial support. The ministers who served it were: Nathaniel Mather to March 1748; John Darbee, 1749-51; Mr. Parkes, 1752-56; Nehemiah Barker, several years; Benjamin Goldsmith, 1764-1810; Benjamin Bailey, 1811-16; Nathaniel Reeve, 1817-23; Abraham Luce, 1825-35; Jonathan Huntting, 1836; Mr. Gilbert, 1837, 1838; Abraham Luce, 1839-45; J.T. Hamlin, for several years, after which the church was for a while without a pastor.

THE LOWER AQUEBOGUE CONGREGATIONAL CHURCH

was organized February 22nd 1854, upon the field of the former Presbyterian church, with 34 members. The new organization gathered strength, and in 1859 the old house of worship was rebuilt and supplied with a steeple 85 feet high. The successive pastors of this church have been Enos H. Rice, Francis Hill, Samuel T. Gibbs, Azel Downs, George L. Edwards, Mr. Parmalee, G.W. Allen, Wooster Parker, John Fitch, and T.N. Benedict, the present pastor. A Sunday-school in connection with this church was organized about 1850. The first superintendent was William Hallock. The present incumbent of this office, J.M. Petty, has occupied it 21 years.

JAMESPORT.

The village of Jamesport is one of modern origin. The historian Prime, writing in 1845, says of it: "In 1833 there was not a single habitation here, now some forty." It is very pleasantly situated on a point projecting into Peconic Bay and bearing Indian name Miamogue. It is regularly laid out, and was designed by its founders as a village of considerable dimensions, but since the first flush of enterprise, which was prompted by the expectation of building here an important maritime village, it has made but little progress. It is located at the head of ship navigation in the bay, which to this point has a good depth of water. A good wharf was built in 1833, and a hotel in 1836. In the days of its short-lived prosperity two or three whaling ships belonged here.

As we have already seen, the neighborhood to which the name Jamesport is now applied really comprises two different settlements, the old one of Lower Aquebogue and the new one which we have just noticed. They are about a mile apart.

METHODIST CAMP GROUND.

Between the two settlements mentioned above, and near the railroad station, lie the grounds on which the first camp meeting was held in September 1834. This land was at that time owned by the Methodists. A comfortable house had been erected in the lower village for schools or religious services irrespective of denomination. In 1854 the Methodists gave the camp ground in exchange for this building, which they then occupied as a house of worship. About twelve years ago the interest in camp meetings revived and the Methodists of this district, after deliberation in special meetings called for the purpose and the report of a committee appointed to select a site, determined to purchase the old camp meeting ground.

The purchase was consummated March 26th 1870, by a committee, who held the title in their own names until it was passed over to the association afterward incorporated. The ground has an area of six acres, and cost $1,000. The association was incorporated by act of the Legislature April 30th 1873. Its charter appointed 27 trustees, viz. George Hill, O.B. Corey, Addison Brown, A.T. Terrill, George W. Raynor, William H. Corwin, Thomas Hallock, S.B. Corey, Charles L. Corwin, William T. Terry. Henry R. Harris, J.L. Overton, Charles Goodall, Nathaniel Fanning, Lorenzo D. Bellows, S.A. Beckwith, Sylvester Downs, Isaac Halsey, John Hawkins, George F. Wells, Albert Benjamin, Minor Petty, John B. Terry, John B. Overton, H.D. Brewster, James Darling and Charles Strong, constituting them and their associates and successors in office a "body corporate and politic, under the name of the Suffolk County Camp Meeting Association of the Methodist Episcopal Church." Improvements have been made upon the grounds at an expense of several thousand dollars. Camp meetings are annually held here.

JAMESPORT M.E. CHURCH.

The first Methodist Episcopal class in this village was organized by Rev. John Luckey, circuit preacher, in 1830. It consisted of 11 members. The first places of meeting were an old school-house and the dwellings of its members. The acquisition of a church edifice by exchange of property has been mentioned. It was fitted up and improved in 1855. Its present estimated value is $1,800. The society has a membership of about 30.

The records contain the names of the ministers who have supplied it, though at first it was part of a circuit comprising several other stations, and later has frequently been connected with Riverhead or Mattituck. The preachers were: John Luckey, 1830, 1831; Alexander Hulin and J.F. Arnold, 1831, 1832; Richard Wymond and James Rawson, 1832, 1833; William K. Stopford, 1833, 1834; John Trippet, 1834, 1835; James Floy, 1835, 1836; William McK. Bangs, 1836, 1837; Theren Osborn, 1837-39; Eben S. Hebbard, William C. Hoyt and Dr. Rowland, at the same time; Orlando Starr, George S. Jayne and Charles B. King, 1839-41; David Osborn, 1841, 1842; S.W. Law, 1843; Oliver E. Brown, 1844; Isaac H. Sandford, 1844, 1845; George W. Woodruff, 1846; Bezaleel Howe, 1847; George W. Woodruff, 1847; Henry D. Latham, 1848, 1849; Frederick W. Sizer, 1850, 1851; Nathan Tibballs, 1851, 1852; F.C. Hill, 1853, 1854; S.F. Johnson, 1854, 1855; F.C. Hill, 1855, 1856; B.F. Reeve, 1857, 1858; N.F. Colver, 1858; Charles Redfield, 1859; B.F. Reeve, 1860, William H. Bangs, 1863, 1864; Thomas N. Laine, 1865; Richard Wake, 1866, 1867; William P. Armstrong, 1868; George Hill, 1869; O.C. Lane, 1871, 1872; George W. Allen, 1873-75; T.G. Osborn, 1877; O.C. Lane, 1878; F.G. Howell, 1879, 1880; J.R. Buckelew, 1881.

A Sunday-school of about 46 scholars is in operation in connection with the church.

RIVERHEAD.

The site of the village of Riverhead appears to have been a locality of no importance until it waas chosen as the spot for holding the county courts, which was done in the early part of the last century. A small frame building was erected in 1728, and the courts were held here for the first time March 27th of the following year. This primitive building answered the double purpose of a court-house and jail. Previous to this the waterpower of the river had been utilized by a saw-mill, the proprietors having as early as 1659 granted to John Tooker and Joshua

Horton the privilege of establishing such a mill, with a small quantity of adjoining land.

OWNERSHIP OF THE SITE.

Hon. George Miller, in his centennial sketch of the history of this village, gives the following outline of the successive transfers of some of the important sections of real estate:

"John Tooker in 1711 conveyed 400 acres of land to John Parker, bounded east by Parker's land, south by Peconic River, west by widow Cooper's land, and north by the sound. Parker owned the land on the south side of the river. In 1726, by deed of gift, John Parker conveyed to Joseph Wickham and Abigail Wickham, his daughter, all his land north of Peconic River, to the said Joseph for life and then to his daughter and her heirs. Her husband died in 1749. His widow died in 1780, and her oldest son, Parker, inherited her estate, which was confiscated after the war and purchased by General Floyd, who sold the property to Mr. Jagger.

"In 1753 Thomas Fanning sold the hotel property, 130 acres, with the dam as far as the saw-mill, to John Griffing for £1,000. In 1775 John Griffing conveyed his land south of the highway, with the grist-mill and his part of the stream, to Nathaniel Griffing, his son, for £500. John Griffing was a patriotic Whig, and went to Connecticut with his family when the war came on, and died there in 1780, intestate, and all his estate descended to his eldest son, John, who occupied the property until he sold it to Benjamin Brewster about the beginning of this century. He, within ten years, conveyed it to Bartlett Griffing, the youngest son of John Griffing the elder, and he within a year conveyed it to his brother, William Griffing, in whose family it ever after remained until it was conveyed to John P. Terry, the present proprietor, in 1864."

HOTELS, ETC.

Notwithstanding it was the site of the "County Hall," no progress toward building a village was made until after the Revolutionary period. The object of courts in those days being simply to dispense justice and settle disturbances as quickly as possible, lengthy terms of court were not required, and the demand for hotel accommodation was not sufficient to warrant any outlay in that direction. Men who were required to attend court, even to the judges, went with their own conveyances, and took with them provisions and provender sufficient for the anticipated needs of the journey. The inhabitants of most of the towns could start from home in the early morning, with their necessary documents and books bestowed in one end of a sack balanced across the horse's back, with a "mess of oats" or corn for the animal in the other end; and, tying their horses under the shade of the trees, attend the session of the court, transact their business and return to their homes at night. Still the need of a "public house" seems to have been noticed, and this want was supplied before any thought of building a village received serious consideration.

In the earliest years of the present century the principal part of the village site was owned by three men, viz., Richard Howell in the eastern part, where cedar trees from which shingles were made were abundant; John Griffing, who then kept a "public house," in the central part, and Josiah Albertson, whose property was in the western part, and included a grist-mill and a fulling-mill on the site now occupied by Perkin's factory.

About the year 1812 the village contained but four dwellings. These were John Griffing's, Joseph Osborn's, David Jagger's and William Albertson's. The grist-mill and the "County Hall" were the public institutions. Not many years later the latter was rebuilt and enlarged, and a separate jail building erected, and the mill, then owned by Benjamin Brewster, was destroyed by fire and another one built in its place. By the year 1825 the village had made some growth. Besides dwellings there had been established a shoe shop by Moses C. Cleveland, a blacksmith shop by Jedediah Conklin, and three stores, kept by Elijah Terry, William Jagger and William Griffing jr.

The three principal hotels of the village were established as follows: The Long Island House, or its original part, by the Griffings, about the middle of the last century; the Suffolk Hotel was built as a dwelling in 1825, and enlarged and used as a hotel in 1834; the Griffing House was built by Henry L. Griffing in 1862, and afterward enlarged.

MANUFACTURING.

Peconic River affords water power for several mills at or near the village. This feature of the locality probably suggested the first steps toward improvement which led to the establishment of a village. A grist-mill was started at the village in the latter part of the last century. A grist-mill, fulling-mill and saw-mill were established at Upper Mills on the stream about a mile above the village. Still farther up the river Jeremiah Petty built a forge for the manufacture of bar iron about the year 1797. The business was carried on by successive owners about twenty years, when it was abandoned. The bed of this pond is now used as a cranberry marsh.

In 1828 John Perkins established a woollen factory at the Upper Mills. A considerable part of the business then consisted of manufacturing the wool raised by the farmers of the surrounding villages for their own home use. The business was carried on by Mr. Perkins during his life, and at his death, in 1866, was assumed by his sons J.R. & J.H. Perkins, by whom it is still continued. The products of this factory are stocking yarn, flannel and cassimere. It is driven by water power, employs ten hands, and consumes annually about twenty thousand pounds of wool.

A planing and moulding mill was started here by Charles Hallett in 1857. It stood just above the bridge, and was driven by water power. A few years later it passed into the hands of other parties, and later still, the business being suspended, the building and power fell again into the hands of Mr. Hallett, who in 1870 appropriated them to the manufacture of strawboard. In 1868 he established a large moulding and planing mill by the river below the bridge, using steam power. This mill is conveniently situated on the river, with a front sufficient to accommodate the landing of lumber from the boats that come up the river. It has had at times fifty men employed, and in some years its business has amounted to more than $100,000.

Among other manufacturing enterprises here may be mentioned the soap factory established a few years since by J.B. Slade; works for the production of fertilizers, by the same, more recently commenced; the manufacture of cigars and tobacco by Newins & Griswold, which has been in operation a few years; of pipe organs by Earle & Bradley, started by George W. Earle in 1868 and closed about 1874; of wagon-jacks by Swezey Brothers; and of chocolate in a mill near the village, which was carried on for a while a few years since. It is estimated that $750,000 is invested in the various manufacturing and mercantile enterprises of the village.

One cause of the slow growth of the village during the first quarter century or more after the Revolution may be found in the general depression of those times and the reduced financial condition of the people. There was but little here except agriculture to support the people, and the soil in this locality, being light and thin, was already well nigh worn out, and so afforded but little promise even to this industry. It is said also that about this time the people were sadly in debt. But in the midst of this depressing condition of things the custom of fertilizing the land with fish came into existence, and the failing energies of the soil were thus revived. This was about the beginning of the present century. Other fertilizers were introduced, and the condition of the soil and consequently that of the people was improved. To Judge John

Woodhull, a prominent man of the town in his day, was given the honor of being first to introduce the use of ashes as a fertilizer.

PUBLIC IMPROVEMENTS .

The river for several miles below the village was naturally shallow and the channel narrow and crooked. A considerable commerce however was from an early date carried on upon it. A few sloops were built on its banks as early as sixty years ago. Vessels of any considerable draft could not come up to the village, but were obliged to anchor below and send their cargoes to the wharf by scows and lighters. In the early part of the last decade improvements were made in the channel of the river which were of great benefit to the village. Attempts had previously been made to effect similar results, but they had fallen short of their mark. As early as 1835 a stock company was incorporated for that purpose and the work was commenced, but for some reason it was discontinued before any considerable progress had been made. In 1870-73 three appropriations were made by Congress to the aggregate amount of $25,000, and the State Legislature appropriated $5,000 to the purpose of opening a channel 75 feet wide at low water from the village down to the mouth of the river, a distance of two and three-quarters miles. This work, nearly completed by the money appropriated, has effected a great improvement in favor of navigation, and it is also said to have wrought a favorable change in the action of the water in the river, causing it to run off nearly a foot lower at ordinary low tides and also preventing its rising so high as it formerly did under the influence of easterly winds. By this means the mills are relieved of what was frequently a serious annoyance, and the lots along the river banks are less liable to inundation.

The village of Riverhead occupies a convenient level site, and is laid out with considerable regularity. Many of the streets are lined with shade trees, and considerable pains is taken to keep the streets and walks in good order. This spirit of public improvement has given birth to a "Village Improvement Society," which was organized in the early part of 1881, with Hon. John S. Marcy president and George F. Stackpole secretary. The object of this society is the improvement of the village generally, as well as its approaches. In the latter direction a very commendable undertaking has already been carried through in the opening and improvement of a new and direct road across the plains southward to Quogue, on the south side.

In connection with the subject of roads it may be noted that Abner street was so named by vote of the town April 2nd 1850, in honor of Abner Howell.

The present population of Riverhead is about 2,000. A small part of the village extends across the river into Southampton. At the census of 1880 that portion contained 218 persons, while the main part had a population of 1,757.

Until within a few years the entire village lay on the south side of the railroad. As lately as 1862 nothing had been done in building on the north. This section was then occupied by cleared fields and groves of native timber. Streets have been opened, shade trees planted, public buildings and many nice residences erected and public and private grounds ornamented and improved.

COUNTY BUILDINGS.

The first court-house, as has already been stated, was erected in 1728, and about a century later was reconstructed and enlarged. This building, located in the center of the business portion of the village, is still standing, though its interior has been rearranged and fitted for various business purposes. A new court-house was erected in 1854-5, on a spacious plat of ground in what was then the northwestern suburb of the village. The building committee, appointed by the board of supervisors, consisted of S.B. Nicoll, of Shelter Island, William R. Post, of Southampton, and Sylvester Miller, of Riverhead. The building is of brick and stone, and cost $17,800. The jail, an octagonal building of stone, occupies a yard in the rear. The jail having been "indicted" by the grand jury 14 or 15 times as insufficient for the purpose, a new building was erected in 1881 in the same yard with it. The court-house is two stories in height, and stands on a basement of stone. The basement and a part of the main floor are occupied by living apartments for the sheriff or jailer. The main floor also contains the jurors' rooms and the supervisors' room. The court-room is on the second floor.

The office of the county clerk was at first itinerant, moving from place to place with each change of incumbent. It was afterward fixed at Riverhead. The first building for the use of this office was erected in 1846. It was a fire-proof structure, about 20 by 30 feet in size and a single story in height, and stood on the west corner of Griffing avenue and Main street. It was sold in 1875, after the completion of the new clerk's office, and is now used as a marble-working shop. The new clerk's office stands on the court-house lot. It is a handsome fire-proof building, of two high stories. The lower story, lined with shelving and a gallery, is occupied by the books and documents belonging to this office, while the upper floor is used as the surrogate's court. In the surrogate's court during the year 1881 99 wills were admitted to probate, three have been contested and are still undecided, and notices of intention to contest have been filed in two other cases. Ninety-eight letters of administration were granted, and there were 40 accountings and 13 cases of real estate proceedings.

The records of the clerk's office begin with 1669. These records for nearly two centuries accumulated very slowly. The first book of deeds, a small volume, contains all that were recorded from 1687 to 1714; the second reaches from the latter date to 1768; and the third from that date to 1804. The first book of mortgages contains all recorded from 1755 to 1775; the second from that date to 1778; and the third from the latter date to 1794. The annual records of mortgages now fill five or six massive volumes of about 600 pages each, while those of deeds fill then of the same sized volumes. It is estimated that the weight of records, books and documents contained in this office is about eight tons, and that the written surface would cover nearly fifteen acres. The office is being rapidly filled with the constant accumulation of matter.

THE RIVERHEAD SAVINGS BANK,

resulting from the discussion and efforts of a number of enterprising citizens led by N.W. Foster and Orville B. Ackerly, was granted a charter April 27th 1872. In accordance therewith the trustees organized at the Long Island House, May 18th 1872, and the bank was opened for business, the first deposit being made on the 31st of the same month. The following gentlemen were the first trustees: James H. Tuthill, John Downs, N.W. Foster, Jeremiah M. Edwards, Gilbert H. Ketcham, Daniel A. Griffing, J. Henry Perkins, Moses F. Benjamin, Edwin F. Squiers, John R. Corwin, Orville B. Ackerly, Richard T. Osborn, Isaac C. Halsey, Simeon S. Hawkins, Richard H. Benjamin, John F. Foster, Thomas Coles, J. Halsey Young, John S. Marcy, Abraham B. Luce, Jonas Fishel, and John P. Mills. The following have since been placed in the board to fill vacancies as from time to time they occurred: Ebenezer P. Jarvis, John A. Monsell, Charles S. Havens, Edward Hawkins, Timothy M. Griffing, George W. Cooper, Thomas G. Osborn, James E. Wells, J. Henry Newins and Clifford B. Ackerly. The first officers were: R.H. Benjamin, president; John S. Marcy and Abraham B. Luce, vice-presidents; O.B. Ackerly, secretary. The present secretary is Clifford B. Ackerly; otherwise the officers have continued to the present time the same as at the first. The prosperity which the institution has enjoyed is shown by the fact that on the first

of January 1882 it had 2,400 depositors, to whom there was due
$581,289.55, to secure which the bank held assets to the amount of
$634,581.85, leaving a surplus or reserve fund of $53,292.30 with
which to meet losses that may occur, or to pay extra dividends to depositors when it shall amount to fifteen per cent. of the deposits.
Through all those years of financial depression which followed so
soon after its organization, as well as during the later years, the growth
and success of the bank have been constant to the present time.

COUNTY FAIR GROUND AND FAIRS.

The Suffolk County Agricultural Society owns a field of 20 acres in the
northern part of the village, where its annual fair is held. This was en-
closed with a board fence in 1868, and the exhibition hall was erected
in 1869. This building cost about $5,000, and at the time was one of the
finest of its class in the State. From its wide northern platform the
lamented Horace Greeley addressed seven thousand people of Suffolk
but a few weeks before his death, on the subject of the waste lands of
Long Island. This was at the annual fair of 1872. The building stands in
the southern part of the grounds. Other buildings, for the use of the officers of the society and for stock, have been erected, and a half-mile
track in the northern part for trotting matches has been prepared.

Though a brief account of this society is given on page 69, our
readers will be pleased with the following fuller history furnished by
N.W. Foster, the secretary of the society:

The first record we find of an agricultural society in this county is
a printed copy of the "Constitution of the Suffolk County Agricultural
Society adopted October 6th 1818"; article 2 of which states the society's object to "be the advancement of agriculture in all its various
branches, by collecting and circulating the knowledge of improvements, and by bestowing premiums for the most successful exertions."
Article 9 provides for "two meetings each year, at the court-house in
Riverhead, in May and in October;" article 10 for "an annual fair and cattle show, time and place to be appointed by the managers." The officers
were: President, Thomas S. Strong; 1st vice-president, Sylvester Dering;
and 2nd vice-president, Joshua Smith; 3d vice-president, Nathaniel Potter; 4th vice-president, John P. Osborne; corresponding secretaries,
Charles H. Havens and Henry P. Dering; recording secretary, Ebenezer
W. Case; treasurer, David Warner. Twelve managers were also elected.
We find no mention of any meetings or fairs.

In Volume I. of the Transactions of the New York State Agricultural
Society for 1841 is found the statement that the Suffolk County Agri-

cultural Society was organized in that year. In the "Transactions" for 1842 are several statements by persons receiving premiums for crops from this county society, of which William W. Mills was then president. In the volume for 1843 is a report by William C. Stout, president, stating that the third annual fair was held November 15th and $186.50 paid in premiums. Richard B. Post was secretary, David C. Brush treasurer, and there was a manager from each town. "The society is not in so flourishing a condition as I would like to see it, owing almost entirely to the immense length of our country, thereby rendering it difficult to fix upon the proper place at which to hold an annual fair and give general satisfaction. Measures are in progress however to correct this evil by organizing two societies."

In the volume of 1846 J. Lawrence Smith, president, writes under date of March 20th 1847, that "the county society was dissolved in 1843, and a new society formed from a smaller and more thickly settled portion of the county." This society was known as the "Western Branch of the Suffolk County Agricultural Society." Its records show that fairs were held each year from 1843 to 1852 (excepting 1844), respectively at Comac, Smithtown, Comac, Islip, Huntington, Greenport, Babylon, Smithtown and Huntington. The officers during this period were as follows, so far as recorded:

Presidents—W.C. Stout, 1843, 1845; J. Lawrence Smith, 1846, 1847; Joshua B. Smith, 1848; Harvey W. Vail, 1849, 1850; Edward Henry Smith, 1851; Dr. John R. Rhinelander, 1852; Edwin A. Johnson, 1853.

Vice-Presidents—W.H. Ludlow, 1845; Lester H. Davis, 1846; Samuel N. Bradhurst, 1847; William Nicoll, 1851; Samuel L. Thompson, 1852, 1853.

Secretaries—Henry G. Scudder, 1845; Nathaniel Smith, 1846, 1847, 1851; Dr. Abraham G. Thompson, 1848-50; Edward K. Briar, 1852; J.H. Carll, 1853.

Treasurers—R.B. Post, 1843; Nathaniel Smith, 1845; Richard Smith, 1846, 1847; Jarvis R. Mowbray, 1848; Elbert Carll, 1849, 1850; William Lawrence, 1851; David C. Brush, 1852; William H. Ludlow, 1853.

At the fair at Comac October 16th 1843 premiums were awarded amounting to $110. At Smithtown in 1845 the premiums amounted to $95. An address was delivered by Dr. John R. Rhinelander. In 1846 the premiums were $79. An address was given by Samuel A. Smith.

At a meeting (date not given) held between the fairs of 1846 and 1847 it was resolved "that this society be hereafter known and called by the name of "The Suffolk County Agricultural Society." At the fair of 1847 mention is made of "corn planted three feet apart, four stalks in each hill, showing that good corn may be produced on much less ground than is usually required;" and "fine flat turnips grown since oats were taken off." The address was by William H. Ludlow, and the premiums aggregated $94. At Huntington October 10th 1848 a new constitution (prepared by the secretary, Dr. A.G. Thompson, as instructed at a previous meeting) was presented and adopted. An address by Dr. Thompson "reviewed the past and present operations of the society, the benefits resulting from the formation of agricultural societies, and urged the importance of system, of industry, and economy in managing agricultural matters."

The first fair held in the eastern part of the county was at Greenport, October 2nd 1849. The address was by John G. Floyd.

At a meeting of the managers, April 6th 1850, it was resolved, "on condition that the residents of Babylon and vicinity pay or secure to be paid to the treasurer of the society, on or before May 1st 1850, the sum of $100, and that the necessary cattle pens be erected, a suitable building or tent be provided, and that arrangements be made for the conveyance of passengers to and from the railroad free of all charge, that the fair will be held in the village September 24th 1850." Also resolved, "in case the residents of Babylon and its vicinity do not agree to the above resolution, the exhibition will be held in Islip in case the said conditions be complied with." In addition to the premiums offered the year before, premiums were offered for crops grown on the "Plain lands." The fair was held at Babylon. "F.M.A. Wicks, of Thompson's station, exhibited cheese, pumpkins, citron, melons, fine potatoes and Isabella grapes raised on the 'Plain lands,' adjoining the Long Island railroad at Thompson's station. Ira L'Hommedieu exhibited tomatoes, blood beets and egg plants raised on land of Dr. E.F. Peck at Lake Road station. These productions showed conclusively the error of the idea that the lands contiguous to the Long Island railroad are worthless." "The society is indebted to Mr. Francis M.A. Wicks and to Dr. E.F. Peck for proving beyond objection that these desolate lands can be made productive under a proper course of cultivation. The perseverance shown by these two gentlemen is deserving the highest commendation, and it is hoped that success may attend their efforts." The annual address was delivered by John Fowler jr.

At the winter meeting, December 4th 1850, a premium was awarded to Samuel S. Thompson, of Setauket, "for 84-1/2 bushels, 4 quarts and 1 pint of Australian or 'Verplank' wheat, raised on two surveyed acres, the weight being 63-1/2 lbs. per bushel; the standard of 60 lbs. per bushel being allowed, the yield of the crop was 89 bushels 2 pecks on the two acres. * * * Deducting the expenses, the net profit was $341.75."

"William Burling, of Babylon, raised 65 bushels of onions on one-eighth of an acre, being at the rate of 520 bushels per acre." The net profit was $24.65.

At Smithtown September 25th 1851 the address was delivered by Dr. Franklin Tuthill, of New York city. Mr. Brush, the treasurer, dying before the next fair, John D. Hewlett was appointed treasurer in his stead. At the fair at Huntington, October 21st 1852, the address was by Henry J. Scudder, of New York city. It is reported that another fair was held in 1852, at Islip, but the record shows no further meeting till February 1st 1865, when the society was reorganized at Thompson's station, with the title "Suffolk County Agricultural Society." The officers elected for the first year were as follows: President, William Nicoll, Huntington; vice-president, Robert W. Pearsall, Islip; secretary, J.H. Doxsee, Islip; treasurer, William J. Weeks, Brookhaven; directors, H.G. Scudder, Huntington; Caleb Smithtown, Smithtown; Robert O. Colt, Islip; Thomas S. Mount, Brookhaven; D.H. Osborne, Riverhead; David G. Floyd, Southold.

The officers from this time have been:

Presidents—William Nicoll, 1866, 1867, 1872-74; Dr. B.D. Carpenter, 1868-71; Henry Nicoll, elected in 1872, not serving, William Nicoll was appointed; Henry E. Huntting, 1875, 1879; 1880; Hon. John S. Marcy, 1876-78; Alvah M. Salmon, 1881, 1882.

Vice-Presidents—Dr. B.D. Carpenter, 1866, 1867; Samuel B. Gardiner, 1868; Henry G. Scudder, 1869-71; Lewis A. Edwards, 1872; Henry E. Huntting, 1873, 1874; R.T. Goldsmith, 1875; Stephen C. Rogers, 1876-78; Alvah M. Salmon, 1879, 1880; George W. Cooper, 1881, 1882.

Secretaries—J.H. Doxsee, 1866, 1867; Thomas S. Mount, 1868-1871, 1875; Henry D. Green, 1872-74; Nathaniel W. Foster, 1876, 1877, 1879-82; J.L. Millard, 1878.

Treasurers—W.J. Weeks, 1876, 1877; Joshua L. Wells, 1868-71; David F. Vail, 1872-74; Samuel Griffin, 1875-82.

The first fair after the reorganization was held at Riverhead, September 27th and 28th 1865. "The board of managers are fully satisfied with the results of the fair, both in the interest manifested by the people of the county and the pecuniary result arising therefrom." The receipts were $1,600, and the disbursements $800. From this time the fair has been held each year at Riverhead, excepting 1867, when it was at Greenport. The addresses have been delivered as follows: In 1865 by Hon. Henry Nicoll, of Mastic; 1866, Hon. William H. Gleason, Sag Harbor; 1867, Hon. Samuel A. Smith, of Smithtown; 1868, Hon. Henry P. Hedges, of Bridgehampton; 1869, William Nicoll, of Islip; 1870, Robert W. Pearsall, of Brentwood; 1871, Hon. Henry J. Scudder, of Northport; 1872, Hon. Horace Greeley, of New York; 1873, General Stewart L.

Woodford, of Brooklyn; 1875, Hon. Townsend D. Cock, of Queens county; 1876, Hon. L. Bradford Prince, of Flushing; 1877, Hon. John R. Reid, of Babylon; 1878, Hon. Nathan D. Petty, of Riverhead; 1879, Hon. James W. Covert, of Flushing; 1880, P.T. Barnum, of Bridgeport; 1881, Hon. R.B. Roosevelt and E.G. Blackford, of the New York Fish Commission, and Barnet Phillips, secretary of the American Fish Cultural Association.

In 1866 the question of permanent location came up, was discussed and laid over; also "the propriety of uniting with Queens county to form a Long Island agricultural society. October 29th 1867 the managers accepted from the citizens of Riverhead a deed donating to the Suffolk County Agricultural Society" land lying near and westerly of the Riverhead Cemetery, for fair grounds, with this condition—if the society shall fail for two consecutive years to hold a fair thereon, the grounds shall revert to the donors." The grounds are pleasantly located, conveniently near to the village and to the depot of the Long Island Railroad, and of very ready access from all directions.

The matter of fitting up the grounds was referred to the president, vice-president and treasurer, and it was "resolved that the sum of $200 be appropriated to pay the treasurer for his extra services in behalf of the society." The first fair on the new grounds was held September 30th and October 1st and 2nd 1868. Again $200 was paid to the treasurer for services.

B.D. Carpenter, Stephen C. Rogers, Joshua L. Wells, John S. Marcy, William Nicoll and Robert W. Pearsall were the building committee that supervised the erection of the Exhibition Hall. The architect was George H. Skidmore, of Riverhead. The contract for building was awarded to Fielder, Skidmore & Co. The building was completed in time for the next annual fair, October 6th, 7th and 8th 1869. In the evening of the 6th a public meeting was held in the court-house, and papers were read by Robert W. Pearsall, of Brentwood, and Hon. Henry P. Hedges, of Bridgehampton, the latter upon "Fertilizers and their Application." "Mr. William Nicoll in a few appropriate remarks called attention to the Exhibition Hall, and, with a view of liquidating the debt incurred by its erection, he moved that a committee be appointed for soliciting life members of the society upon the payment of $10 each. The motion having been passed and the committee appointed, Mr. Nicoll manifested his earnestness in the movement by the payment of $70, making his wife and children life members. Others immediately followed the example, till $400 had been contributed." The annual meeting in the evening of the 7th was addressed by Mr. Nicoll.

On June 22nd and 23rd 1870 occurred the first horticultural exhibition, a festival and reunion, which was very successful, bringing together a very large and pleasant company. Others were held June 14th 1871 and June 19th 1872. There being few if any professional florists in the county, and the strawberry growers being particularly busy marketing their fruit, it was found to be impracticable to attempt at present more than one fair each year.

In 1876, besides the usual annual meeting on Wednesday evening during the fair, meetings were held at the court-house on Tuesday and Thursday evenings for discussion of matters of interest to the county and its people; but the attendance was so small that no encouragement was felt to repeat the experiment.

During this year the grounds were improved by planting trees, which were donated to the society by Isaac Hicks & Sons, of Old Westbury, Queens county. P.H. Foster, of Babylon; E.F. Richardson, of Brentwood, and Israel Peck, of Southold. Adjoining Exhibition Hall was built a cloak or package room, which was proved a great convenience to visitors and a source of profit to the society. New features were introduced into the exhibition, viz. "Centennial relics" and "a display of antiquities." This being the Centennial year this feature seemed to touch every heart, bringing out a warm response throughout the county, and, not stopping with county limits, was similarly responded to in several other counties as a striking feature in their fairs. The suggestion, coming as it did from this county, at once introduced this society to many sister societies that before hardly knew of it. A display of "plans" for farm buildings, etc., by Suffolk county architects (which has been of much service by favorably introducing to visiting strangers such architects as exhibited, and also by elevating the standard of architecture in the county) and a "collection of foreign curiosities" were very successful in themselves and added much to the exhibit. A new and notable feature of the fair was the gathering of the children of the public schools of the county,—teachers and pupils being admitted free on one specified day,—the effect of which was so gratifying that it has become one of the fixtures of each fair, thereby cultivating in the rising generation an interest in the society. This year, too, more largely than ever before, was the power of the county press shown in arousing throughout the county a new and general interest in the society, and a strong desire to attend the fair. All together, notwithstanding the greater attraction offered by the Centennial Exhibition at Philadelphia, this year seems to have been a turning point in the history of the society. Partly from the geographical situation of the county, partly from the difficulty experienced in reaching the fair with articles for exhibition, and from various other reasons, a feeling of more than indifference seemed very largely to have possessed the people of both east and west. This now gave place to a desire to promote the success of the fair.

In 1877 the new features of the preceding year were retained and a new department, an "exhibit of school work," was introduced, whereby the public schools became interested in the society, also exhibits of minerals and Indian relics. This fair was made more attractive by a fine display from the Long Island Historical Society of Brooklyn, through the kindness of Elias Lewis jr. The attendance was larger, by reason of the improved railroad connections and facilities, whereby people were brought from all parts of the island and returned at reduced rates. Not only the society, but many people throughout the county were much benefited by a donation from J.N. Hallock, formerly of Suffolk county, now publisher of *The Christian at Work*, New York city, of subscriptions amounting to $100, which were largely used as premiums. This year $600 was paid on the debt, and in 1878 $400.

In 1879 more new features were introduced—displays of decorated pottery, rare china, native woods, and leaves and nuts of trees growing in the county. Among the cattle exhibited were a pair of immense oxen, weighing over 4,600 pounds, exhibited by Elbert Rose of Bridgehampton, and some superior Jerseys from the well known stockyards of William Crozier of Northport. Point judging on cattle and horses was now introduced. The exhibit of school work, first introduced in 1877, showed gratifying progress. The hall was made more cheerful by the exhibit of a large number of the bills and posters of the different county societies of the State. The debt was reduced $250 this year.

A very important feature of the fair of 1880 was the addresses of P.T. Barnum, at the hall in the afternoon and at the court-house in the evening, replete with humor and wisdom. Some very fine Early Rose potatoes, that took the first prize, were grown in beach sand. One man reported a crop of 500 bushels of potatoes raised on an acre of ground. This year the debt was again reduced $250.

At a meeting of the board of managers held at Riverhead January 27th 1881 Austin Corbin, the newly elected president and receiver of the Long Island Railroad Company, and several of the directors were present; also reporters from the city papers. Mr. Corbin and others explained the condition of the road and the company and their plans and intentions for the future. Mr. Corbin, as a Suffolk county farmer, made a donation to the society of $250.

Before the fair the railroad company offered $500 in special premiums for stock, grains, fruit, etc., which greatly stimulated the exhibitors and added much to the interest of the exhibition. H.W. Maxwell, one of the directors of the railroad company, offered five gold medals, of the total value of $100, to be competed for during the fair by the pupils of the public schools of the county, in reading, arithmetic, United States history, geography and English language. Three of these were taken by pupils of the Greenport school, one by a pupil at Yaphank, and one by a member of the school at Patchogue. During this year the grounds were improved by planting more trees. The addresses at the fair were on fish culture, out of the regular course, but of great interest to the whole county. The debt was still further reduced $500.

Again a new departure: The officers of the society, not content with showing their county's products to those that might come to the county fair, proposed to the farmers and others of the county an exhibit of their good things at the State fair at Elmira, which exhibit, although an experiment, was very encouraging in its results, the first premium ($25) being awarded to R.O. Colt, of Bay Shore, for the best collection of vegetables besides other premiums to different exhibitors; while a new wagon gear invented and exhibited by C.M. Blydenburgh, of Riverhead, attracted great attention, as did also the wood of which the wagon was built—Suffolk county oak. The exhibit brought the county into very prominent and favorable notice.

SCHOOLS.

The public school of this village occupies a handsome building standing on a lot which adjoins the Methodist Episcopal church grounds on the east. The building is two stories high, and it reached its present size by an enlargment in 1867, and another in 1871. The school was organized as a union school in April 1871.

In view of the particular neglect of female education, which seemed to be a conspicuous fact half a century ago, two enterprising citizens of the village, Dr. Joshua Fanning and George Miller, undertook the task of establishing a female seminary here. In 1834 they erected a commodious building, for the times, and in the spring of 1835 the school was begun. Miss Leonard, of Massachusetts, was employed as the first teacher, and she occupied the position at different times afterward, making an aggregate term of 21 years. Later she became the wife of George Miller, and whether actively engaged in teaching or not she held the supervision of the seminary during its entire existence, which closed some ten years since. During this term the school had an average attendance of from thirty to forty pupils. It was said of this school by one who knew its history well:"Its object was to give thorough instruction in all the primary branches of an English education, with Latin and mathematics. The effect of the school was almost magical upon the community. The ideas of people in regard to thorough primary education soon became great, and told upon the academies of the country, and the examination day at the close of the terms was for years among the proudest days of Riverhead." The seminary building still occupies its site, beside the Congregational church, which may be called its offspring, as for many years before the erection of the church religious services were conducted in the lower room of the seminary.

THE VILLAGE CEMETERY

lies in the northern part of the village, adjoining the fair grounds on the east. It contains about ten acres, and was opened for burials in September 1859. A considerable part of it is occupied by a grove of native oaks. The grounds were laid out at considerable expense by a professional landscape artist of repute, and abound with graceful curves and varying effects. There are many neat and elaborate monuments, and well kept burial plats. Near the entrance stands the soldiers' monument, erected through the generosity of Hon. John S. Marcy, as a tribute of honor to the soldiers of the village who joined in the war of the Rebellion. It occupies a circular enclosure by an evergreen hedge.

THE CHURCHES OF RIVERHEAD.

Congregational.—The people of this village in their religious connection had been united with the church at Upper Aquebogue, and were mainly among the seceders from the old church, who in 1829 formed a new congregation and built a church between the two villages mentioned. About the year 1825 the minister of the Aquebogue church preached in the court-house on alternate Sunday evenings, at 5 o'clock. In 1827 regular weekly prayer meetings were commenced and a Sunday-school established, with nearly 100 scholars, both of which have since been steadily maintained. At that time a Methodist "circuit rider" also preached in the court-house, his appointment being Friday afternoon or evening once a fortnight. After the secession above spoken of services were conducted in the court-house regularly at 11 o'clock on Sunday morning for several years. The seceding congregation, which consisted mainly of the people of Northville and Riverhead, in 1834 divided harmoniously, and, the church being removed to Northville, the congregation of Riverhead established its place of worship in the seminary, then just built. At that time the society consisted of about 20 members, among whom were some of the leading men of the village. The congregation being strengthened, a church was erected in 1841, which still remains. It was enlarged in 1868, and further repairs and improvements were made in 1880 and 1881. John Moser was pastor of this church from its organization to 1836; his successors have been: Ashley M. Gilbert, 1836, 1837; Charles I. Knowles, 1837-44; Mr. Brooks, a short time in 1845; Mr. Knowles again from June 1846 to his death, in October 1850; Clarke Lockwood, 1853-57; George H. Entler; Henry Clark, 1861-65; Mr. Hoover, till 1870; Samuel Orcutt, 1871, 1872; William I. Chalmers, July 1872 to the present time. Since its organization 332 persons have united with this church, and its present membership numbers about 150. A flourishing Sunday-school is connected with it, of which Hon. James H. Tuthill has for many years been the superintendent. The school numbers 200 pupils, and has a library of nearly a thousand volumes.

Riverhead M.E. Church.—Regular services by the Methodist Episcopal Church were established here about the year 1825. In 1828 or 1829 services were held by this denomination and the Congregationalists in the court-house on alternate Sundays. A church with nine members was organized in April 1833. In 1834 a house of worship was erected, the size of it being 34 by 42 feet. This was dedicated the following year. In 1845 the number of members had reached 100. In ministerial service this was at first a part of the Suffolk circuit. Afterward it was for several years connected with Jamesport. The present church, a stately edifice, was commenced in 1869 and completed and dedicated in the following year, at a cost of about $12,000, all of which was paid soon after its completion. It occupies the site of the first church, which was sold and removed to the opposite side of the street, not far away. A burying ground, established about the time of the first church, occupies the yard about the church. The following are the ministers who have served this church since its organization:

Richard Wymond, 1833; William K. Stopford, 1834; John Trippett, 1835; James Floy, 1836; William McKendree Bangs, 1837; Orlando Starr, 1838, 1839; Theron Osborn, 1840; David Osborn, 1841, 1842; Samuel W. Law, 1843; Oliver E. Brown, 1844; Isaac Sandford, 1845; George W. Woodruff, 1846, 1847; Henry D. Latham, 1848; Federick W. Sizer, 1849; David Robinson, 1850, 1851; Nathan Tibbals, 1852; Francis C. Hill, 1853; Samuel F. Johnson, 1854, 1855; Nicholas Orchard, 1856, 1857; Justus O. Worth, 1858; John S. Haugh, 1859; Daniel F. Hallock, 1860; D.A. Goodsell, 1861, 1862; Samuel M. Hammond, 1863, 1864; Thomas N. Laine, 1865, 1866; Thomas G. Osborn, 1867, 1868; E.F. Hadley, 1869-71; J. Cromlish, 1872, 1873; J.S. Mitchell, 1874; L.P. Perry, 1875, 1876; Thomas G. Osborn, 1877-79; B.T. Abbott, 1880, 1881. The membership at present is about 200, and the church and parsonage are valued at $15,000. The Sunday-school connected numbers about 230.

The New Jerusalem (Swedenborgian) *Church* of this village was established mainly by the efforts and influence of Elijah Terry, a citizen of the village who joined the church of that sect at Baiting Hollow in 1831. A church consisting of ten members was organized here May 12th 1839. Public worship was at first conducted in a school-house, then in a private hall built by Mr. Terry, which was also used as a select school room. In 1855 a house of worship was erected in the central part of the village. It is a creditable structure and its tall spire looks far out over the surrounding settlement. The adherents of the church number about 35 families. There is a Sunday-school connected with it, numbering about 40 pupils. A burying ground belonging to this church lies in the northern part of the village, adjoining the Roman Catholic church grounds on the northwest. The regular ministerial supply of this church began in 1844, when M.M. Carl divided his time between this and the Baiting Hollow church. He was succeeded by Revs. George F. Stearns, C.C. Lord and Charles A. Dunham, the service of the latter reaching to May 1880. The present pastor is Rev. Benjamin D. Palmer.

St. John's Roman Catholic Church.—The first movement of the Roman Catholic church in this town was in 1844. In that year mass was celebrated here for the first time. The ceremony took place at the house of James Magee, at Upper Aquebogue, being conducted by Father Curren of Astoria. There were in attendance on that occasion four persons. In 1848 Father McGiness of Jamaica began visiting here twice a year, and afterward Father McCarthy of Hicksville received it with some other parts of Suffolk county into his charge, visiting and celebrating mass here once in three months until 1856. His successors were: Father O'Neil, 1857; Father Brunneman, 1857-67; Father McKenna (once in six weeks), 1867; Father Cassella, of St. Peter's, Brooklyn, placed in charge of Smithtown, Patchogue and Riverhead in 1868, on the division of the parish of Suffolk county, living at Riverhead; Father Kearney, who succeeded to the position in 1872 (since which time mass has been said once a month) and remained until December 23d 1878; Father Hanselman, till May 1880, and Father McNulty, who still remains in charge. A small house on East street, in the eastern part of the village, was purchased for use as a chapel in 1860. This, having become too small to accommodate the increasing congregation, was sold in 1870 and a new church edifice erected. This is a handsome building , located on a spacious lot in the northern part of the village, and a parsonage adjoins it. A part of the lot, which is about two acres in size, contains the denominational burying ground. The church was consecrated by Bishop Loughlin in 1871; it is called St. John's church. The house will seat three hundred persons, and its cost, with that of the personage, was about $6,000. There are said to be about 450 Roman Catholics in this town. A Sunday-school of 60 scholars is connected with the church. The facts in this sketch of St. John's Church were furnished by Samuel Tuthill of Northville.

A church of Free Methodists was organized here January 20th 1870, by Rev. William J. Selby. It occupies a neat chapel on Concord street, in the eastern part of the village, built in 1869. The congregation is not large. Three years after its organization it numbered only 30 members. The following ministers have supplied it: John Gimson, 1870; William Dixon, 1871; Thomas Ross, 1871, 1872; Lewis Hough, 1873.

Grace Episcopal Church. —Worship according to the Protestant Episcopal form was commenced in this village in 1870. A house of worship was erected in the northern part of the village, between Washington and Roanoke avenues, fronting the latter. The parish is prosperous. Rev. Thomas Cook is the rector.

The church edifice is a neat and beautiful structure, 60 by 26, roofed with slate, and furnished with a lofty belfry and spire surmounted by a gilt cross. The inside is tastefully ceiled with narrow pine. It has a recess chancel, with a beautiful center window of stained glass, with appropriate emblems. The other windows are of ground glass, with suitable colored borders. The church is capable of seating 250 persons. It was built in 1872, chiefly by the efforts of othe Rev. Thomas Cook, head of the Associate Mission, and cost, with the grounds, $6,000.

ASSOCIATIONS.

Riverhead Lodge, No. 465, F. & A. M. was organized in March 1867, with 14 charter members. Its first officers were: N.S. Woodhull, M.; B.V. Chase, S.W.; D.A. Vail, J.W.; J.H. Terry, treasurer; Wesley Fanning, secretary. Succeeding masters of the lodge were: N.S. Woodhull, 1868; E.F. Squires, 1869; J.H. Perkins, 1870; N.S. Woodhull, 1871; George H. Skidmore, 1872, 1873; H.H. Benjamin, 1874, 1875; W.E. Gerard, 1876, 1877; O.A. Terry, 1878; J.E. Young, 1879; George H. Skidmore, 1880-82. The lodge meets in Terry's Hall, on Griffing avenue, every Tuesday evening, except during the months of July and August, when it meets only on the fourth Tuesday of each month. It has a membersip of over 100.

Peconic Division, No. 101, *Sons of Temperance* was organized here in the early days of the order, and for many years exerted a wholesome influence over the morals of the village. In 1875 it reported 112 members. After an existence of more than a quarter of a century it surrendered its charter in 1879.

The people of this village and town have maintained a good character for sobriety, and have been active in the interests of the cause of temperance. Prime, in 1845, said of it: "There are few places in the land in which the efforts of the friends of temperance have been crowned with more triumphant success. Most of the hotels or taverns are conducted on temperance principles." At the special election held May 19th 1846 to decide the question of granting licenses the town of Riverhead gave 221 votes for "no license" against 82 for license. Hon. George Miller said in reference to the same subject:

"In 1828 the liquor drunk in the town was five times as much as it was two years afterward. The first temperance meeting in Riverhead was held late in January 1829, when 17 signed the pledge. At the next meeting, a fortnight later, the signers were doubled, and the consumption of liquor was undoubtedly lessened one-half in three months. Before that liquor was almost everywhere. Every merchant and man of business kept his open bottle. But as soon as the principles of total abstinence were adopted a change came over the community. At the very next town meeting the people all went home before night, sober. At the next launching, of Captain Henry Horton's vessel, no liquor was used." Fishermen abandoned it; merchants who sold other goods quit the sale of it. The people soon saw clearly what fifty years has proved to be true, that even the moderate use of liquor is not necessary but hurtful, and that sound morals and good government require that its habitual use should be abandoned. It would be hard to estimate the amount of temporal blessing this great reformation in principle and practice has caused to households and individuals."

By the town election of 1881 the board of excise commissioners became anti-license, so that no licenses are now granted in the town.

The Suffolk County Mutual Benefit Association, organized a few years since, has its headquarters in this village, and is in a prosperous condition. Its report for last year showed an increase in membership from 172 in the previous year to 284 in the year 1881. Thus during the latter year the membership increased 112. As there were no deaths during the year there were no assessments. The assets for 1880 were $401.75, and for 1881 they were $801.15. The present officers are: W.E. Gerard, president; John M. Price (of Patchogue) and George H. Skidmore, vice-presidents; David F. Vail, treasurer; Ahaz Bradley, secretary.

Two fire engine companies have been organized in the village. Of these the first was Red Bird Engine Company, No. 1, which was organized in 1836. It has two hand engines and several hundred feet of hose. The company consists of about forty members. The second fire company, Washington Engine Company, No. 2, was organized June 1st 1861. Besides an elegant large hand engine which it already had, a new steamer was purchased for it in 1875. This company has also several hundred feet of hose. It has about forty members.

THE PRESS OF RIVERHEAD.

Being the county seat this village has been a favorable field for the location of a weekly newspaper. The first one started here was the *Suffolk Gazette*. It was established by John Hancock, in August 1849. It was moved to Sag Harbor in the early part of 1851, and back again to Riverhead in December 1854. Its publication was soon after suspended. The *Suffolk Union* was started here in 1859, by Washington Van Zandt. Its publication was continued until the winter of 1862-3, when the officer was destroyed by fire, and the paper was discontinued.

In 1865 Buel G. Davis started the *Suffolk County Monitor*, the publication of which ceased in the following year.

The *Riverhead Weekly News* was started by James B. Slade March 3d 1868, and was continued by him till its ownership was transferred to William R. Duvall, May 26th 1875. The latter still continues its publication. It is the only paper published in the village.

GEORGE MILLER.

George Miller, of Riverhead, perhaps more widely known than any other resident of the county of Suffolk, is the son of Timothy Miller. He was born at Miller's Place, on the 16th of March 1799. His mother was Mehetabel, daughter of Joseph Brown, of Rocky Point. His health has always been delicate. At Clinton Academy, East Hampton, be acquired a good knowledge of the classics.

He studied law first with the late Judge Selah B. Strong, and afterward with Caleb S. Woodhull in the city of New York. In the year 1825 he came to Riverhead and established his law office; he was then 26 years old, and for 57 consecutive years he has steadily resided there. He succeeded Samuel B. Nicoll, who a few years before had taken the place vacated by the removal of Hall Osborn.

His reputation for honesty, industry and capacity was early established, and he was overrun with official business at the very outset of his career. Other lawyers soon opened offices there, but he commanded a large share of all the practice, and in important cases he was sure to be retained by clients from every part of the county. He was very thorough, and not less persevering; once convinced that his position was right he never abandoned it till he succeeded, or was reduced to submission by the decision of the court of last appeal.

During the 20 or 25 years he has practiced chiefly in the higher courts, and this has been especially the case since about that time he associated with him James H. Tuthill as a law partner. In the face of strong competition the firm has maintained its original reputation and been eminently successful.

Mr. Miller's time and strength have been greatly taxed in the conduct and defense of suits originating from defective titles, etc., to an entire township of valuable timber land in the State of Maine, which he and a few associates had purchased. He also had a long and vexatious contest with the merchants Griswold of New York, in relation to the ownership of some lots at the Atlantic Dock in Brooklyn.

As a speaker his addresses are always to the judgment and without the least attempt at oratory; yet in the courts, and on occasions of religious revivals and temperance gatherings, where his whole heart was absorbed, he has made some very pathetic and touching appeals. The charm of his forensic efforts consists not in their brilliancy and show but in their logic and power.

The Congregational church at Riverhead owes its early origin chiefly to his labors and contributions, and to it he has ever rendered a hearty and cordial support.

He married, about 1836, Miss Eliza Leonard of Massachusetts, for many years a teacher in the Riverhead Academy.

He represented the county of Suffolk in the Lesiglature in 1854, and was county judge and surrogate in 1857.

N. W. FOSTER.

Nathaniel Woodhull Foster was born in Riverhead, September 24th 1835. His father, Herman D. Foster, a native of the town of Southampton, was one of the pioneer merchants of Riverhead. His mother was Fannie, daughter of Nathaniel Woodhull of Wading River, a near relative of General Nathaniel Woodhull of Revioluntary fame.

The subject of this sketch was early trained to "tend the store," and there studied his lessons for the school. On the site of the old store, owned and occupied nearly forty years by his father, he has recently erected a handsome and substantial brick store, greatly improving the appearance of the village.

His school life was mostly spent at the public school in the village, but later he studied two winters at the Franklinville Academy.

While in the store with his father he accepted the local agency of the Equitable Life Assurance Society of New York, then just beginning its operations. A while afterward he took up the business of fire insurance. In 1867 the officers of the Equitable asked him to take the general agency for Suffolk county, and in 1870 added Queens county. In 1874 he sold out his mercantile business.

Mr. Foster married Fannie, daughter of Sylvester Miller, of Wading River, in 1858. He is a member of the Congregational church, and active in all its meetings and in the Sunday-school. In early life he was earnestly interested in the temperance work, and was connected from time to time with the different organizations, particularly with the Sons of Temperance. In 1865 he was, quite unexpectedly to himself, called to the head of that order for eastern New York. Politically Mr. Foster is a thorough Republican.

Always desirous of seeing progress and improvement, he has ever been active in any movement that promised for the good of Riverhead. He has been a trustee of the village cemetery association from its organization, freely giving thought, time and money for its success, working night and day to establish it in such shape that it might forever be a credit to the village. He was the originator of the Riverhead Savings Bank, and one of its trustees from the start.

As secretary of the Suffolk County Agricultural Society he introduced several new, attractive and important features in its annual fairs, and, with the assistance of the county press, succeeded quite largely in arousing a new interest therein, not only in the county, but throughout the State.

CAPTAIN EDWARD HAWKINS.

Captain Edward Hawkins was born in Stony Brook, town of Brookhaven, January 21st 1829. His father, Daniel Shaler Hawkins, was for many years a resident of Suffolk, and an active and successful business man. For many years he was engaged in the coasting trade, being the builder and owner of a number of vessels. The later years of his life he spent at his residence at Stony Brook. He raised a large family and trained them to habits of industry and independence. Believing that success can be achieved by honest effort, he early taught them to make efforts for their own advancement in life. It is not surprising therefore that at the early age of 15 the subject of this sketch entered upon his chosen seafaring life, quitting the paternal roof to seek his fortune unaided except by the good advice and training secured at home. Mr. Hawkins was educated at the common schools, never having the advantages for higher education that our colleges and universities now afford. When he left home it was with the determination to become master of his profession, and we find him at the age of 21 in command of a vessel, and a few years later both a commander and an owner. Captain Hawkins has spent many years of his life on the sea, engaged in the coasting trade, principally in southern waters; and has at various times made voyages to the West Indies, Mexico and many southern ports. During the war of the Rebellion he was in government employ, using his vessel for transport service.

At the close of the Rebellion and at the age of 36 Mr. Hawkins retired from seafaring life, never having met with an accident during his experience on the water. Immediately after his retirement from the sea he purchased a farm in the town of Riverhead, which he is successfully cultivating and where he continues to reside, making his home one of the most attractive in the county. In company with three brothers he engaged extensively in the manufacture of fish oil and fish guano, having extensive factories at Gardiner's Island and Barren Island employing 150 men and 5 steamers.

In politics Mr. Hawkins has always taken an active interest, and he is an earnest worker for the Democratic party. He has at various times been nominated to positions of trust by his party, unsolicited, being named as a candidate for supervisor of his town and later for sheriff and county treasurer; but, his party being in the minority, he was not elected to the positions which his friends tendered him and which he is by their nomination judged well qualified to fill. He is a director of the Riverhead Savings Bank, and is interested in all measures for the advancement of the public good.

Mr. Hawkins was married in 1855 to Miss Susan C. Smith, daughter of Israel Smith of Lake Grove, Suffolk county. They have had seven children, of whom five are now living.

Mr. Hawkins has always been an active and independent business man and eminently successful. He takes decided views on all subjects, and is an independent and fearless advocate of what he believes to be right. Socially he is highly esteemed, and he is justly termed one of the Suffolk county's representative successful citizens, among whom he takes high rank.

SIMEON S. HAWKINS.

Simeon S. Hawkins was born at Stony Brook, in the town of Brookhaven, March 30th 1827. At the age of 15 he entered upon a seafaring life, in which he made so rapid advancement that in 1847, at the age of 20, he became captain of the schooner "Charles D. Hallock," engaged in the coasting trade. Although the burden of this boat was only 200 tons, she was considered a large schooner at that time, and attracted a good many visitors when lying in New York harbor. The general verdict was that she ought to be called a ship and rigged accordingly. After this Captain Hawkins was master of various vessels, some of which were engaged in the southern trade. During his stay in southern ports he saw and heard things that led him into a train of serious thought. The nation was being agitated about this time by the "Free Soil" movement, and he repeatedly heard the declaration from the mouths of hot-blooded southerners that no Free Soiler could ever take his seat as president if elected. This he thought a flat denial of, and a rebellion against, the fundamental idea of democratic government, viz., a willing submission to the will of the majority. Up to this time he had been a Democrat, but the attitude of the south, which was the backbone of the Democratic party, changed him, and he has ever since worked and voted with the Republican party. At Charleston, South Carolina, there was a public reading room, to which all captains while in port were nominally invited. Captain Hawkins, supposing the invitation meant what it said, went to the reading room, but when it became known that he was a northern man he was unceremoniously ordered out. This was another eye-opener, a novel applications of the institutions of a free government. Ever since then he has had a new conception of the sacredness of the principle that, however high party strife may run, the majority must be sovereign at last. This he believes to be the theory and principle of the Republican party. As a member of that party he has given special attention to the town primary meetings, believing that the real authority of the "government of the people by the people" begins here. He feels that a reform in these meetings has been effected in his own town through the efforts of himself and a few friends who hold the same views.

Mr. Hawkins has served his town and county as an office-holder on several occasions. The first was in 1866, when he was elected county superintendent of the poor, which office he held three years. In 1870 he was elected supervisor of his town, his brother Edward being his competitor on the Democratic ticket. The contest was warm but perfectly friendly. He was a delegate to the State convention that nominated Reuben E. Fenton for governor. He was also a delegate to the great Republican convention at Chicago that nominated James A. Garfield for the presidency. At that convention Mr. Hawkins was one of the original bolters of the "unit rule," believing it to be a sacred principle that the voice of the people should be heard in the national as well as in the State convention. He was one of the immortal "19" who voted as they had been instructed by the authority which they represented—their constituents at home. He says Roscoe Conkling took them into a committee room and openly threatened every man of them with political annihilation if they bolted the "unit rule." They chose to obey the people rather than the machine.

When the war broke out Captain Hawkins was trading at ports on the coasts of Georgia and Florida. In 1862 he was in command of the bark "Hannibal," an assistant to the naval store ships at Port Royal, S.C. After that he came home and began trading in coal and lumber at Jamesport. He bought the schooner "Anna D. Price" and placed her in this service. In 1870, wishing to extend his operations, he formed a partnership with three of his brothers in the mendaden [sic] fishery business. Theirs has become the largest concern engaged in this line of enterprise; owning five steamers and nine other vessels, some of which are double gang boats. The amount of Capital invested is $175,000. Their works are on Barren Island. They are among the pioneers in utilizing the "scraps" that used to be thrown away as worthless.

The Hawkins family is of English extraction, three brothers of that name having emigrated from the old country at one time and settled in the new. Edward Hawkins, grandfather to the subject of this sketch, was a direct descendant of one of the three brothers. He married MIss Olivia Shaler, a school teacher from the State of Connecticut, and settled at Stony Brook when that was the most important seaport and the liveliest village in the town of Brookhaven.

Daniel Shaler Hawkins, the father of our subject, was one of Edward's sons. His first wife was Sophia Smith, daughter of Simeon Smith. They raised five sons—George, Ebenezer, Simeon S., Edward and Jedediah; and three daughters, one of whom is dead. Simeon was the third son and the third child. He was married in 1852 to a daughter of Albert Youngs, of Jamesport, by whom he has four children.

Mr. Hawkins is still a middle aged man, full of vigor and usefulness, having accomplished vastly more than the average of men 55 years old. He has a beautiful home in the village of Jamesport, and bids fair to furnish from the next twenty years' achievements material for another biographical sketch, in a second Illustrated History, that the growth of Suffolk county may demand within that period.

CHAPTER VII

DEVELOPMENT OF AGRICULTURE IN SUFFOLK COUNTY

Written by Henry P. Hedges in 1883

Henry Hedges died in 1911 at the age of 93. Born on a farm in Wainscott in the Town of East Hampton, he entered Clinton Academy and later became a student in Yale College. He practiced law in Sag Harbor and Bridgehampton. He was elected to the Assembly on the Whig ticket and later, was District Attorney of Suffolk County and for many years a County Judge. But what separated him from his fellow public servants was his abiding life-long interest in local history. His first major lecture was in 1849 at the age of 32 when he delivered the Oration at the celebration of the Bicentennial Anniversary of East Hampton Town. Little about the history of East Hampton had seen its way into print prior to 1849. It was a time when books were leather-bound and somewhat scarce. Hedges broke new ground in providing historical facts and figures to residents in the community who cared about local history. His orations were printed in pamphlet form or printed in local newspapers for wide dissemintation to the public. While, at times, Hedges' prose becomes florid, it was delivered at a time when oratory was one of the main entertainments of a small community. There were no movies, TV, or magazines. What Hedges provided in lecture was a level of primary-source research using Town and Trustee records not used in prior histories. He was systematically providing access to local hsitory in a style and language local people enjoyed—something unique until then on the East End.

IN these centennial exercises the subject assigned to me was "The De-velopment of Agriculture." Agriculture, new and old, what it was two hundred years gone by, and what is now in Suffolk County. From 1639, when Lyon Gardiner made the first English settlement in the County of Suffolk, and within the present bounds of the State of New York, other colonies were founded at Southampton and Southold in 1640; in East-Hampton in 1649, and extending to Shelter Island, Setauket, Smithtown and Huntington, soon thereafter covered by charter the territory of the county of Suffolk. At the organization of the county in 1683, forty-four years had passed since Gardiner came to his island. This county com-prised about two-thirds of the territory of Long Island. The census of 1875 gives the area thus:

	IMPROVED	WOODLAND	OTHER	TOTAL,
Kings county, acres,	9,110	600	1,174	11,090
Queens county, "	117,686	29,736	24,561	171,983
Suffolk county, "	156,760	102,550	129,135	388,445

TOTAL AREA, 571,518

One-third is 190,506

Area of Kings and Queens is 183,073

Area of Suffolk over one-third is—acres 7,433

The precise population of the State or county in 1683, I have not ascertained. There was a partial statement in 1693, and the apportion-ment of militia to each county, thus:

City and county of New York,	477
Queens county,	580
Suffolk "	533
Kings "	319
Albany "	359
Ulster county and Dutchess,	277
Westchester county,	283
Richmond "	104

Total, 2,932

Special thanks to the following individuals and organizations for generously providing the photos, postcards, and other memorabilia that made the 32 pages of black-and-white pictures and 16 pages of color pictures that follow possible:

Color pictures courtesy of:
Town of Riverhead

Black-and-white pictures courtesy of:
Tom Twomey
Katherine Kalanz, The Riverhead Free Library
Georgette Lane Case, Town of Riverhead, Office of the Historian

Pair of horses in plow

Woman mowing farm with horse drawn clipper

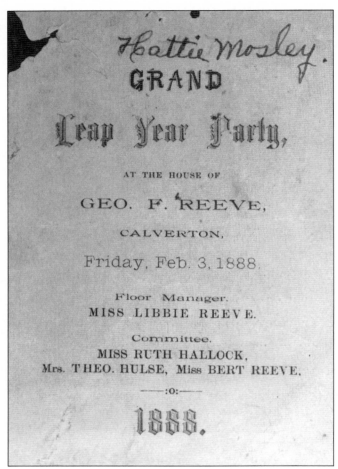

Leap Year Party Invite, 1888

BOARD OF EDUCATION, SCHOOL DISTRICT NO. 5,
TOWN OF RIVERHEAD.

No. 1526   Riverhead, N. Y., *November 6* 1888

To *James Nail*   Treasurer,

Pay to the order of *Silas C Beebe*

Two 25/100 — Dollars,

For *Labor*

$2.25/100   *Thos C Davis* Clerk.   *Jas E Wall* President.

Board of Education School District #5 paycheck, 1888

Riverhead High School Girls Basketball Team, 1909

Howard Camp of Sons of Veterans, from left to right: Howard V. Lane,
George (Widgens) Brown, Lane, Henry Daton, John Oliver, John S. Conklin,
Fred Corwin, Nat Corwin, Elmer G. Conklin, Edwin Benjamin, Ernest Conklin

Quogue-Riverhead Motor Transit Bus

Hudson Cultivator, Talmage Farm

Barber Shop: One chair, no waiting

Croquet on the lawn, Jamesport, 1886

Judge Griffing at Lotus Pond
Postmark date Sept. 7, 1919

Fishing at Wildwood Lake
Postmark date Mar. 31, 1917

Racing at Suffolk County Fair

Watching the Ball Game
Postmark date Sept. 18, 1913

Published by J. H. Brown, Riverhead, L. I.   Photo by Spooner & Wells, New York

FAST SPEED ON THE STRAIGHTAWAY—THE LONG ISLAND AUTO DERBY OVER THE RIVERHEAD-MATTITUCK COURSE

Fast Speed on the Straightaway—The Long Island Auto Derby over the Riverhead-Mattuck Course

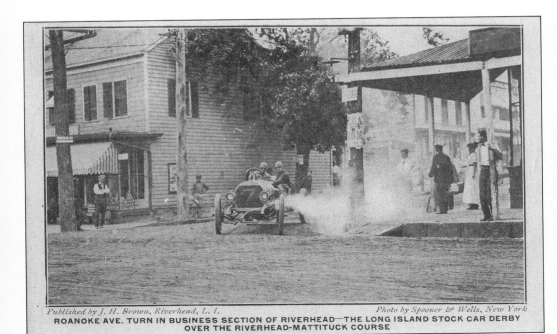

Published by J. H. Brown, Riverhead, L. I.   Photo by Spooner & Wells, New York

ROANOKE AVE. TURN IN BUSINESS SECTION OF RIVERHEAD—THE LONG ISLAND STOCK CAR DERBY OVER THE RIVERHEAD-MATTITUCK COURSE

Roanoke Ave. turn in business section of Riverhead—
The Long Island Stock Car Derby over the Riverhead-Mattuck Course

Young Soap Box Entrants line up on Main Street—Prize winners have prizes on hoods, 1910

Bridge at the head of Peconic River

Main Street, 1912

Main Street, from Peconic Avenue corner.
Large building on left side still stands as Star Confectionery.

Main Street

West Main Street looking East

33 East Main Street

East Main Street

3235   MAIN STR., RIVERHEAD, L. I.   ILLUST. POST CARD CO., N. Y.

Main Street
Postmark date June 30, 1913

Corner of Main Street & Grilling Avenue
Postmark date Nov. 6, 1921

SCENE on GRIFFIN AVE. RIVERHEAD, L. I.

3234

&LUST. POST CARD CO., N. Y.

Griffin Avenue

3328   GRIFFING AVE, LOOKING SOUTH, RIVERHEAD N. Y.

Griffing Avenue looking South
Postmark date Sept. 3, 1907

Second Street looking East
Postmark date Feb. 17, 1911

Griffing Avenue from Main Street

Lovers Lane
Postmark date Sept. 30, 1909

Roanoke Avenue looking North
Postmark date Apr. 3, 1920

ROANOKE HEIGHTS, RIVERHEAD, L. I., N. Y.

Roanoke Heights

Published by G. H. Downs & Sons
Main Street, looking east, Aquebogue, L. I.

Main Street looking East, Aquebogue

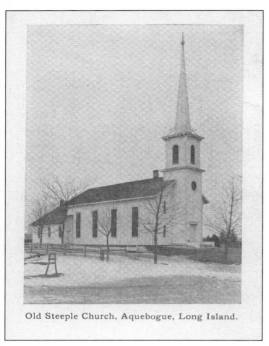

Old Steeple Church, Aquebogue, Long Island.

Old Steeple Church, Aquebogue

St. Isador's Polish Catholic Church

The First
Congregational
Church

Kosciol Polski Sw. Izydora w Riverhead, N. Y., w Stanach Ziednvczonych Pol Nocnej Ameryki.
St. Izydora's Polish R. C. Church, Riverhead, N. Y., U. S. A.

St. Izydora's Polish Roman Catholic Church

Riverhead Firehouse
Postmark date Sept. 18, 1933

Riverhead Rail Road Station

Rest-A-While, Flanders

Suffolk County Court House
Postmark date July 24, 1941

Joshua L. Wells House

Great Peconic Bay House and the Miamogue, South Jamesport

The Griffin House
Postmark date Nov. 17, 1916

Women's Building, Fair Grounds
Postmark date Sept 5, 1913

The Old Woolen Mill, Upper Mills

The Hallet Mills
Postmark date Jan. 26, 1911

Old Landing Club House on Reese Farm—washed away in hurricane, 1944

11353 Riverhead Yacht Club Dock, Riverhead, L.I.

Riverhead Yacht Club Dock (Pre-1915)

Looking towards waters edge in South Jamesport

The Old Bridge, Grangebel Lake
Postmark date Nov. 17, 1916

Water Tower & Mill.   Riverhead, L.I.

Tack för korten många hälsningar från E. J.

Water Tower and Mill
*Postmark date
Jul. 24, 1905*

3238   THE OLD RED MILL, RIVERHEAD, L. I.   ILLUST. POST CARD CO., N. Y.

The Old Red Mill

On Peconic Bay, Aquebogue

Trout Brook Mill, Aquebogue

Peconic River

Bird's eye view of Peconic River
Postmark date Oct. 25, 1905

Peconic River
Postmark date Sept. 25, 1906

Near Head of Peconic River
Postmark date Oct. 14, 1912

The Sound Cliffs, near Roanoke
Postmark date Mar. 2, 1911

Lovers Rock
Postmark date Nov. 9, 1915

Sound Beach Scene

The Sound Shore looking East, Roanoke
Postmark date Nov. 17, 1916

TOWN LANDMARKS

The following pages relate to the historic sites that were designated by Town Board Resolution. Please note: the information that each caption provides may not be completely accurate, since our researcher relied not only on Town records, church records, and newspaper articles, but also on personal memoirs and best recollections. Such sources may also have conflicted with one another.

BANK BUILDING Located at 34, 38 and 42 West Main Street, Riverhead. The Bank Building was erected in 1892 specifically for the Riverhead Savings Bank.

THE WADING RIVER CONGREGATIONAL CHURCH Located at 2059 North Country Road. This building was erected in August 1835 to replace the original 1740 church. The 1837 call to worship bell is still in use today.

DAVIS-CORWIN HOUSE Located at 133 East Main Street, Riverhead. This house is probably the oldest house in the village of Riverhead. Built by Chapman Davis, Jr., the exact date of construction is unknown, but it was not much later than 1835.

CARRIAGE HOUSE Located behind the Davis-Corwin House, has been converted into a garage and caretaker's quarters.

BENJAMIN HOUSE Located at 141 East Main Street, Riverhead. Built prior to 1870, this was one of the early residences on Main Street. Moses Benjamin, proprietor of Benjamin's Drug Store, built this unpretentious and roomy house. The Town of Riverhead purchased this building and the Davis-Corwin House in 1996 from Northville Docks.

FRESH POND SCHOOLHOUSE Located behind the Benjamin House, was a one-room school which was built in Baiting Hollow in 1821, was moved to the George Sabat Farm in 1918, and used for storage and farm housing. In 1977, the Sabat family donated the schoolhouse for preservation, and it was moved to its present location.

BARNES HOUSE
Located at 224 Griffing
Avenue, Riverhead.
Built between 1858
and 1873 for A.G.
Moore, it was later
sold to the Barnes
family.

CAPTAIN DIMON
HOUSE Located at 370
Manor Lane, Jamesport.
Captain Dimon, a whaling captain reputed to
be the founder of
Jamesport hamlet,
erected this Gothic
style house in the
1850's. It was believed
to be haunted.

CENTERVILLE CHAPEL Located
at 3718 Sound Avenue,
Riverhead. Built in 1888, it was
last used for regular worship in
1926 and sold to private owners
in 1976. The present day First
Baptist Church used Centerville
for prayer services from 1916 to
1926.

CHARLES HALLETT HOUSE Located at 218 Griffing Avenue. This house shows on the 1873 map of Riverhead and is believed to have been built in the 1860's. It was the first house in Riverhead to have electricity.

CHESTER HOUSE Located at 179 Sound Road, Riverhead. Originally constructed about 1790, it was substantially rebuilt by the Tuthills and later enlarged by the Davis family.

EVERETT CONKLIN HOUSE Located at 206 Lincoln Street, Riverhead. This house, and its workshop in the rear, were built about 1870. At the time the house was built, the area was considered a prime residential area. Mr. Conklin used the workshop for picture framing and other small fine cabinet making.

BRIAN J. TRAFFORD HOUSE Located at 216 Lincoln Street. Built in 1870, this house is one of the several original Conklin family homes on Lincoln Street.

CORWIN-YOUNG HOUSE Located at 445 Griffing Avenue, Riverhead. The exact date of this house is unknown, but it was sometime in the mid-1800's, possibly as late as 1891. The Corwin family was in the building and lumber business. This shows in the fancy porch turnings, the design of the shingles and the turns of the moldings.

DeLAGERBURG HOUSE, also known as FOUR CHIMNEYS. Located at 126 Sound Road, Riverhead. The original part of the house was built about 1760 by the Woodhull family. It was enlarged in 1845 with the addition of a section reputed to have been brought from Connecticut.

EASTLAWN HOUSE Located at 540 East Main Street, Riverhead. Built by Hubbard Corwin in 1855, in the Italianate style, the flat-roofed cupola and front porch remained unaltered until 1990 when the porch was changed.

FENIMORE MEYER HOUSE
Located at 18 First Street, Riverhead.
This is believed to be an early- to mid-
1800's building with a stone foundation. It has had two additions.

GEORGE TUTHILL HOUSE Located at 5412 Sound Avenue, Riverhead. The original 4-bay cottage was built about 1760, making it the oldest house still standing in Northville. In 1901 it was remodeled, the roofs raised and peaks added.

HALLOCKVILLE MUSEUM FARM Located at 6038 Sound Avenue, Riverhead. The main building of the Hallockville Museum Farm, known as Miss Ella's House, was built in 1765 by Reuben Brown. It was sold to Ezra Hallock after the American Revolution. The old farmhouse, its barn and outbuildings are the oldest farm buildings still standing in Riverhead Town.

IRVING DOWNS SCHOOL AND FARM HOUSES Located at 941 Manor Lane, Jamesport. Constructed in 1860, the house is considered to be a typical Long Island farmhouse. The small schoolhouse dates from 1836 and originally was at the northwest corner of Pier and Sound Avenues. When the new school was built on Sound Avenue, the old schoolhouse was moved to the Downs farm.

JAMESPORT CONGREGATIONAL CHURCH
Located at 1590 Main Road, Jamesport.
Constructed in 1731, it is the oldest
Congregational church building still in use
anywhere. The original building still stands
on the original foundation. The actual cash
outlay in 1731 was $18.00 for metal work
such as nails. All timbers, boards and shingles were hand cut from local trees.

JEREMIAH EDWARDS HOUSE
Located at 193 Griffing Avenue,
Riverhead. A white clapboard, modified Victorian House, the Edwards
House featured very ornamental window treatments. It was built in 1873,
in what was then considered to be an
exclusive residential area.

MILLER COTTAGE Located at 2078 North Wading River Road, Wading River. The cottage was built in 1932, near the Miller Homestead, in a typical farmhouse style.

MILLER HOMESTEAD Located at 2098 North Wading River Road, Wading River. A store and tavern, this building was built in 1799 by Zophar Miller. It also served as the first post office, with Zophar, Sylvester and Elihu Miller holding the position of Postmaster over a period of 60 years.

FENTON HOUSE Located at 5298 Sound Avenue, Riverhead. The original building was constructed in 1803, with extensions added later. It still stands on its original foundation and has a birthing room.

ROBERT PALMER HOUSE (also known as the Reuben Wells House) Located at 5130 Sound Avenue, Riverhead. It is not known how old the house is, but there is evidence that a David Wells lived on the site in 1790. Whether or not he lived in this house remains a question. The house is now a part of Palmer Vineyard.

PAUL HULSE HOUSE Located at 3060 Wading River Road, Wading River. The Hulse family first built along the North Wading River Road in 1810. This house is believed to date from 1812 or 1822.

PETER J. LUCAS HOUSE Located at 939 Main Road, Aquebogue. The main section of the house was built about 1817 in Greek Revival style. The western section, added later, is a mixture of Federal or Sheraton motif and Greek Revival. In the late 1800's there was a final two-story addition.

THE PUMP HOUSE located in Grangebel Park, downtown Riverhead. Although the date of the Pump house is unknown, it is considered the last visible edifice of our pioneering forefathers' mill industry.

REPPA "1812" HOUSE Located at 144 Sound Road, Wading River. This home is said to have been built by Benjamin Glover for Ellsworth Tuthill. It was modernized in 1858 and again in the 1900's.

RIVERHEAD NEWS BUILDING Located at 215 Roanoke Avenue, Riverhead. A Greek Revival–style building, it was built prior to 1858.

SLADE-HALLETT
HOUSE Located at 214
Griffing Avenue,
Riverhead. The house
was built for J.B. Slade
about 1860. It is
shown on the 1873
map of Riverhead and
was sold to A. Hallet
(sic) in 1916.

SOUND AVENUE CON-
GREGATIONAL
CHURCH Located at
5267 Sound Avenue,
Aquebogue. The pres-
ent church building
dates from 1904. It
was built on the foun-
dations of an earlier
church, which had
been struck by light-
ning and burned
down. It is now offi-
cially named First
Parrish Church.

PARRISH HALL Located at
5268 Sound Avenue,
Aquebogue. Also known as
Grange Hall. Built as a
church in Aquebogue in
1831, it was moved to its
present location in 1834. It
was converted to the
Northville Academy in 1859
and subsequently changed
to the Grange Hall and
Parrish House. A belfry and
steeple were added in
1859, but destroyed in the
1938 hurricane. The Parrish
Hall served as a meeting
house for Quakers for a
number of years.

TAFT CANDY STORE Located on Peconic Avenue, Riverhead. The candy store stood on Main Street from 1892 to 1915, in front of the old Riverhead Savings Bank building. It sold apples and penny candy. After Judge William Taft died, the building was moved to a backyard on Roanoke Avenue. It was later moved to the rear of the Benjamin House on East Main Street. In 1978 it was moved to its present location.

TUTHILL-LAPHAM HOUSE Located at 342 Sound Road, Wading River. Known as Friendly Hall, the house was built by Bartley Fanning Tuthill about 1820. Much later, it was sold to the Lapham family.

WITCH'S HAT Located at 347 Main Road, Aquebogue. This roadside stand was built in the late 1920's by a Mr. Fleming (first name unknown), and was used as a vegetable stand. Through the years a variety of items were sold there, from vegetables to penny candy to hot dogs and soda. It was even used by the Girl Scouts to sell cookies.

VAIL-LEAVITT MUSIC HALL Located at 18 Peconic Avenue, Riverhead. Built in 1881 the music hall occupied the second and third floors of the building. A men's clothing store was on the first floor at the time. Its design was modeled after Ford's Theatre in Washington, D.C. Shortly after WWI, it was closed and remained closed until June 2003.

VAIL-LEAVITT MUSIC HALL Interior stage

Suffolk was the third county in the colony in the Quotas. I 1698, 1703 and 1723, the population is thus given:

	1698.	1703.	1723.
New York,	4,937,	4,436,	7,248.
Queens county,	3,565,	4,392,	7,191.
Suffolk "	2,679,	3,346,	6,241.
Kings "	2,017,	1,915,	2,218.
Albany "	1,476,	2,273,	6,501.
Ulster " }			
Dutchess " }	1,384,	1,669,	1,083.
Richmond,	727,	504,	1,506.
Orange,	———	268,	1,244.
Westchester,	1,063,	1,946,	4,409.
Total,	17,848	20,749	40,564

These results show that Suffolk County in population was the third in the State in 1693 and 1703, and the fourth county in 1723. A similar comparison will show that by the census in 1731 and 1737 this county held the same rank. In 1746 and 1749 it was the third; in 1756 the fifth, and in 1771 the sixth county of the State in numbers. In these periods reaching over almost one hundred and forty years, when the State was largely agricultural, the population of this county, chiefly so sustained, was nearly one-sixth of that in the entire State. In 1790 it was the eighth county, and contained 16,440 out of 340,120 in the State—a little under one-twentieth of the whole amount. On the 17th day of May, 1683, the tax of the province of New York was fixed at £2556 4s. 0d., and was apportioned thus:

		£	s.	d.
The city and county of New York to pay		434	10	00
County of Westchester,	"	185	15	00
City and county of Albany,	"	240	00	00
County of Richmond,	"	185	15	00
County of Ulster,	"	408	00	00
Kings County,	"	308	08	00
Queens County,	"	308	08	00
County of Suffolk,	"	434	10	00
*Dukes County,	"	40	00	00
County of Orange	"	10	00	00

*The County of Dukes comprised Nantucket, Martha's Vineyard and the Eizabeth Islands.

Thus at the organization of the county its farmers were taxed to pay over one-sixth of all the taxes paid in the then ten counties of the province of New York, and as much as the city and county of New York, and more than any other county that alone excepted. Unless the county of Suffolk was then a productive territory, agriculturally, the tax was unequal, oppressive and unjust. Assuming its equality, it is given as an evidence that even then agriculture had so far progressed that in wealth, in substantial comfort, in ministry to the necessities of mankind, this county as an agricultural county stood even with the then commercial metropolis of the province, and second to none in the province. In 1693 Queens County furnished the highest number of militia men by 47, Suffolk County the next highest number by fifty-six over the number assigned to New York, which latter county came then third on the list of Quotas.

In the Journal of the Legislative Council of New York, under date of September 28, 1691, I find a memorandum of the Address of the House of Representatives, setting forth their sense of the displeasure of Almighty God for their manifold sins "by the blasting of their corn," etc., and an order that the first Wednesday of every month, until the month of June following, be observed and kept a fast day, and that proclamation be issued through the government to enjoin the strict observation thereof, and that all persons be inhibited any servile labor on the said days. Thus the uncertainties of unfavorable seasons, sometimes occurring now, clearly prevailed widely at that early day.

In the Journals of the same Council, under date of October 16, 1738, among the bills read before the Council is one entitled "An act to encourage the destroying of wild cats in Kings County, Queens County and Suffolk County." By an act of February 16, 1771, a like provision applied to Suffolk County, and later, up to the first constitution of the State and acts passed under it, similar provision was made, until the matter was, after the Revolution, devolved, by statute passed March 7th, 1788, upon the several towns in the State. Thus, for nearly one hundred and fifty years, the agriculture of the county, from its infancy, contended against the depredations of wild animals, as well as the blights and mildews of adverse seasons.

Through all this period it encountered a greater obstruction in the method of conducting it. In all early settlements, when the axe clears the forest and the plow inverts the virgin soil, where ages of repose have stored up treasures of fertility, those treasures appear for years unexhausted and inexhaustible. It so seemed to the first settlers on the Mohawk Flats, in the Genesee Valley, in the vales of Ohio, on the prairies of the far West—and it so seemed to our ancestors on the shores of

Long Island. They cropped field after field with little, and oftener no manure; they fenced large farms; they plowed, and raising more oats, and little wheat, and more rye, left the land unseeded with grass for eight, ten or fifteen years, hoping that rest would restore the exhaustion of cropping. Up to the time, and long after the Revolution this skinning process went on all over this county and Island. What manure was made, and that was small in quantity and poorly cared for, was applied on the few acres of mow land, and was thought to be wasted if put on pasture. The vast old pasture lot, comprising often one-half the area of the whole farm, impoverished and skinned, produced a few wild bayberry bushes, such few weeds as worn out land could grow, and everlasting five-fingers and briers. Nine pasture lots in ten were blackberry lots in my early days. This skinning process, that run down the averages of wheat per acre on the Mohawk flats, in the Genesee Valley, and through Ohio, to twelve or thirteen bushels, was perpetuated here for nearly two hundred years. The pasture where I, when a child, was sent to bring home the cows, was such a vast waste that often in a fog I was lost for a time and could find neither cows nor the way to them or to my home. With all the abundance of fish in the waters, I find no evidence that they were caught and applied as a fertilizer to any noticeable extent until after the Revolution. The application of fish, ashes, bone dust and other fertilizers, to any considerable extent, upon the farms of this county, with few exceptions, dates within the last sixty years. Within that time the production of grass, grain and root crops in the county, I think, must have been more than doubled by the increased and increasing application to fertilizers.

So little change occurred in the modes of farming and farm life that the farm and farmer of 1683 might well stand as a picture for those of 1783—the same tools, the same methods, the same surroundings. Grass was cut with the scythe, raked by a hand-rake, pitched by the old heavy iron fork; grain was reaped with the sickle, threshed with the flail and winnowed with a riddle; land was plowed with a heavy wooden framed plough, pointed with wrought iron, whose mole board was protected by odd bits of old cart wheel tire; harrows were mostly with wooden teeth; corn hills were dug with the hoe; the manure for the hill was dropped in heaps, carried by hand in a basket and separately put in each hill. The farmer raised flax and generally a few sheep. Threshing lasted well into the winter, and then out came the crackle and swingle, knife and board. The flax was dressed, wool carded, and the wheel sung its song to the linen and woolen spun in every house. The looms dreary pound gave evidence that home manufacture clad the household. From his feet to his head the farmer stood in vestment

produced on his own farm. The leather of his shoes came from the
hides of his own cattle. The linen and woolen that he wore were products that he raised. The farmer's wife or daughter braided and sewed
the straw-hat on his head. His fur cap was made from the skin of a fox
he shot. The feathers of wild fowl in the bed whereon he rested his
weary frame by night, were the results acquired in his shooting. The
pillow-cases, sheets and blankets, the comfortables, quilts and counter-
panes, the towels and table cloth, were home made. His harness and
lines he cut from hides grown on his farm. Everything about his ox
yoke except staple and ring he made. His whip, his ox gad, his flail, axe,
hoe and fork-handle, were his own work. How little he bought, and
how much he contrived to supply his wants by home manufacture
would astonish this generation.

The typical farm house of 1683 and 1783, were much alike. It was
a single house unpainted, the front two, and the sloping rear roof made
that one story. Four Lombardy poplars, tall, slim and prim, its sole ornament in front. The well pole, a few feet in the rear of the kitchen,
pointed 45 degrees towards mid heaven—underneath swung the
bucket, "The old oaken bucket," immortal in song. Two small windows,
of 6x8 glass, dimly lighted his front room. A large beam ran across its
upper wall. Houses then were built to stay. The floor was uncarpeted.
The chimney and fire-places were capacious masses of masonry, looking with contempt upon the Lilliputian proportions of like structures
of these modern times. The mass of chimney and oven and fire-places
contracted into an entry what would otherwise be a hall. The front
stairs zig-zagged and turned, and wound and squirmed towards the
upper rooms. Over the fire-place hung the old King's Arm, with flint-
lock wherewith he had brought down deer and wild ducks, and brant,
and geese in no small numbers. Outside hung his eel spear, clam and
oyster tongs. Close at hand was the upright hollow log that was his
samp mortar. The barn-yard was near, and in view of the kitchen, and
on the farther side his small barn. One roof sloped down low in the
yard, and on that in the cold winter's day he spread his sheaves of flax
to dry for crackling. All day he labored in the fields. In the long autumn
and winter evenings he husked corn and shelled the ears over the
edge of his spade. No horse-rake; no corn sheller, no horse pitch-fork;
no horsemower or reaper—the life of the farmer was literally a battle
against the forces of nature for little more than the actual necessities of
subsistence, and with the most rude and unwieldy supply of weapons
for the war. The monotony of his life was relieved by hunting and fishing in their season. The farmer raised rye and corn, rarely wheat, for
bread. He ate fresh pork while it lasted, and salt pork while that lasted.

Corn was pounded into samp; ground into hominy and meal; baked or boiled into johnny-cake, Indian bread, griddle-cakes, pudding, or what the Dutch called "suppawn" and the Yankee "hasty pudding;" and in a variety of ways eaten with or without milk. In some shape corn was a chief article of diet. Rye bread, the chief bread, and wheat bread a rare luxury. Oysters, clams, eels and other fish, with game of the forest or fowl of the air, helped out the supply of food in the olden time. The statistics of ancient agriculture, if to be found at all, are not accessible to me. I turn to the State census reports of 1865 and find:

Improved acres in New York State,		14,827,437
" " " Suffolk County,		148,661
Unimproved acres in New York State,		10,411,863
" " " Suffolk County,		230,556 1-2

Showing that Suffolk County contains a trifle less than one-hundredth part of all the improved lands in the State, and over one-fiftieth of all its unimproved lands. The extensive beaches and woodlands of the county constitute its unimproved lands.

The same census reports thus:

	CORN.	BUSHELS HARVESTED.	BUSHELS AVERAGE.
New York State acres plowed	632,213 1-4	17,987,763 1-4	28
Suffolk County, " "	16,460 1-4	580,015	35
	WHEAT.		
N.Y. State, " "	399,918 3-4	5,432,282 1-2	14
Suffolk County, " "	10,563 1-4	199,941 1-4	short 19
	OATS.		
N.Y. State, " "	1,109,910	19,052,833 1-4	over 17
Suffolk County, " "	10,945	289,575	over26
	RYE.		
N.Y. State, " "	234,689	2,575,348-304	short 11
Suffolk County, " "	5,353	61,555 1-2	over 17
	BARLEY.		
N.Y. State, " "	189,029 3-4	3,075,052 3-4	over 16
	CORN.		
Suffolk County, " "	498	14,095	over 28
	TURNIPS.		
N.Y. State, " "	8,123 7-8	1,282,338	over 157
Suffolk County, " "	689 1-4	160,457	232

		POTATOES.	BUSHELS HARVESTED.	BUSHELS AVERAGE.
N.Y. State,	" "	235,058 1-4	23,236,687 3-4	over 98
Suffolk County,	" "	3,439 1-2	292,738	over 85

	ACRES OF GRASS CUT	TONS CUT.
N.Y. State,	4,237,085 3-4	3,897,914 1-8 short 1 ton.
Suffolk County,	34,577 3-4	34,758 over "
New York State, neat cattle,	1,824,221	
Suffolk County, "	18,792	

	HOGS SLAUGHTERED	LBS.	AVERAGE.
New York State,	706,716	128,462,487	181
Suffolk County,	13,942	3,060,602	219

CATTLE SLAUGHTERED FOR BEEF.

New York State, 221,481 1-4.   Suffolk County, 2447

VALUE OF FARM IMPLEMENTS AND MACHINERY.

New York State, $21,189,099.75.   Suffolk County, $407,257.

FERTILIZERS PURCHASED.

New York State, $838,907.52.   Suffolk County, $294,429.40

The value of poultry owned in 1865, and of poultry and eggs sold in 1864, in twelve counties, is thus:

	VALUE.	POULTRY SOLD IN 1864.	EGGS SOLD IN 1864.
Albany,	$52,466.30	31,016.40	34,957.61
Cayuga,	52,911.75	41,696.50	44,772.00
Columbia,	59,816.00	31,195.05	33,125.14
Dutchess,	77,194.00	76,326.50	52,059.50
Monroe,	53,977.33	38,706.05	33,743.98
Onondaga,	49,251.05	34,607.28	45,978.84
Orange,	63,410.00	32,101.24	36,858.36
Queens,	79,597.00	80,035.00	45,960.00
Saratoga,	52,576.53	36,500.81	45,082.91
Ulster,	55,292.12	29,277.20	36,601.30
Westchester,	75,643.75	45,068.46	41,346.53
Suffolk,	47,708.75	47,120.00	57,003.13

The results of these figures make this showing a fraction less than one-hundredth part of all the improved lands in the State lie in the county of Suffolk. If that county produces one-hundredth part of all the aggregate product of the crops in the State that shows, other things being equal, that the farmers of Suffolk County understand their business at least as well as the average farmer. If the land of our country be reckoned poorer than the average in the State, that fact will not lessen the force of the figures, or detract from the greater credit due to Suffolk County farming, provided that production comes up to the average State production. At the outset it appears that of all the tools and machinery used in farming in the State, Suffolk County held in value about one-fiftieth part—showing that the Suffolk County farmer was up to the average twice over in the value of mechanical appliances in his business.

Suffolk County purchased over one-third of all the fertilizers in the State, and more than any other ten counties. Suffolk County kept over one-hundredth of all the neat cattle in the State, and slaughtered over that proportion of all the cattle slaughtered therein, showing that her system of agriculture returned to the soil very largely the products, and was no skinning process; that the corn, oats, roots and grass were fed to domestic animals, and thereby the elements of fertility were restored to the soil.

Although these figures show an average for the county per acre of 13 bushels of potatoes less than the State average, they show more on all other productions. The average of the county over the State is, per acre in corn, 7 bushels; wheat, 5; oats, 9; rye, 8; barley, 12; and turnips 75 bushels. This county raised nearly one-thirtieth of all the corn raised in the State more than one-thirtieth of all the wheat, over one-seventieth of all the oats, nearly one-fortieth of all the rye, over one-eighth of all the turnips, and nearly one-eightieth of all the potatoes. It produced nearly one-fortieth of the total pork, and our average weight of hogs exceeded that of the State by 38 pounds. Suffolk County is credited with less poultry in 1865 than any of the twelve counties I have named, but sold more in 1864 than any counties in the State except Queens and Dutchess. Suffolk County beat all other counties in the State on eggs, and sold nearly $5,000 more than Dutchess County, which is the next highest on the list.

The census of 1875 gives these figures.

Improved lands in the State, acres,	15,875,552
Unimproved lands in the State, acres,	9,783,714

Suffolk County, improved lands,	156,760
" " unimproved lands,	332,685

The relative proportion of lands in the State and county remained nearly as in 1865:

Value of all stock in the State,	$146,497,154
" " " " " " County,	1,879,073
" " tools and implements in the State,	44,228,263
" " " " " " Suffolk County,	541,158
Value of all farm buildings other than dwellings,	
In the State, $148,715,775.	In Suffolk County, $2,161,675
Value of all fertilizers purchased in the State,	$1,767,352
" " " " " " Suffolk County,	316,737
Area mown in the States—acres,	4,796,739
" " " Suffolk County,	38,744
Hay produced in the State, tons	5,440,612
" " " Suffolk County	41,980

CORN.—The State produced 20,294,800 bushels; Suffolk County produced 582,690.

OATS.—The State produced 37,968,429 bushels; Suffolk County produced 280,566.

WINTER WHEAT.—The State produced 9,017,737 bushels; Suffolk County produced 182,867.

POTATOES.—The State produced 36,639,601 bushels; Suffolk County produced 405,237.

Number of cattle slaughtered in the State,	85,571
" " " " " Suffolk County,	889
" " hogs " in the State,	521,490
" " " " " Suffolk County,	11,585
Pork made in the State, lbs.,	121,184,622
" " " Suffolk County, lbs.	2,708,759
Gross sales of farm produce in the State,	$121,187,467
" " " " " " Suffolk County,	1,019,617
Apples produced in the State, bushels	23,118,230
" " " Suffolk County, bushels	308,315
Poultry sold in the State, value	$1,772,084
" " " Suffolk County, value	$65,572
Eggs sold in the State, value	2,513,144
" " " Suffolk County, value	118,049

Two counties sold more poultry, and two only, viz.:

Dutchess County sold $77,188; Queens County sold $88,403.

Onondaga sold eggs in value next to Suffolk, and to the amount of $91,818.

A careful comparison of these tables show results not unfavorable to the agriculture of Suffolk County, and the average of crops of the State and county are these:

AVERAGES OF STATE AND COUNTY PRODUCTION COMPARED.

		BUSHELS PER ACRE.		BUSHELS. PER ACRE.
Corn,	New York State,	32.	Suffolk County,	35.
Barley,	" "	22.	"	25.
Oats,	" "	28.	"	28.
Rye,	" "	11.	"	12.
Potatoes,	" "	102.	"	96.
Hay,	" "	1 ton.	"	1 ton.
Hogs,	" "	223 lbs.	"	233 lbs.

All fractions are rejected in the foregoing figures.

Suffolk County contained in value one-seventieth of all the farm buildings, exclusive of dwellings in the State of New York. Its farmers owned in round numbers one-eightieth of all the farm tools and machinery in the State. They purchased one-sixth of all the fertilizers purchased in the State. The value of the stock in the county was over one-eightieth part of all owned in this State. The acres mown to feed that stock was less than one-hundredth of all mown in the State, and the average cut of hay was within a fraction of the State average per acre.

The number of cattle slaughtered in the county was over one-hundredth of all slaughtered in the State. The pork made in the county was over one-fiftieth of all made in the State, and the average weight of hogs in the county beat the State average ten pounds. Of all the corn raised in this State, Suffolk County produced over one-fortieth; of winter wheat over one-fiftieth, and of potatoes about one-ninetieth. The proportion of oats raised in the county was about one hundred and thirty-fifth of the State production.

It was thought Suffolk County would be a poor county for the production of fruit, and yet the apple crop of the county was over one-eightieth of the whole State production. In the amount of poultry sold Suffolk County stands third in the list of counties in New York State. In the value of eggs sold this county stands first, beating every county, and beating Onondaga by over $26,000.

The results of the oat crop of the county as reported in the tables were a disappointment to me. I knew that in 1865 our average and aggregate product put this county among the foremost. Why in 1875 it was among the hindmost seemed unaccountable. The census of 1875 reports the product of 1874. Consulting my record of 1874, I found that I had ten acres in oats. I remembered that the crop never promised better for from 50 to 60 bushels per acre than then. I threshed 50 bushels, and the army worm threshed the rest. That clears the mystery.

The loss on oats that year in the best oat region of the county on the south shore was ten times more than the amount harvested. Generally in my section none were threshed. In round numbers 10,000 acres were sown in the county. I estimate the loss by the army worm to be not less than 100,000 bushels, of the value of 55 cents per bushel, and in the aggregate $55,000. This loss should be credited to the county in any fair calculation of averages with other counties not so ravaged. This is pre-eminently the age of criticism. Moses and the Pentateuch are questioned.

All the old foundations are pried up to see if they have good cornerstones. Men build capitols, and monuments, and bridges, and hotels by the job, covering up vast frauds. Practical men, and literary men, and mechanics, and the professions, believe nothing until it is demonstrated. The whole earth is a war of question and denial and call for proof. I anticipate this question: If Suffolk County is the purchaser of one-third of all the fertilizers sold in the State in 1865, and one-sixth in 1875, it must be a poor county; if not, why not?

Other counties purchase little or none, while Suffolk is so poor it must purchase to produce, and unless the production is increased so as to pay the cost of fertilizers, Suffolk County is still in arrears.

All that may be said regarding the necessity of restoring fertilizers to a soil long abused by the skinning process in this old county and the like necessity that will come to other counties will avail nothing. All that may be said showing that feeding produce to animals on the farm while in the main good farming lessens the amount of sales and apparent profit, will avail nothing. More largely than in other counties Suffolk fed on the farm the hay, corn, oats and roots, and sold proportionately more meat, lessening not really but apparently her farming profits. All this is apparent, but still the demand comes and must be met or avoided.

The excess and value of county over State averages may be thus stated for 1865:

	ACRES.	TOTAL.	PRICE PER BUSH.	VALUE.
Corn, 7 bushels	16,460 1-4	115,221 3-4	$1 00	$115,221 75
Wheat, 5 "	10,563 1-4	52,816 1-4	2 60	137,322 25

		ACRES.	TOTAL.	PRICE PER BUSH.	VALUE.
Oats, 9	"	10,945	98,505	0 80	78,804 00
Rye, 8	"	5,353	42,824	1 10	47,106 40
Barley, 12	"	498	5,976	1 10	6,573 60
Turnips, 75	"	689	51,675	0 40	20,670 00

The like excess for 1875.

		ACRES.	TOTAL.	PRICE PER BUSH.	VALUE.
Corn, 3 bushels		16,304	48,932	$1 00	$48,932 00
Wheat, 3	"	9,388	28,164	1 25	35,205 00
Barley, 3	"	186	568	1 00	568 00
Rye, 1	"	4,333	4,333	1 00	4,333 00
Apples 1	"trees 130,406		130,406	0 50	65,203 00
Loss on oat crop by army worm,					55,000 00

Total value of county excess,	$614,939 00
Add for permanent improvement of land by fertilizers,	100,000 00

Total,	$714,939 00

Deduct for less county average.

	ACRES.	TOTAL.	PRICE.	
1865.Potatoes 13 bu.3,439 1-2		44,713 1-2	$0 80	$35,770 80
1875. " 6 " 4,208		25,248	0 50	12,624 00

Total to deduct,	$48,394 80
Balance of county over State production,	$666,545 20
Cost of fertilizers in 1865, $294,429 40	
" " " " 1875, 316,737 00	
Amounting to	611,266 40

Balance credit to the county over the State average after deducting cost of all fertilizers,	$55,278 80

In this calculation I have disregarded the item of fertilizers purchased by other counties and have under-estimated the amount of permanent improvement which I believe the land derived from the large application of fertilizers. No account is made of any extra straw or stalks thereby grown, and none of the extra market value of Long Island potatoes.

All these items in the statement would make it still more favorable to the county, and would add force to he demonstration that Suffolk County can afford to purchase, and actually profits by the large application of fertilizers. It is usually the farmer who purchases judiciously the most manure who makes the most profit.

J.H. Wardle, Esq., has kindly sent in advance sheets of the census of 1880, from which I give these figures:

No. of farms in the State of New York,		241,058
" " " " Suffolk County,		3,379
" " acres improved in the State,		17,717,862
" " " " " " County,		156,223
" " " unimproved in the State,		6,062,892
" " " " " " County,		152,694
" " " woodland in the State,		5,195,795
" " " " " " County,		134,836
Value of farms in the State,		$1,056,176,741
" " " " " County,		17,079,652
" " farm tools and machinery in the State,		42,592,741
" " " " " " " " County,		563,225
" " live stock in State,		117,868,283
" " " " " County,		1,359,047
" " fertilizers purchased in State,		2,715,477
" " " " " County,		272,134
" " farm productions in State,		178,025,695
" " " " " County,		2,198,079

	BUSHELS.	ACRES.
Barley, in the State,	7,792,062	356,629
" " " County,	5,459	199

	BUSHELS.	ACRES.
Indian corn, in the State,	779,272	25,690,156
" " " " County,	18,097	624,407
Oats, in the State,	1,261,171	37,575,506
" " " County,	9,556	311,581
Rye, in the State,	244,923	2,634,690
" " " County,	3,931	47,471
Wheat, in the State,	736,611	11,587,766
" " " County,	5,660	182,537

	AREA MOWN ACRES.	CROP, TONS.
Hay, State,	4,644,452	5,255,642
" County,	33,197	40,111

NUMBERS POULTRY.		
6,448,886,	Eggs Produced, in the State, dozens	31,958,739
160,173,	" " " Suffolk County, "	910,848
214,595,	" " " Erie " "	1,116,191
194,950,	" " " Cayuga " "	932,947

183,395,	Eggs Produced, in Oneida	"	"	1,008,330
204,295,	"	"	"Onondaga " "	972,206
199,840,	"	"	"St. Lawrence Co."	1,073,385
217,826,	"	"	"Steuben Co. "	1,037,509

	BUSHELS.	ACRES.
Irish potatoes, State	340,536	33,644,807
" " County,	3,796	493,078
Orchard Products value, State		$3,409,794
" " " County		17,248
Market garden products sold, State value		4,211,642
" " " " Co. "		118,293

Amount of cord-wood cut.

State, 4,187,942.   County, 34,228.

Value of fruit products sold.

State, $8,759,901.   County, $127,960.

The results of the figures of the census of 1880, are these:

| The area of farms in the State averages over acres, | 73 |
| " " " " " " County " " " | 45 |

measured by the acres of improved lands.

Less than one-hundredth of all the improved lands in the State lie in Suffolk County, yet the county has nearly one-seventieth in number of all the farms, showing thereby a more general distribution of land among the masses of people. Suffolk County contains about one-fortieth part of all the unimproved lands in the State, and a fraction over that proportion of all the woodlands. The farms of this county in value aggregate over one sixty-second part of the whole State valuation.

Suffolk County owns over one-eightieth part of the farm tools and machinery in the State, and over one-eightieth in value of all live stock in the State. Suffolk County purchased over one-tenth of all the fertilizers purchased in the State. The aggregate farm production of the county was over one-eightieth of all produced in the State. This county raised over one-fortieth of all the corn raised in the State, nearly one-hundredth part of all the oats; over one-sixtieth of all the rye, and over one sixty-fourth of all the wheat. Suffolk County mowed less than one-hundred and fortieth of all the acres mown in the State. It produced nearly the one-hundred and thirty-first of all the hay crop cut.

The State average per acre was a little over one and one-tenth tons, and the county average per acre a little over one and two-tenths tons. Suffolk County produced nearly one-thirty-fifth of all the eggs in the State, from less than one-fortieth of all the poultry, ranking the seventh in product of eggs, and holding in number of poultry by over twenty thousand less than any of the six counties which produced more eggs. In acreage Suffolk County had of potatoes a fraction less than one-ninetieth contained in the State, and produced therefrom a fraction over one-seventieth of all the bushels produced. In value of orchard product the county, compared with the State, fails to come up to anything which might in former results have been reported.

In value of market garden products sold, the county sales were over one thirty-fifth of all sales made in the State. Suffolk County cut less than the one hundred and twenty-second part of all the wood cut in cords in the State, but sold in products of the forest over one-seventieth of all sold in the State.

The State and county averages compare thus per acre:

		BUSHELS.		BUSHELS.
Barley,	State,	21.85	County,	27 3-10
Indian corn,	"	32.97	"	34 4-10
Oats,	"	20.79	"	32 6-10
Rye,	"	10.76	"	12
Wheat,	"	15.73	"	18 8-10
Potatoes,	"	98 6-10	"	129 8-10

In all these products the county, rejecting fractions, exceeded the State averages thus: Per acre, on barley, 6 bushels; on corn, oats and rye, two bushels each; on wheat, three; and potatoes, twenty-one bushels. The deficiency of the county in potatoes in the years 1865 and 1875, is more than offset by its surplus per acre in 1880. The former surplus reported for the State in oats, in 1875, when our county suffered by the army worm, does not continue in 1880.

In the great staples of corn and winter wheat the surplus average of this county continues through all these years, to the credit of the county. It will be observed that while Suffolk County purchased in 1865 one-third, in 1875 one-sixth, and in 1880 one-tenth of all the fertilizers purchased in the State, other counties were increasing their proportion of fertilizers after her example, and following more closely her methods.

I introduce this account to show that such purchase pays:

The whole farm products of the State in value are	$178,025,695
" " " " " " County, " "	2,198,079
The county owns less than 1-100 of all the improved lands of the State, and measured thereby, 1-100 of the products is,	1,780,256
Credit of surplus product to the county is	$417,823
Cost of fertilizers purchased in the county is	272,134
Excess product,	$145,689

These figures add force to all former statements favorable to the quality of land or purchase of fertilizers to make farming pay in the county or State. The variety of soil in Suffolk County is seldom found elsewhere. For corn, no land on the continent is better suited. Midway between the cold blasts of a northern climate and the extreme heat of a southern, it is peculiarly adapted to the growth of that crop. In the production of wheat its conditions are favorable. The low, moist lands of the southern sea coast are well suited to raise oats. For vegetable growth and root crops, both the variety of its soil and temperature of its climate are favorable.

The hardier fruits, like apples and pears, flourish here. The cauliflower and strawberry are so extensively cultivated that for the transportation of both crops extra railroad trains are specially run, and for the latter steamers from Greenport to Boston. The tables of the census demonstrate much of these remarks. But those of 1875 were compiled before the culture of these crops had reached their present very large proportions, or become a largely developed industry and been proved to be so profitable in pecuniary results. It is a matter of regret that no records exist whereby the precise extent of production in these crops can be ascertained. Yet it is significant that as New York city has judged the flavor of Long Island potatoes to be so superior as to command a premium in her markets, so Boston seeks in preference the strawberry that grew in Suffolk County.

How this old county from the acorn grew in wealth and comfort to the solid oak; what changes occurred from its primitive government, jurisprudence and the administration of justice; how the light of education, intelligence and literary culture shone from its early dawn to the brightness of the present day; what progress it has made reaching for the wisdom that comes from above; how its commerce, navigation and fisheries were pursued by its adventurous citizens. All these are subjects assigned to other speakers and prohibited to me. Of that glad acclaim which echoed from the shores of this county in exultation to Heaven, when in 1783 the last British soldier evacuated forever its soil—even to speak of this is to tread on ground dedicated to another. But in all these historic events the farmer of Suffolk County was the central figure, and the tillers of the soil the prominent actors.

The first settlers derived their subsistence chiefly from the farms they cleared in the wilderness. The early primeval government organized was instituted, and perpetuated, and developed by farmers. The diffusion of the light of education, intelligence and literary culture was mainly due to the farmer. If true devotion spoke anywhere to the power on high, it spoke at the hearthstone and fireside of the farmer. If commerce and navigation carried adventurous enterprise to the remotest sea, the sons of the farmer manned and sailed the ship. If fisheries were followed on stream or bay, on harbor, or sound, through strait or ocean, his hardy sons cast the net, threw the line or harpoon with the foremost pioneers. In colonial conflicts with the Indians or with the French, or both, the yeomanry of this county contended side by side with their compeers of other counties. The numbers they armed and the tax they paid were often among the largest contributed by any county in the State.

In the long Revolutionary war, from the first, the farmers of Suffolk County were solid in resisting the oppressions of the Crown. In the disastrous battle of Long Island her sons bled in defence of the country. The seven dark years of captivity and desolation that followed, what historian can record! what pencil can paint! Abandoned by countrymen, oppressed by foe, plundered and derided by both, this county suffered its long hours of agony, upheld by the hope that the power that rules the universe would bring deliverance to them. From its household altars ascended in devotion the thought in a later day beautifully embodied thus:

> *"If for the age to come, this hour*
> *Of trial hath vicarious power;*
> *And blest by thee our present pain*
> *Be Liberty's eternal gain—*
> *Thy will be done!*
> *Strike; Thou the Master, we thy keys,*
> *The anthem of the destinies!*
> *The union of thy loftier strain;*
> *Our hearts shall breathe the old refrain,*
> *Thy will be done!*

In every line of the record of the historic past; in every great crisis of the colony or State, the farmers of Suffolk County have imperishably recorded their names with the illustrious dead. Go to the Declaration of Independence, and with the signers to that indestructible landmark of the Nation is written the name of William Floyd, a farmer of Suffolk County!

Look for the consecrated dust of those who fell martyrs in the Revolutionary struggle, and within the limits of this county find buried one of her farmers over whose memory broods unceasing regret, and over whose name burns the undying fire of patriotism. Monuments may perish; age may obscure; yet after monuments have vanished, after ages have passed the name and memory of General Nathaniel Wood-hull will remain in the minds of his countrymen linked forever with the remembrance of that great contest in which he fell.

For the farmers of Suffolk County I might and I must say more. But for them there had been no Suffolk County as it now is. The bed rock of Agriculture underlies all other occupations; is the mother of all arts, of all manufactures, of all navigation, subsisting on the products of the prolific earth, all these may flourish. Thereby manufactures may expand; the mechanic arts make progress, and commerce be carried, for exchange of products over every ocean. But for Agriculture there had been no planting of colonies on these shores; no commerce over her waters; no United States on this Continent.

The farmer made all this possible. Mainly by his strong arm; the feeble colonies grew in numbers and power, into States, and fought successfully the great Revolution that made them free and independent of all other nations. All honor to the farmer! all praise to agriculture! Not least of all to the agriculture and the farmer of Suffolk County.

The mariners who from this county traversed every sea; the mechanics who wrought in all the arts of industry; the professions which shone as lights in theology, in medicine, in jurisprudence; the Legislators who sat in the halls of the State or Nation, were born and reared on the farms of Suffolk County. Therefrom came her Senators in both. Thenceforth marched that wondrous tide of emigration from colonial days to other counties of this great State, north and west, and to east and west Jerseys, as then known; and through after ages to the expanding West and the remotest Pacific coast. That mighty tide, enlarging, enriching, augmenting the population and power of other counties and States and territories, diminished the growth of this county while it enlarged theirs.

The proximity of Suffolk County to the large cities of the continent attracted visitors from the earliest days. The invalid and wayworn found its ocean breeze bracing in summer and mild in winter. The sportsman found game running in its forests, swimming in its abounding waters, and flying in its air. The lover of quiet and repose found it here. The good cheer and substantial comfort of its old taverns and farm houses were widely and well known. From the tip ends of Orient and Montauk Points to its western limits, in early, and increasing in later days, Suffolk County was the resort of hundreds now grown to thronging thousands.

Dominy's and Sammis' hotels were almost as well known as the Astor House and Delmonico's; yet Fire Island and Bay Shore were but two, out of scores of other resorts where, on both shores of the county, and extending eastward, then and now the interior and the cities pour their residents on the sea coast of this county. The products of its soil were largely consumed by boarders in farm houses, and hence the returns of those products foot up relatively less for this than other counties in the census reports.

If elsewhere the farmer communes with nature and comes nearer her gates than other industrial classes; if elsewhere the contest to overcome the obstacles nature interposes to impede the fruition of his desire, is waging; if elsewhere the study of her laws and mysteries awakes close observation, minute search and absorbing thought; if elsewhere conformity to her laws by the requirement of success in the battle of wrestling from the soil its products; if elsewhere the vastness of her range, the uniformity of her constitutions, the precision of her methods, the inexorable power of her elements, the evidences of design in her arrangements, reveal the hand and mind of a mighty Maker.

In all these surroundings the Suffolk County farmer lives within a field as vast, as varied, as full of all that animates observation, impels to study, excites to wonder or elevates to devotion as his brother farmer in other locations, here the fields of green grass or waving grain are varied with the growth of the forest. Here the parching droughts of summer's long day are relieved by the munificent dews of the evening. Here the oppressive heat of winds from north and west is overcome by the breeze of ocean. The glimmer of stream and creek, of harbor and bay and Sound, add to the charm of rural landscape—and over all the sound of ocean's wave.

Since 1683, when under Governor Thomas Dongan, Suffolk County as a county was organized; six generations of its farmers have passed away. The simple funeral rites of those times strangely contrast with the pomp, display and pageantry of the present.

"The Power incens'd the pageant will desert." On the bier on the shoulders of the living the dead were reverently carried to their final rest. The stars of heaven shine upon their graves as they shone then; the blue vault that o'er arches us, hung over them; the anthem of ocean that sung their funeral dirge, age after age, rolls on, and will sound in our expiring breath and over our crumbling dust.

Celebrating this day that great event that two hundred years gone by organized the then living generation in one compact body as a county; paying our tribute to them and their descendants; honoring their virtues and their patriotism; blessed with the results of their toils, their fortitude and their courage, as if standing beside their opened graves, we bear our unworthy offering to their memory and their solid worth.

They built this time-honored county and made it what it is; sire and son, after each other, transmitted to coming posterity the fruits of their industry, the immunities they gained, the free institutions they formed possessing this fair inheritance from them, let our thanks be given from age to age, constant as the lights or the voices that Nature gives. In this let us not fail, as these never fail.

"The harp, at Nature's advent strung,
Has never ceased to play;
The song the stars of mourning sung
Has never died away;
And prayer is made, and praise is given
By all things near and far;
The ocean looketh up to heaven
And mirrors every star.
Its waves are kneeling on the strand
As kneels the human knee;
Their white locks bowing to the sand,
The Priesthood of the sea.
The winds with hymns of praise are loud,
Or low with sobs of pain;
The thunder organ of the cloud,
The dropping tears of rain.
The blue sky is the temple's arch;
Its transept earth and air;
The music of its starry March
The chorus of a prayer.
So Nature keeps her reverent frame
With which her years began,
And all her signs and voices shame
The prayerless heart of man."

CHAPTER VIII

CELEBRATION OF THE 100ᵀᴴ ANNIVERSARY OF THE ORGANIZATION OF THE TOWN OF RIVERHEAD, SUFFOLK COUNTY, N.Y.

Written by Orville B. Ackerly, Esq. in 1892

Orville B. Ackerly, a former prominent citizen of Riverhead, was born at Patchogue, in Suffolk County, February 7, 1842, being the oldest son of Samuel and Charlotte (Burnell) Ackerly. His early education was obtained in the district schools of Patchogue and at Bellport Academy. At the age of seventeen he was a clerk in the store of Terry & Wood at Sayville, and when, in 1864, John Wood, of that firm, was elected clerk of Suffolk County he selected Mr. Ackerly as his deputy. This position he retained for two terms. During his residence in Riverhead he was considerably interested in the cause of education, serving for several years as a member of the Board of Education. He was connected with the Suffolk County Historical Society, of which he was corresponding secretary.

Mr. Chairman, Ladies and Gentlemen:

We have been passing through a period of centennial anniversaries, the first in our history as a nation.

Beginning with the celebration of the Declaration of our Independence at Philadelphia in 1876, which must always remain the greatest event in our national life, our birth; hardly a week, certainly not a month, has passed, that has not witnessed in some part of the territory comprising the original thirteen States the centennial anniversary of some important event; the battles on land or sea, victories or defeats of the Revolutionary War, the final surrender of Cornwallis, the evacuation of New York, the adoption of the Constitution, the inauguration of President Washington, and like events, so that, as much as possible, we have lived over again the stormy scenes of our early history, and we appreciate more than ever before what it cost to make us a free and independent nation.

In many places, celebration of events that took place two hundred years ago have occurred. The county celebrated its bi-centennial nine years ago, and the towns of Southold and Southampton only two years ago rejoiced over the fact that they had lived two hundred and fifty years. Last autumn the churches at Upper Aquebogue and Baiting Hollow invited their friends to enjoy with them in the festivities that appropriately marked the conclusion of one hundred years of useful existence, and now the Town of Riverhead finding itself one hundred years old, proposes to celebrate the fact, selecting the glorious national anniversary day, that the fires of local pride and national patriotism may mingle and make brighter and more memorable the happy occasion.

Next year this notable period of anniversaries may be said to close with the celebration of the greatest event known to modern times, that which made all the rest possible—the discovery of a new world by Columbus. Occurring somewhat tardily, it may be all the more successful. No lover of his kind and of his country but rejoices over the fact that the public enters so heartily into the spirit of these celebrations.

Let us consider briefly the condition of our own country and the world at large at the time this town was organized. The new constitution was almost an experiment, for less than four years had passed since it had been made the supreme law of the land. No addition had been made to our territory. Maine was still a province of Massachusetts, and Vermont had just been made a State only to prevent it from any longer being debatable ground between New York and New Hampshire.

The vast valley of the Mississippi was a part of France, while Florida and the immense region north of the Rio Grande were still under the rule of Spain. Thanks to enterprising and intrepid explorers, we to-day know a great deal about Central Africa. But the generation that lived when this town was established knew nothing of the unknown land beyond the Mississippi. In all maps of the world at that time the region was a blank.

It was, of course, supposed that there must be rivers and mountains there, and so they were put down apparently at random and by guess-work. It was the custom of geographers to people these unknown wastes with strange and uncouth animals, or monsters rather, which makes one of the poets of that day declare,

"Geographers on Africa maps
With savage pictures fill their gaps;
O'er uninhabitable downs
Place elephants for want of towns."

And it was so on the maps of America. The "western country" meant then the middle of the State of New York. New York was a respectable sized city of about 30,000 inhabitants, where everybody knew everybody, and on the east end of Long Island there were many who had heard of the great city and longed to see it, but "died without the sight," for want of courage enough to brave the long and dangerous journey. George Washington was serving his first term as President, and "His Excellency, George Clinton, Esq.," was our Governor.

The great men of state were Alexander Hamilton, Aaron Burr, Robert R. Livingston, John Jay and Gouverneur Morris; De Witt Clinton was but a young lawyer only five years out of college. Fulton had not yet made the dream of his life a reality; the sloop on the river and the stage coach on the land were the means of conveyance, and the only means. Political parties had no platforms, at least no written ones, but the dividing line between the Federalists and Republicans were as strongly drawn as any party lines at the present time.

The followers of Jefferson and Burr denounced Washington and Hamilton in terms which would be considered outrageous even to the political rancour of to-day, while they in return were accused in most vehement language of a base conspiracy to destroy religion, the Bible and all that respectability then held dear, and to emulate the Jacobins of France in their deeds of blood. George III. was still the King of Great Britain, and destined to continue so for a score of years to come.

Louis XVI. and his ill-fated Queen, Marie Antoinette, were still the rulers of France, but only in name, for the time was brief indeed before they would leave the palace for the prison, and the prison for the scaffold. Robespierre was but a young attorney, and had not yet made his name infamous for all coming time. Mirabeau, whose power and political genius might have turned the tide of revolution into more peaceful channels, had but lately passed away. The French philosophers, who had done their best (or their worse) to destroy all faith in religion and the Bible, and had conjured up in their place atheism and anarchy, were destined soon to be among the first victims of the fiends they had raised. Among the spectators of the events that "passed with giant steps" was a young man named Napoleon Bonaparte, then twenty-three years old, a captain of artillery, who was shortly to change the map of Europe and make the earth shake with the tread of his armies. Wellesley, afterwards the Iron Duke, Napoleon's conqueror to be, was twenty-two years of age and preparing for service in India.

Spain was then but a shadow of the power that had been, but even then how vast was its territory. Prussia had become powerful through the mighty military genius of Frederick the Great, but what is now the German Empire was then but a group of petty States powerless for want of union. Italy, partly ruled as "the States of the Church," partly under independent rulers, and all overshadowed by Austria. The only place in Europe where freedom was enshrined was on the mountain top of Switzerland.

Turkey was not then the "sick man of Europe," but a power fully capable of taking care of itself. Greece was but a name on the map; it had its ruins and its records of the past, nothing else. It now seems hardly credible that the piratical fleets of Algiers, Tunis and Tripoli were then the terror of the seas, and the most powerful nations of Christendom were compelled to pay them tribute as a protection for their commerce. It was the beginning of a new order of things when the young nation beyond the Atlantic returned as an answer to their demands, "Millions for defense, but not one cent for tribute."

Lastly there was Russia, vast in its extent of land, great in the numbers of its people, but as a nation just emerging from barbarism, and with a young Alexander for an Emperor. We might add as an item of interest, that when this town was established, the first newspaper on Long Island was but a year old, *Frothingham's Long Island Herald*, established at Sag Harbor, May 10, 1791.

Seventeen hundred and ninety-two seems to have been a year prolific of events worth nothing. Kentucky, created a State out of Virginia's large territory, was that year admitted to the Union, becoming the fifteenth State. The manufacturing city of Paterson, N.J., was founded that year and is now celebrating the fact. A Boston captain, cruising in the Pacific, by accident discovered the largest river on the coast, and named it after his ship, the Columbia.

The New York Stock Exchange was started that year; coal gas was first used as an illuminant, and the canal system of this State originated in 1792. And down at East Hampton, in a very humble dwelling, on the 9th day of June, in that year, to the first teacher of Clinton Academy, the first academy in this State, there was born a son, who, in a wandering, checkered career covering sixty years, as clerk, actor, manager, playwriter and diplomat, achieved nothing else of note, but made himself famous as long as the English tongue shall last, as the author of "Home, Sweet Home"—John Howard Payne.

On January 11, 1792, there was presented to the Assembly, then in session in New York City, the petition of Peter Reeves and others that the town of Southold be divided into two towns. At the same time, the petition of John Wells, Justice of the Peace, and others praying for a postponement of such action by the Legislature, until the next session, was read.

Benjamin Horton, Jr., Henry Herrick and others also prayed for an Act authorizing town meetings to be held alternately at the old Town Meeting House (the First Presbyterian Church at Southold) and the Aquebogue Meeting House. The last refers doubtless to the old church, 24x33, which then stood on the south side of the road, nearly opposite the present church at Upper Aquebogue. The petitions were referred to the appropriate committee, which reported on the 16th of the following month in favor of an Act dividing the town, and the Assembly concurred. The Act passed the House March 3, and passed the Senate five days later. The law was approved by the Council of Revision, a feature in our first constitution, and Riverhead became a town March 13, 1792. These petitions cannot be found, and we are left to surmise the reasons for and against the change.

No matter what they were, the town became a fact, and she has no doubt as to the date of her birth, unlike her mother, Southold, and her aunt, Southampton; for these dear old sisters, having long passed the period when ladies expect to be thought young, are now claiming, each that she is older than the other. On this question Riverhead is neutral; in fact, we do not want it settled; it keeps alive interest and stimulates inquiry, benefiting us by increasing our knowledge of the beginnings of history on the east end of Long Island.

The first town meeting was held at the Court House (the old Court House) April 3, 1792, and Daniel Wells was chosen Supervisor; Josiah Reeve, Town Clerk; John C. Terry, Joseph Wells and Benjamin Terry, Assessors; Jeremiah Wells and Spencer Dayton, Highway Commissioners; Deacon Daniel Terry, Zachariah Hallock and Daniel Edwards, Overseers of the Poor; Nathan Youngs, Eleazer Luce, Rufus Youngs, John Corwin, Zophar Mills, Peter Reeve and Merrit Howell, Overseers of Highways; Sylvanus Brown, Collector, and David Brown, Abel Corwin and Benjamin Horton, Constables.

These names sound familiar; for although all long since dead, others bearing the same names, certainly same surnames, are among us today. In later years new and strange names have appeared on the town tickets, like Perkins, Millard, Stackpole, Homan and Bagshaw, but only because the people are hospitable, unselfish and like to encourage immigration. Daniel Wells, the first Supervisor, was re-elected the next year, but died before completing the term of office. Josiah Reeve continued to be Town Clerk for four years, and was succeeded by John Woodhull (afterwards Judge John Woodhull), who held the office for eleven years.

In the early days the circumstances and conditions of establishing a new village or settlement were very different from those of the present time. The main points to be considered then were: How near to a bay or harbor? Is there plenty of meadow land? This was a most important consideration, for the crop of meadow hay which, without care or cultivation, came with annual regularity, was a thing of the greatest value. And last, not by any means least, "Is there a stream for a mill?" How greatly times have changed may be known by the fact that when a country place is now spoken of as a desirable place of residence the very first interrogatory is, "How far from a railroad station?"

The main settlement of Setauket, the parent hive of the town of Brookhaven, soon sent out small swarms of inhabitants to establish new villages. The native Indian inhabitants have a right to the soil, which, to their credit be it said, the settlers of the towns in Suffolk County never failed to recognize, and under date of June 10, 1694, we find that the Indian Sachem, "John Mayhew, doth freely give, grant and surrender, unto the Committee of Connecticut for settling business on Long Island, for the use of the town of Seatalk, the feed and timber of all ye lands from ye Old Man's to the Wading River." This was signed by the Sachem and duly witnessed by John Cooper and Richard Howell, who were prominent residents, of the village of Southampton. This John Mayhew, an Indian with an English name, must have been a powerful chief and well recognized as one in authority, for we find him giving to the original purchasers of Moriches their right and title to the land, and his name is connected with other transfers on the south side of the land.

In 1669 and 1686 the settlers of Setauket obtained from the Royal Governor patents for "all the lands, bays, harbors and streams between the Stony Brook River on the west and the head of Wading River or Red Creek on the east," "and from the head of the Wading River their eastern bounds were to be a straight line running due north to the sound and due south to the sea or main ocean." Our first knowledge, then, of the Wading River and the settlement near it, finds it as a part of the town of Brookhaven. The spot which was then designated as "the head of the Wading River," was marked by a large pepperidge tree which after standing for more than a century and a half fell to decay, and the

site it occupied was in 1840 marked by a stone bearing the initial letters of the adjoining towns. It stands at the northwest corner of the
church lot and will doubtless remain for long years to come.

The land at the Wading River having been fairly bought, next
comes the settlement, and as the record states, "At a lawful town meeting 17 November, 1671, it was voted and agreed upon that there shall
be a village at the Wading River or thereabouts of eight families or eight
men. It was granted and agreed upon by a vote that Daniel Lane, Jr.,
shall have a lotment at the Wading River convenient to the water for
his calling (they do not tell us what that calling was), and at the same
time allotments were granted to Thomas Jenness, Elias Bayles, Joseph
Longbottom and Thomas Smith, and Francis Muncy had a lot granted
there with the rest upon condition that he lived there himself!" Was
this a shrewd dodge to get Francis Muncy (who may have been an un-
desirable neighbor) as far off from Setauket as they could, or was it an
equally shrewd dodge on his part to get a lot free without ever having
to live on it?

There are questions upon which history throws no light and we
cannot assume to answer them. From that time the village was an established fact. The Wading River is certainly the smallest stream ever
dignified with that title, for its entire length from mouth to fountain
head cannot much exceed a mile, but the place has always been one of
the most important portions of our town, though comparatively far
greater in the past than in the present; but that it will have a prosperous future no one who sees its natural beauties can doubt.

In 1675 there is another Indian grant to the patentees of
Brookhaven, ratifying and confirming all former purchases of land between Stony Brook and the Wading River, and by the same grant all
lands not before purchased were conveyed to Richard Woodhull. This
grant was signed by the Sachem, John Mayhew, and his associates Mass-
tuse, Nascenge and Achedouse.

On November 23, 1675, Richard Woodhull relinquishes all the said
lands to the towns and under the same date we find the following: "At
a town meeting was voted and given to Richard Woodhull a farm at the
Wading River, that is to say, ten acres upland where it is most convenient to set a house on, and three score and ten acres most of upland
where the said Richard Woodhull shall choose it, lying together adja-
cent to the said Wading River, and half the meadow that belongs to us
this side of the creek, being divided, and to draw cuts for it, and this is
given in consideration of land that was given by the Indians and assigned over to the towns."

To locate ancient landmarks is one of the duties, and we need not say one of the greatest pleasure, of the antiquarian, and our researches lead us to believe that the place mentioned as the "ten acres where it is most convenient to set a house up" is the present homestead of Charles Woodhull, the descendant in the eighth generation from Brookhaven's most illustrious founder.

On May 4, 1708, we find that upon application of John Roe, Jr., in behalf of himself and others of the Wading River, that "they may have liberty to set up a grist mill at the Red Brook there, and to take up— acres of land adjoining to it for the use of the said mill or miller, on condition they set up a mill as aforesaid and support the same continually." The Red Brook, so called from the color of the sands over which it flows, still "goes on forever," and the mill, under a long succession of various owners, still grinds as it did in days of yore.

How Wading River came to be a part of Southold is a curious episode in our local history. It seems that about 1708, one John Rogers, who had been a townsman of Brookhaven, had removed to the town of Southold and by various misfortunes had become a public charge. Southold claimed, and with justice, that the cost of his support was chargeable to the neighboring town whence he came. A letter was sent by the authorities of Southold calling attention to the matter, and on October 7, 1708, a reply was ordered to be sent. This elicited another letter from Southold, and on December 9, another reply was sent. The evidence was plainly against Brookhaven, for, at a Trustee meeting in June, 1709, we find the following resolution:

> "Upon the application of James Reeve, in behalf of the town of Southold in reference to defray the charge of keeping John Rogers, it was agreed upon between the said James Reeve on the one part in the part of Southold and the Trustees of Brookhaven on the other part, that the town of Brookhaven shall be acquitted and fully discharged from all charges whatever that now is or shall hereafter be concerning the said John Rogers, his keeping or care, on the condition that the town of Brookhaven do assign unto the town of Southold all their patent right of the land and meadow on the east side of the Wading River, and also pay unto the said James Reeve, four pounds in current money at his house, for the use of the town of Southold, at or before the 29th day of September next ensuing the date hereof."

Now, we think our readers will, one and all, agree that Southold, through James Reeve, its agent, made a pretty profitable bargain, and this is the first instance on record where a pauper added to the wealth of a town. And so it happened that the due north line from the pepperidge tree to the sound ceased to be a boundary and the river itself became our western bounds.

Our limits will not permit us to dwell too long on the ancient history of this village; let it suffice to mention some of the names of men who were prominent, and of places that were well known localities at the time when our town was established. We might say that from the earliest settlement the Woodhull family were the bone and sinew of the village. Here was the homestead of Joshua Woodhull, who died in 1787 at the age of fifty-two years. He was well known here during the days of the Revolution, and on the top of his house was built a lookout from which the watcher could descry and give timely warning if marauding bands from British vessels on the sound were seen approaching the shore.

Not far from him, on the present homestead of Mrs. Thomas Coles, and what was in the very early days the home of Robert Terry, lived his son, Nathaniel Woodhull, a true and worthy representative of a noble race, a strong supporter of the church, a good, substantial citizen, and in all the relations of life a useful and honored man. He was the maternal grandfather of our worthy chairman, Nathaniel Woodhull Foster, and from whom he derives his honored name. On the east side of the street, in the centre of the village, was the homestead and extensive farm of Major Frederick Hudson, a wealthy and influential citizen, but of Tory proclivities, and the officers of the British army found a warm welcome at his house. His son, Oliver Hudson, sold the estate to Zophar Mills, who was one of the largest land owners in the town.

To all lovers of local history there is a peculiar interest connected with this farm, from the fact that it was the early home of the famous Indian preacher, Paul Cuffee, who was the bound servant of Major Hudson till his twenty-first year. Strange change of circumstances. The grave of the master is somewhere unmarked and unknown in a dense thicket of weeds and briars. The grave of the servant, fenced and guarded with pious care, by the roadside at Good Ground, is visited by hundreds who revere his virtues and honor his name. Further east is the well-known homestead of Zophar Miller, whose son, Sylvester, and grandson, Elihu, are names "whom not to know argues a Riverheader unknown."

In front of this house, and a few feet north of the road, stood the old meeting house built about 1785. It stood till 1838, when it was sold and removed, and is now a barn on the premises of Alonzo Hulse, about two and a half miles east of the village. When the new church was built in 1857 it was Zophar Miller who gave the lot for the new edifice. It was in the house of the Miller family that the post-office was kept for sixty-one years. It was removed in 1886 to its present location.

One of the conspicuous features of the place is the ancient house of Stephen Homan (of an old East-Hampton family), who came here in the latter part of the last century, married a daughter of Zophar Mills, and was store-keeper, tavern-keeper and farmer. A brown tombstone tells us he died in 1816 at the age of forty-nine. His son, Benjamin Homan, who never tires of talking of the past, inherits his name and place. There, too, in old times, was Isaac Reeve, a noted boatman and great judge and prognosticator of wind and weather. For aught we know he may have been a descendant of James Reeve who drove so sharp a bargain for the town. And also Nathaniel Tuthill, a well known citizen, and as one of the old residents said, "a mighty smart man," and father of our honored townsman, Hon. James H. Tuthill.

What shall we say of Jonathan Worth, who for long years ran the mill, and then left it to his son David, who sold it to a company consisting of the minister, Partial Terry, Deacon Nathaniel Tuthill, Deacon Nathaniel Woodhull and Deacon Luther Brown. Church and State might be separate, but church and mill were pretty closely connected in those days. The sentiment of the people may be imagined when we learn that when Washington was a candidate for re-election to the Presidency he had only three votes in Wading River, and these were cast by Rev. David Wells, Stephen Homan and Benjamin Worth. New York took no part in the election of the first President.

The changes which are apparent in every part of Long Island, are especially evident in the relative importance of villages in the present compared with the past. At the time when this town was established let us suppose a stranger had asked, "What is your most important place?" The answer might have been, "Wading River or Aquebogue," but it most assuredly would not have been "Riverhead." In the olden time to live on the post road had a certain advantage. There would always be more or less passing.

The stage coach with its weekly or semi-weekly mail was the only communication with the outside world, and its arrival would be looked for with an interest which we can now scarcely realize. The taverns at intervals of a few miles with their swinging signs announcing "Accommodations for Man and Beast," were welcome sights to the belated traveler. But the greater part of the people did not travel; many of them scarcely ever went beyond the bounds of their native village, and it is safe to say that hundreds lived, and lived to a good old age, who never saw anything outside of Suffolk County. The foundation for a village was a fertile soil where good crops would be raised.

Means of communication with other villages were of little importance. As one old man expressed it, "A place is made to stay in, not go away from." It was the boast of some old-fashioned farmers that they did not go off their farm any day of the week except Sunday. The railroad changed all this. The whole section of country in the neighborhood of Riverhead was known to the old settlers by the name of Occobog, a name common to both sides of the river, and meaning in the Indian language, "the place at the head of the bay, or the cove place."

Previous to 1659, John Tucker, a very prominent man in the early days, and who was dignified with the title of Deacon, Captain and Esquire at a time when they meant something, presented a petition for the privilege of building a saw-mill within the town bounds near the head of the river. It was granted with liberty to "cut all sorts of timber," but with the condition that he should "cut no more oak than fell in the common track of getting pine and cedar, which was the chief inducement of getting a mill there to saw." This would seem to indicate that oak was comparatively scarce. He also asked for "ten acres of land for himself and such partners as he should take in to himself," which was granted. He seems to have found a partner in the person of Joseph Horton, for on February 7, 1659, we find that "John Tucker with Joseph Horton desire the five men to enlarge the grant to the effect that they should have the privilege of building the saw-mill and of cutting timber for twenty-one years without molestation, nor any inhabitant to set up another mill by them." This also was granted on condition of their completing the mill within three years.

A writer in the Genealogical and Biographical Record (Oct., 1882) claims that Joseph Carpenter of Maschete Cove, Long Island, who built a saw and fulling mill in 1677, "was the first man on Long Island, New York, Connecticut or New Jersey, to set up a saw-mill run by water power," but here was a mill running more than fifteen years before, and the credit of being the first to establish a mill of this kind must now be given to John Tucker and Joseph Horton and to Riverhead. Tucker lived here in 1665 and was no doubt the first settler, but we cannot be certain of the exact location of his house.

The town of Southampton, on April 14, 1693, granted to John Wick, "serge dresser," "the use of the stream called the Little River, on condition of setting up a fulling mill, and fulling cloth for that town and Southold." It is doubtful if he complied with the conditions, for two years later we find that Southampton voted that John Parker and his heirs and assigns should have the stream and the privileges granted to John Wick, on condition of his building a good fulling mill, and that he should full cloth there "forever." John Parker also had land granted to him in 1700 to build a house on, and he probably did build a temporary residence at that time, but in 1713 he built a far more substantial mansion, which is yet standing on the south side of the river, and which in after years passed into the hands of his son-in-law, Wm. Albertson, and continued in his family for three or four generations. Since then this house was owned and occupied by the Sweezy family and is now the residence of Sylvester H. Woodhull. On May 15, 1715, we find that "the Justices of Suffolk County met at Parker's to ascertain the amount of arrears of taxes."

All the lands of Peconic River which are included in the village are a part of the original division of the lands of Southold, called the second Division of Aquebank lands. The lots were of large extent and ran from the river to the sound. In 1711 John Parker purchased from John Tucker, a grandson of the original John Tucker who died in 1690, one of the original lots containing 400 acres, bounded west by land of Widow Margaret Cooper and east by land of John Parker, which seems to have been another original lot of the same size, and which he had bought from its former owner. These two lots, with a lot of Widow Cooper on the west, embrace the entire business portion of Riverhead.

In January, 1727, about a month before his death, John Parker gave a deed of gift to his daughter Abigail and her husband, Joseph Wickham, Jr., for their lives and then to her heirs, for all his land north of the river, and this tract in course of time came into possession of Parker Wickham, their eldest son and heir-at-law, whose loyalist proclivities caused his estate to be confiscated after the Revolution and sold to Nathaniel Norton, who sold a part of it to Stephen Jagger, and it is well known in recent years as the "Jagger farm."

There are missing links in the chain of title which more extended investigation may supply; but it seems as if at some time previous to 1727 a tract of 130 acres on the western part of this land had been disposed of to other parties, for in 1753 Thomas Fanning sold John Griffing "a tract of land at a place called Acaboug, bounded north and east by the lands of Abigail Wickham, south by and with Peconick river, together with the dwelling thereon, so far as the saw-mill, and west by the land of Christopher Young, containing by estimates 130 acres, reserving one-half acre of land at and about the place where his mother lies buried, with free passage in and to the same."

This burial place, doubtless the first in the village, is situated just north of and adjoining the stable on the lot of Mrs. Louisa Howell on the east side of Griffing Avenue and next south of the railroad. The dwelling house mentioned is the first of which we have any positive knowledge in the village, and the Long Island House now occupies its site. The deed evidently includes the stream.

This John Griffing, the first of his name to settle in Riverhead, was a prominent Whig. At the request of his neighbors he became a "tea-spy," as they called men whose business it was to detect and prevent the use of tea and other imported articles upon which the English Government levied duties of the inhabitants here. When the British forces got possession of Long Island after their victory over the Colonist forces at Brooklyn in August, 1766, Mr. Griffing and many others fled to Connecticut. He died there October 18, 1777, in the sixty-first year of his age. As he died without will his property descended to his son and namesake.

The mother of the late Charles and Gamaliel Vail was one of his daughters, and we well remember hearing them comment on the injustice of the English law of primogeniture. His grave is at a place called Cromwell, on the west side of the Connecticut River, about three miles from Middletown. Near it is the grave of Martha L'Hommedieu, the mother of Ezra L'Hommedieu, one of the most prominent men in the State 100 years ago, and a resident of Southold until his death in 1811.

The land next west of the Griffing farm, the original lot of Widow Margaret Cooper, descended to her grandchildren, the children of Stephen Bailey and Elnathan Topping of Southampton. Upon a division of her estate the land above mentioned fell to the latter, beyond which we cannot trace it, but in 1753 it was owned wholly or in part by Christopher Young. For long years the place was isolated from the rest of the town. No direct road connected it with the "Middle Road," then the principal thoroughfare.

The fulling mill, the grist mill and the Court House and jail were the only things to call any of the people from the neighboring region, and the people whose business called them there did not come to stay. It was recognized as a very central locality in the county, and this is doubtless the reason why the place was selected for the county seat. On November 25, 1727, an Act was passed by the Governor and Provincial Legislature to enable the Justices of the Peace in the County of Suffolk to build a "County House and Prison." Riverhead was chosen as the most suitable place, and the building was erected and the first court held in it on March 27, 1729. Previous to that the jail seems to have been the basement or cellar of the old church at Southold.

On July 12, 1729, an Act was passed reciting that "there had been of late some dispute among the Supervisors of the County of Suffolk," and hence it was enacted "that the place and time of the Supervisors' meeting forever hereafter should be at the Court House on the last Tuesday in the month of October, and that their pay should be 9 shillings (or $1.12 1-2) a day." For a period of more than seventy-five years the place remained stationary, and from the best authorities we learn that for nearly thirty years after the Revolution there were but four houses, the Griffing tavern, Joseph Wickham's house, afterwards that of David Jagger. David Horton lived in the Court House and kept the jail. Stephen Griffing occupied the place late of Dr. Thomas Osborn, and besides these there was the old Parker house, then owned by William Albertson on the other side of the river.

It may perhaps be needless to state that till within comparatively recent times the village was surrounded by a dense forest. One of our best known citizens, John P. Terry, says: "When a boy (sixty years ago), I set snares and caught quails where the house of Hon. James H. Tuthill now stands. All the land north of Main Street was covered with woods, except in a few spots." He adds as a curious illustration of the changes in social life: "Sixty-one years ago my father died, one of the well-known men of the place. His funeral expenses were a dollar and a half. The remains, and the mourners, the members of his family, all rode to the grave in the same box wagon. The grave was dug by neighbors who volunteered; and this was the general custom at the time." He adds: "I saw ten deer, which had been caught in the woods south of the river, confined in a pen where Riverhead Hall now stands.

The first store was in the northeast corner of the house of the late Judge Miller. It was kept by Stephen Griffing, who afterwards moved to West Hampton. Seventy years ago, Jasper or 'Jep' Vail lived at Riverhead, but kept a store some miles east, opposite the Steeple Church, thinking that a far better location for business than this place. He had some peculiar methods: for instance, if a customer tendered a dollar bill for fifty cents worth of goods he would cut the bill in two, keep one-half and tell the customer to bring the other half some other time, and he would take it for fifty cents. He thus secured that man's custom for so much trade anyhow, and then he would paste the two halves together.

The use of liquor was general. All storekeepers kept it and everybody drank it, and to expect a workingman to live without rum was the same as expecting him to live without air." For nearly a century and a half the Griffing family had been part and parcel of the place, and none have been more closely connected with its business and social interests. One of our largest hotels, kept by a member of the family, stands on the land bought by his ancestor in 1753, and one of the finest streets is justly named in their honor.

Dr. Thomas Osborn was the first physician in the village and is well remembered by the older citizens. He commenced practice very early in the present century, and died here in 1849. Sixty years ago there was but one mail a week, brought here in a one-horse wagon. If a person wished to go to New York he must cross over to Quogue, take the mail stage which came from Sag Harbor, and he would reach the city at the close of the second day.

A newspaper clipping tells us that "on the 25th day of July, 1844, the first train passed over the Long Island Railroad from Brooklyn to Greenport, and the event was duly celebrated." Well it might be. It was the commencement of a new order of things. Since then Riverhead has been a part of the world.

At the Upper Mills there had been at various times a grist mill, saw-mill, and a fulling mill, all owned by Richard Albertson, and his son after him, and built in the latter part of the last century. In 1828 John Perkins became the proprietor of the water-power and established a business there that has been for long years one of the most important industries. With that honesty and enterprise that have ever distinguished them, the name became a household word in all parts of Suffolk County. "If you buy Perkins' cloth," said an old farmer, "you know what you have got, but if you buy this store cloth it will like enough drop off of you in the street." No such catastrophe ever occurred with cloth that was made at the Upper Mills.

Sixty years ago there were about thirty houses in all scattered along the main road, and outside of the main street there was not a dwelling of any description. Cutting wood and shipping it on small vessels was the most important industry and employed more men during the winter than any other enterprise. As the level of the street was much lower then, it was no uncommon thing for the tide to come up to the old Court House: and there are now living in this village two ladies who, when young, picked huckleberries in a swamp where Bridge Street now is—Mrs. Daniel R. Edwards and Mrs. Noah W. Hallock.

Some seventy years ago the house of the late David Jagger was moved from the "Middle Road." To accomplish this it was necessary to move it east to the fork of the roads and then west to Riverhead. It was quite an event and required a great many yoke of oxen.

It can be readily understood that the population here was far too small to constitute a church or to justify the erection of a meeting-house. As late as 1828 the people from Flanders, Riverhead, Baiting Hollow, Northville and east as far as Mattituck, went to the Steeple Church at Upper Aquebogue to worship. But a volume could be written to tell the lives and labors of a class of reverent preachers who, with small reward for constant labor, made it the object of their lives to do good. Their meetings were held in barns, schoolhouses, private residences, and even in the open air, and their coming was anxiously awaited.

The Steeple Church might be called the mother of churches. It was a portion of this congregation that in 1829 built a small meeting-house about two miles east of this village. In 1834 this congregation was also divided, one portion taking the meeting-house, removing it to Northville. The remainder established a church in Riverhead, and at first worshipped in the lower room of the Seminary building, till the erection of the Congregational Church in 1841. But prior to this came the Methodist Church, with its untiring ministry. This society was organized in 1833, and the first meeting-house built in 1834, to be succeeded in 1870 by the present elegant edifice.

The followers of Emanuel Swedenborg organized a society in 1839 and built a house of worship in 1855. The old Court House, or County Hall, as it was generally called, might, in the early days, have well been called a church of all denominations. The Congregational Church of Upper Aquebogue always claimed this neighborhood as a part of their parish, and every other Sunday Mr. Sweezy, the pastor, would preach in the building. Next came the Methodist circuit rider, who would preach on Friday afternoon or evening, making his temporary home (for he had no abiding one) at the house of Dr. Osborn; and at a later day, the service of the Roman Catholic Church would be conducted in the same place, their church being built in 1870. The Free Methodists built their church in 1872. The Episcopalians commenced stated worship in 1870, and erected a chapel in 1873. So far all these varied denominations have lived in harmony, which we trust will never be interrupted.

For long years the schools were of the most inferior description; the only ones that had the slightest claim to being educational institutions being schools kept at Upper and Lower Aquebogue, the former by Josiah Reeve, who was afterward Sheriff of the county, and the latter by Judge David Warner. These had a well-deserved reputation, and their influence for good was felt far and wide.

Riverhead, and indeed Suffolk County, is indebted to the late Judge George Miller for much that is good, but in nothing is it under greater obligation that [sic] for the seminary established by him in 1834 to advance the cause of female education. It was from the commencement a complete success, and its influence for good can be hardly expressed in words. It is fortunate for the present generation that the days of the old-fashioned district school have passed away, and it is to be hoped that the entire community fully appreciates the advantages of the Union School and the tireless labors of our well-trained and efficient teachers.

We must not fail to give our due need of praise to the followers of the "art preservative of arts." Our first newspaper, the *Suffolk Gazette*, was started in August, 1849, under the editorial management of John Hancock. The next year it was removed to Sag Harbor, but came back to its native place in 1854, and ended its career shortly after.

Then came the *Suffolk Union*, with Washington Van Zandt as editor, in 1859, a very fearless paper during the early days of the Civil War. The office, which stood on the south side of Main Street, just west of the residence of the late Dr. Luce, was burned about thirty years ago and publication stopped. A few years afterward, Buell G. Davis, an energetic young man from Greenport, started the *Monitor* here, but it did not continue long, being purchased by James S. Evans, who merged it in a paper he was publishing in Setauket, which establishment was afterwards removed to Patchogue and survives to-day in the *Patchogue Advance*.

Then James B. Slade, started in a very modest way what he called an advertising sheet, which grew into the *Riverhead News*. In 1875, Wm. R. Duvall purchased the *News* and continued it till the time of his death in 1882. Mr. Duvall was a witty, sarcastic and effective writer, and humorous as well, though, strange to say, he seldom smiled. He had traveled a great deal and had a wide knowledge of the world and men. His son and namesake succeeded to his work and well maintains the character and influence of the paper.

We cannot do better than to present a picture of Riverhead as it was fifty years ago, as taken from notes kindly furnished by Hon. Henry P. Hedges, who has been so long identified with the public life of Suffolk County, and who came here fresh from college to study law with Judge Miller. He says:

"I went to Riverhead in October, 1840, when the Harrison campaign 'log cabin and hard cider' cries were heard. At that time Henry T. Penney and John Corwin kept the hotels. Penney was Deputy Sheriff and kept a hotel in an old-fashioned house formerly of his father-in-law, William Griffing, the father of Wells and Hubbard Griffing. At that time there were about forty houses in Riverhead. Dr. Osborn's was almost the extreme west, only one or two houses beyond it. The avenue to the railroad station was then a cart path, and where the Court House now stands was thick woods. My solitary walk was often that cart path, north to where is now the cemetery.

At that time the Griffings were shipping wood to Providence; Judge Miller was in the thick of his professional fight; Sidney L. Griffin was the only other lawyer in Riverhead; Dr. Thomas Osborn was in active practice as a physician and so was Dr. Doane; Capt. Edward Vail was running a vessel, also Capt. Harry Horton and James Horton; William Jagger and David Jagger were advocating temperance; their father, David, was then living; Herman D. Foster, Elijah Terry and Nathan Corwin were selling goods in country stores; David Davis was building vessels; Timothy Aldrich was building the church; Rev. C. J. Knowles was minister; Clem. Hempstead was painting houses and wagons; Mulford Moore was blacksmithing; Geo. Halsey was tailoring; Titus Conklin was making shoes; and Aunt Polly Griffing was doing then, as always, the work of the good Samaritan; Daniel Edwards, was keeping the jail; John Perkins was manufacturing cloth at the Upper Mills; Isaac Sweezy, across the river, was grinding grain, and John P. Terry, now of the Long Island House, was living with him and threshing rye with a flail.

"The County Courts were held three times a year. Hugh Halsey was first Judge. Henry Landon, Judge Gillett and Richard M. Conkling were among the Associate Judges, and Selah B. Strong was District Attorney. The principal lawyers who came to court were S.S. Gardiner of Shelter Island and Samuel L. Gardiner of Sag Harbor, and Abraham T. Rose. These were the only ones from the east. From the west were Selah B. Strong, Judge Buffett, Charles A. Floyd, and a little later John G. Floyd.

The old Court House and jail is now occupied by the Perkins Bros. as a clothing store. Charles Vail and his brother Gamaliel were old residents in the same house, where they continued for many years; now the house of D.F. Vail. North of the Main Street there were no houses, nor on any street parallel with the Main Street. The religious meetings were held in what was called the lecture room, where the Congregational Church now stands. The Ladies' Seminary was taught by Mrs. Miller, and was located on the same lot. In 1841, the 3d of April, I find a memorandum: 'Day before yesterday raised meeting-house in Riverhead.' On December 1, same year, it was dedicated. Mr. Badger, Secretary of the Home Missionary Society, spoke from the text, "It is none other than the house of God.' Hubbard and Wells Griffing were among the most munificent contributors to that church.

There came from Flanders to trade the peculiar characteristic people from that section—the old preacher, Nathaniel Fanning, who built his own church, old Major David Brown and 'Uncle Joe' Goodale. These two were rivals for the control of Flanders. At that time David Edwards was Justice, a very competent man and so mild-mannered that he never offended anyone. In some cases there would be testimony absolutely conflicting, and plain perjury on one and sometimes on both sides. He would allude to this in his charge as 'a little discrepancy between the evidence for plaintiff and defendant.' He was a great admirer of the works of Pope, especially the 'Essay on Man.'

One of the men of stronger intellect, and who impressed his opinions, very largely upon his companions, was Elijah Terry. Johnson was the first man that I saw hung in the county. He did not look like a malicious man. I think Judge Rose defended him. I remember Judge D.G. Gillett of Patchogue, who came to Riverhead and attended conventions. He was a large, thick-set man and of very impressive appearance; and also Dr. Fred. W. Lord, a man of powerful intellect and pre-eminent as a public speaker. In 1840 Judge Abraham T. Rose was the most accomplished speaker, politically and as an advocate before a jury, in this county. It was said that Chancellor Kent once came down to Riverhead to hold a court of Oyer and Terminer, but found no lawyer, no cases, no prisoner, and adjourned for want of business.

Titus Conklin was very intelligent, benevolent, and an active man in the church and business, and he had as fellow workers Deacon Hubbard Griffing, Wells Griffing, Isaac Sweezy, Herman D. Foster and first of all, Judge George Miller, who for a long time had meetings in the Court House and conducted the services. He was the founder and upholder of the Congregational Church; the Methodist Church was upheld by John Perkins and his family, and Dr. Osborn, who were its main supporters.

Jonathan Horton preached in the Swederborgian Church, and was the heart of that organization. Sells Edwards employed him to draw his will. It was intended to give a life estate to a prodigal son, but by a mistake he gave him the whole fee of his portion. Judge Miller used to say Sells Edwards saved 50 cents in writing a will and lost $10,000. Sylvester Miller was a man of excellent understanding. He was Justice of the Peace and Supervisor for many years. He was prudent, with a strong sense of justice, and was fully competent to control and direct. Judge John Woodhull was a man rather intelligent, cautious and discreet, not disposed to yield to the popular current, and more disposed to row against than with it. He was thoroughly honest and very careful and deliberate. He had the confidence of all. In personal appearance he was tall, spare, bent, lean, angular, blue-eyed, and wore blue spectacles, owing to weak eyes. He was a strong Federalist. He lived to be 100 years old.

David Warner was a very large and tall man. He was a man of strong understanding, and he well knew it, and was somewhat above his contemporaries in reading, intelligence, in thought and in position. In later life his mind became unbalanced. He died nearly ninety years of age."

At what time settlements were first made in the eastern part of the town is unknown, but is probable that they are at least as old as the settlement of Wading River. At the location called in early days the "Fresh Ponds" and now "Baiting Hollow," a settlement is believed to have been, as early as 1719, and in 1792 a church was organized with a few members. Previous to that the people had doubtless been connected with the church at Wading River, said to have been old in 1750.

We may add here that the churches which were known as the "Strict Congregational," had their origin in the famous "New Light" movement that originated in New England about 1744; their leader on Long Island was Rev. Elisha Payne, who was pastor of the "New Light" church at Bridge Hampton, and whose tombstone may be seen in the Hay Ground cemetery near that village. In 1803 a small meeting house was built at Baiting Hollow, which was succeeded by the present edifice, built in 1862.

Time fails us to give due justice to the memory of Rev. Manly Wells, Nathan Dickinson, David Benjamin, Azel Downs, and their successors, whose names are identified with the history of this church. The village and country round has been the home of thrifty citizens, whose family names are among the oldest in our town. It was here that the first Swedenborgian church was organized, whose leader and teacher for many years was Jonathan Horton, its chief supporter.

An important item in the history of Northville is the memorable repluse of a party sent from a British squadron to capture several sloops lying near the shore, on May 31, 1814. The American militia (a small company of thirty) was under the command of Capt. John Wells, a man of resolute will and great courage, a member of the Legislature in after years, and who has left many prominent descendants, among them the late Alden Wells, a son. The attack was met with so vigorous a defense that the enemy soon withdrew, their errand unaccomplished.

Doubtless the most ancient settlement in the town is the region known as Upper and Lower Aquebogue; the latter portion being now generally known as Jamesport. From the fact that this latter region was frequently spoken of as "Old Aquebogue," we may conclude that it may claim priority of settlement, and with the more reason as it was nearer to the parent village of Southold. When these settlements were actually begun, we have at present no knowledge, but it is hoped that a more thorough investigation will eventually throw light upon the subject. From our present information, we conclude that it was about 1690. It is believed that a church was established here in the early part of the last century, and a meeting-house built on the cemetery lot, where the first interment is said to have been made in 1775. This church was doubt-less an offshoot or a branch of the old church at Southold, but on the 26th of March, 1758, a "New Light" Church, or as it was called, "The First Strict Congregational Church of Southold," was organized by Rev. Elisha Payne. From the fact that they occupied the old meeting-house, we conclude that it absorbed the former organization, or at least a ma-jority. We may say here that the "New Light" bore the same relation to the old Congregational Churches that the Puritans did to the Church of England; their motto was "Come forth from the world and be ye per-fect." At intervals of a few years large numbers were added to the church by revivals of religion, and among them was Manly Wells, Daniel Youngs and David Benjamin, who, as preachers, were afterward known throughout the country.

In 1797 the old church at Upper Aquebogue was replaced by a new and larger one, rebuilt in 1833, and a tall steeple, which from the peculiar nature of the country was visible for a great distance round, and gave to the building and also to the neighborhood, the name of "Steeple Church;" and this, in 1863 was replaced by a still larger build-ing. The old one was removed to Riverhead, by the late George N. How-ell, and converted into two stores, now owned by John Robert Corwin, and occupied by Davis & Son and Lee & Bunce. The names of Timothy Wells, Daniel Youngs, Moses Sweezy and Parshall Terry must ever be identified with its history.

In 1829, about sixty members of this church withdrew and built a new one about half way to Riverhead, and a few years later this again was divided, part with the church building removing to Northville, the remainder to Riverhead.

The great success of Sag Harbor, as a part for whaling ships, prompted a few men, among whom the foremost were James Tuthill, of Southold, and James Halsey, of Bridge Hampton, to purchase Miamogue Neck, and establish a new seaport, which from the names of its princi-pal founders was called Jamesport. Its rapid growth at first is men-tioned by the historian Prime, who in 1845 says:"In 1833 there was not a single habitation here, now some forty."The place was well started by building a hotel and a good wharf, and at one time two or three whale ships sailed from here, but the failure of the whale fishery ended its prosperity.

In 1849, James Halsey, one of the founders, started for California overland, but never reached the land of gold. The future of Jamesport is doubtless to be a summer resort, for which it is well adapted. In Lower Aquebogue, the oldest church in this town was established, it is believed as early as 1728. It was Presbyterian, and a church building was erected in 1731, and a hundred years later was repaired and enlarged. It was eventually merged into the Lower Aquebogue Congregational Church.

We cannot fail to mention the Camp Meeting Association which annually in August attracts crowds of worshipers from all the country around. Jamesport will long be distinguished as the home of two brothers, Messrs. Simeon S. and Edward Hawkins, both of whom have represented the First Senatorial District at Albany, and who, belonging to different political parties, are notable illustrations of a fact which politicans sometimes forget, that men can be good representatives and not belong to your party.

A fact but little known and proper to be stated here, is that in 1793 Mrs. Phebe Wickham, at her house, near Mattituck, established the first Sunday-school in Suffolk County, only eleven years after Robert Raikes, the father of Sunday-schools, began them in London. Mrs. Wickham was a half sister of the famous traveler, John Ledyard. She died in Groton in 1840.

There are many persons besides those we have mentioned of whom extended notice should be given, like the Hon. John S. Marcy, a genial and generous man; Rev. Thomas Cook, public-spirited and of great energy; Nathan Corwin, long a leader in town matters and who in his person always seemed to us as the incarnation of Riverhead Town; his long-time partner, John C. Davis, Member of Assembly thirty years ago; Silas S. Terry, a man greatly beloved by a wide circle of acquaintances; his partner, Joshua L. Wells, in early life a successful school teacher; Dr. R. H. Benjamin, a zealous supporter of his church and the public school, and who, as first president of the Savings Bank, laid broad and deep the foundations of its great success; his successor, Dr. A. B. Luce; John Corwin, the popular landlord; and scores of others, useful, prominent citizens of this town, who have gone to their reward; but the limit of time and space forbids; nor can we attempt to add the names of those who, natives here, have achieved honorable name elsewhere.

There is one name, however, that must be mentioned. Tappin Reeve, son of Rev. Abner Reeve, a clergyman of this town, became famous as a lawyer and founder of the celebrated law school at Litchfield, Conn. He was the first eminent lawyer in this country to arraign the common law of England for its cruelty in cutting off the natural rights of married women and placing their property entirely within the control of their husbands. This year is the 100th anniversary of the passage of the first Act in our Legislature looking to the liberation of married women from this bondage, and by a law passed at our last Legislature the reform which Mr. Reeve first preached is thoroughly effected. He died in 1823, but he lived long enough to see his principles gain a footing in Connecticut, though at first they did not meet with much favor.

A book should be written to preserve the memory of what Riverhead Town did to aid in the war to preserve the Union. She promptly voted down all disloyal resolutions offered by the few sympathizers that rebellion had here, and supplied all the moneys necessary to do her part, while one hundred and twenty-two of her citizens went to the front, of whom ten never returned. Of those who did return, sixteen have answered to the last roll call here, and time is reducing the ranks of the remaining.

> *Then honor to the brave who nobly died;*
> *And honor to the men who by their side*
> *Survived the canon's hail*
> *With hearts that did not quail*
> *When all our country's fate was cast*
> *For life or death in War's fierce blast.*
>
> —DR. WHITAKER.

The time and space we have devoted to the past forbids our entering upon extended remarks as to the future. We have endeavored to give a picture of the times that are gone; but the things that are, surround us now, and they speak for themselves. The unpainted and unsteepled meeting-house is succeeded by the elegant church edifice. The little rustic schoolhouse of the rudest kind, and for whose maintenance every dollar was grudged, is supplanted by the Union School, for which no expense is too great and no ornament too good.

Compare the private dwelling of to-day with the homes of our best citizens of generations past, and how great the contrast. To-day a good selection of books and the weekly or daily newspapers are found in every household; then the Bible and the almanac comprised almost their only library, and of newspapers their [sic] were none. In matters of decoration, how great the change. There is not a house that has not a multitude of things which the good people of the past would have called the "superfluities of life."

The chromos and engravings that now adorn the humblest homes would have been miracles of art a century ago. The increase of means of communication with the outside world are too apparent to require mention. Where the thrifty village was in the early times we find it more thrifty still; and where once was an unbroken forest we see around us all the evidences of prosperity and happiness.

If towns and villages have their periods of decline it is nothing strange, for cities and nations have the same; but the general progress is still onward. The traveler who ascends a lofty mountain will not find his journey one regular ascent from the base to the summit. For a long distance he will be traveling over apparently level ground; then he will ascend a slight elevation, then he will descend into a valley, and for a part of his journey he will actually be going down hill; but as he travels on he will find that the valley of the present moment is higher than the hill on which he stood an hour before. At one time he will be as completely hidden from the goal of his hopes as if he were in the center of the earth, and again he will be in full view of the object of his aspirations.

And so he goes on and on, through all changes of climate and varieties of vegetation, till he reaches that chill region of mist and cloud, where no life exists and which marks the border line of perpetual snow. But beyond all these, the cloud and darkness left behind, he enters a region of perpetual light and his feet at length tread the summit where the sun shines forever with unclouded glory.

The band here played again, and then Chairman Foster presented Prof. Joseph M. Belford of Riverhead, who delivered the following address:

What man has done, how he has done it, and what results have followed his action, are questions that not only powerfully appeal to the imagination, but engage the intellect as well. There is probably no field of investigation into which the human mind can enter that in a greater degree stimulates the curiosity, and arouses and sustains the interest, than that of human history. With unwearied patience, in the face of difficulties that seemed unsurmountable, we find man feeling his way through the past, reading its cuneiform inscriptions, deciphering its Babylonian bricks, exploring its pyramids, studying its art, its architecture, its literature, anything and everything that might throw any light upon the life of a people that had played its part in the solemn drama of history.

And there is no field of study that is more fruitful of solemn lessons than this, for as man comes to study the facts of the past, not as isolated phenomena, but in their obvious and necessary relation to each other, as so many successive links in the great chain of historic evolution, he is overwhelmed with the fact that here as everywhere in the universe he is within the domain of law; that there is just as absolute and fixed an order of sequence in the phenomena of history as there is in the phenomena of nature; that the scientific observer can with no more certainty lay down the law of sequence in the facts he observes in nature, than the historical observer can lay down the law of sequence in the facts he observes in history; that things no more happen fortuitously in the growth of a nation than they happen fortuitously in the growth of a plant; that nations have a law of life and decay, just as trees have a law of life and decay; that a nation can no more grow in contravention of law than an oak can.

And whether we study the civilization of Greeks or Aztecs, of Persians or Indians, of English or French, we find the *law* of their development always the same. The reason why one nation attains a higher point of civilization than another is not that it had a *different* law of development, but that the *same* law had a freer scope and a wider range. And along broad lines these laws are very distinct. Every one, for example, recognizes that there is a necessary relation between the character of a people and their external surroundings.

The student of history isn't surprised to find the Greek mind and temperament one thing, and the Asiatic mind and temperament quite another thing. The conditions of their life makes this imperative. It isn't a matter of accident, it's the outworking of a fixed law. Every one of us is familiar with the law of supply and demand; the law of ratio between the wages of labor and the cost of food. These are things that we can't escape. They inhere in the very constitution of society. Have you ever reflected that there is a fixed ratio between the number of marriages that occur in any given year and the price of corn in that year—the higher the price of corn the fewer marriages, the lower the price of corn the more numerous the marriages? So that if the young men of Riverhead Town seriously wish to multiply their chances in this direction, let them set about lowering the price of corn.

But, seriously, when once this idea of law has possessed us, when we can see everywhere the silent, resistless play of unseen forces, working their way on and through and over all obstructions, to the final destiny which God has marked out for nature and man, "that one far-off divine event to which the whole creation moves," not only will we come to study the facts with a deepening interest, but with a deepening reverence as well, and we will come to see that history is something more than a mere catalogue of events, something more than a record of sieges and battles and crusades.

We will see in it all and through it all the Divine purpose with regard to man, ever unfolding, ever ripening, through shadow and through sunshine, through the inky darkness of mediaeval [sic] ignorance and the meridian splendor of Nineteenth Century knowledge, ever approaching the splendid fulfillment of which the law of development—which is stamped upon all that God has made—gives us certain assurance.

It is this conception of history that brings order out of chaos. The scientific student assures us that in the whole realm of natural phenomena there is no such thing as catastrophe; that what we are accustomed to look upon as sudden upheavals or violent cataclysms in nature, are in reality only the necessary and orderly giving way of old to new conditions under the direction of law. So, too, the historical student, from this higher standpoint of observation, assures us that there are no catastrophes in history; that amid all those social and political upheavals which threaten to disrupt society, throughout all the conventions or congresses or parliaments with their fury of debate, amid all the battle fields with their clangor of arms and their groans of the dying, always, always there has been an imperative law higher than all these things and regulating them all and evolving from them new and higher social conditions and possibilities.

Now, so much for the way in which we ought to study history. And if we are to hope for any higher or larger development in the future it must come from such thoughtful study of the past, of the causes which contribute to its growth, of the law underlying its development. For law, my friends, can never change; it's the same for all times, all seasons, all conditions; the same for the falling apple and the blazing meteor; the same for the dew-drop and the ocean; the same for the dust molecule that noiselessly settles on your parlor mirror and the cruel avalanche thundering down the sides of the mountains; law everywhere and always the same. Conditions change, phenomena change, environment changes, but law never.

So that under whatever law of life and development your ancestors lived one hundred years ago you live to-day, and you can hope for no change or advantage in this regard. It's true, the conditions of your life are widely different; it's true that your environment has been much enlarged, but be convinced of one thing, that if there was any law of relation between the means at your ancestors' command and the use they made of those means you live under the same law, and you can neither escape nor modify its operation.

Now, however complex an organization society may seem to be, yet the great principles underlying social growth are simple and obvious, and easy of statement. In the first place, man can never separate himself from nature, and it must be apparent, as I have already hinted, that very largely social development must depend on the character of our relation with the external world. Think what a wondrous storehouse this nature is. It stands for something more than a moving panorama of light and beauty, delighting the eye and feasting the imagination, something more than a treasury of wealth in precious metals and precious stones. It stands for us too as a wondrous depository of forces, ever present and always potent, from whose play we can never escape, and from a proper utilization of which it is probable there arises more substantial and permanent social development than from any other cause.

I think it is not an extravagant statement to say that civilization is advanced or retarded, suffering diminishes or increases, according as man dominates or is dominated by these forces. We see him go into nature's forest, hew down her trees, transform them into dwellings, multiply these into villages, into cities, utilize her forces to do his work, to light and heat his houses, to propel his machinery, to elevate his grant, to carry his burdens, turning her to a thousand noble uses, and we cry, Behold the wondrous impetus given to the social movement!

See how man is lord and master of nature! But look again. From out the summit of Vesuvius a little cloud of smoke begins to rise. The scientists watch it with interest as an evidence that other of the internal forces of nature are at work; the smoke becomes flame, the flame becomes lava and ashes; down the mountain sides it streams, burying houses, burying people; Herculaneum and Pompeii nothing more than a mighty sepulcher, entombed for hundreds of centuries. Look again. This nature denies the fruit of the earth for a reason—famine comes, plague comes, and we hear the cry of anguish from starving millions in Russia and India. No, No! Any philosophy of social development that would ignore this relation of man to the world in which he lives would be singularly inadequate and incomplete.

Out of this relationship spring the most magnificent discoveries of science; and along the line of scientific discovery lie some of the grandest possibilities of civilization. You don't light your houses with pine knots and tallow dips any more. Why? Because the student of nature has been abroad and has caught the lightning from the clouds and has given you it as a means of light. You no longer spend weary days jolting and bumping and exasperating yourself and your neighbor passenger in going from point to point over roads almost impassable. Why? Because scientific discovery has found in nature another mode of motion. Look where you will you find the fruits of this spirit of discovery.

And as Henry Thomas Buckle says, "The discoveries of great men never leave us. They are immortal. They contain those eternal truths which survive the shock of empires, outlive the struggles of rival creeds and witness the decay of successive faiths. All these have their different measures and different standards, one set of opinions for one age, another set for another. They pass away like a dream; they are as the fabric of a vision which leave not a rack behind.

The discoveries of genius alone remain. They are for all ages and all times; never young and never old, they bear the seeds of their own life. They flow on in a perennial and undying stream; they are essentially cumulative and giving birth to the additions which they subsequently receive, they thus influence the most distant posterity, and after the lapse of centuries produce more effect than they were able to do even at the moment of their promulgation."

Your ancestors of a hundred years ago hardly felt the impress of this current of discovery. But we feel it now, we are a part of it. For it is of the essence of scientific discovery that you can't limit its application as to time or place. We may say that a great deal that is going on in the scientific world is of no immediate interest or concern to us; that it can neither directly or indirectly advance or retard our development. But we're wrong if we say that.

A new scientific truth is the possession of the world. It enlarges by so much our knowledge of the world in which we live, and our command of the forces by which we are surrounded. Says the same learned writer whom I have already quoted: "In a great and comprehensive view the changes in every civilized people are in their aggregate dependent on three things: First, on the amount of knowledge possessed by their ablest men; second, on the direction which that knowledge takes, that is to say, the sort of subject to which it refers; thirdly, and above all (mark that), above all on the extent to which the knowledge is diffused and the freedom with which it pervades all classes of society." And in our day, with a telegraph system girdling the earth, no sooner is a fresh scientific discovery made than it becomes the possession of every race and every clime.

In our age there is no such thing as a monopoly of knowledge. You may effect a corner in wheat, but you can't effect a corner in brain product. That immediately becomes the property of inquiring millions, going by so much to enrich their intellectual possessions, and so contribute to their social development. Now in the next hundred years we are to live right in the flood-tide of this tremendous impulse that has been given to scientific study and discovery. And if you will compare, and I need not make this comparison for you, the multiplied blessings

which have followed these discoveries, the beneficent uses to which
they have been turned—if you will compare these things with what
you recollect or what you read of the conditions of life that confronted
your ancestors, you may find some just basis of speculation or
prophecy as to what the next hundred years may develop.

But it isn't alone in the way of outward material advantages that
the spirit of scientific discovery enriches us. It does something more
for us than to give us devices for lighting and heating our homes or giving us labor-saving machines. It brings within the reach of every one a
literary product of which our ancestors never dreamed. I know that a
great many bad books are written. I know that very much that passes
under the name of poetry and romance is fit for nothing but for bon-
fires, and that it would make uncommonly poor material for that. I
know that many of the utterances of the so-called realistic school reek
with moral filth and every form of literary abomination.

But I know, too, that all over the world there are intellects all
aflame with the fire of genius and hearts all aglow with love to God
and man, that are pouring out a stream of mental health and moral
strength and spiritual beauty that must enrich the age in which they
live and form a precious heritage for the future; writers whose sentiment is so pure and whose moral tone is so lofty that it finds its way as
a mighty potential force into the hearts and lives of those who are aim-
ing to make the age in which they live a better age, whose aspiration is
to help on the social movement along the line of loftier, purer character and an enlarged manhood and womanhood.

Don't let me be misunderstood. I have no purpose to disparage the
libraries of one hundred years ago. I fear we are a little too much given
to patronizing our forefathers. We are apt to institute unfavorable com-
parisons between their rather limited opportunities and the almost
boundless resources of the modern student. We are apt to think that
they didn't have many books, and that we ought not to expect them to
know very much. Well, I presume they didn't have very many books;
but then I'm not sure that the value of a library is measured by the
number of volumes on the shelves.

There is another and a higher test than that. A book is valuable not
so much for the knowledge it gives as for the character it develops. And
from this higher standpoint possibly their libraries were not so meagre
after all. If they had not many books they had good ones. Now and then
you found Burns there—sweet, gentle Robert Burns, who has found a
voice for every human sorrow, a cry to the pitying Father for every
human need; whose sympathy was aroused alike by the daisy care-
lessly upturned by his plow and by the sorrows of struggling men and

women, toiling on in obscurity under a burden of poverty. And they had their Shakespeare, to whose affluent genius all knowledge and all experience seemed an open secret; who read the human heart and unfolded its workings as astronomers read the stars and tell us their elements.

And, above all and grander than all, they had their Bible, not as a text-book for critical study, but as a veritable fountain of life, drawing from its sustenance and strength, and the amplest equipment for their daily duties. To them the songs of David meant more than the rhythm or cadence of Hebrew poetry; they meant actual power to uplift and sustain. To them they turned when the burden grew too heavy or the sorrow pressed too sorely, and they found in them—not words, but the Lord God himself, a tower of strength in the hour of need. And before the type of manhood and womanhood that they evolved from these elements you and I must stand to-day with uncovered heads in reverent homage.

It was a manhood and womanhood that would have graced any time and any civilization. Heroic in self-sacrifice, large in charity, lofty in ideal, affluent in all the graces that adorn and dignify the human character, it ought to move you with pride to look back upon such an ancestry. In contemplation of this larger worth we lose sight of oddities of manner or extravagances of dress. These are accidental, adventitious, the creature of the hour, the whim of the moment, liable to constant change and fluctuation, but character is an undying possession, and for it we can have nothing but the deepest reverence. We may smile at the bonnet as capacious as a Saratoga trunk, or at the bodice as stiff and as unyielding as the laws of the Medes and Persians, but we don't smile at the large hearts and the generous souls which gave to Riverhead Town such a history as it has had for a hundred years.

Yet granting all this, and not losing sight for a moment of our obligation to the past, what of the future? I find it impossible to cherish the belief that the past is exhaustive of high possibilities of life and character. You may say that it is of the essence of lofty character that it be developed by hardships; that it is born in travail, nourished and perfected in suffering, and that an amelioration of the conditions of life naturally tends to an emasculation of the moral fibre, a general lowering of the moral tone. But in so saying don't you neglect another obvious arrangement in the moral economy of the universe, namely, that these very changes create new hardships, and that, however great may be the change in the condition of life, there can never be any change in the law of character?

Be sure of this: God never leaves any age without the proper and necessary conditions of development. Nay, more; all history proves that He provides for an ever loftier standard of character, and places man in the very conditions which make the attainment of that standard possible. A great deal of the apprehension that is expressed for the present and for the future has its foundation in a false philosophy, and a neglect of the most obvious teachings of history. We need not fear man nor his work. Whatever obligation the future may lay upon him we will manfully meet. And this brings me to the principal purpose of my address to-day.

If we look backward we see the noble line of patient men and women, working out, in the face of discouragement and difficulty, the history which is theirs and ours to-day. Their work is completed, at least so far as their active participation in it is concerned. But in the sense of there being in every good and generous deed, and in every noble life, a power of reproduction and perpetuation, that work can never die. It must form an integral part of the future history of the town by whomsoever that history shall be made. Looking forward, our eyes rest upon the youth to whom is committed the future destiny of Riverhead Town. All it is ever to become they must make it. It is an obligation that can neither be eluded nor shifted. It is an obligation that is individual and personal, it is yours and mine, and it cannot be relegated or assigned to other hands.

I have hinted at the aides we are to have from the outside, in the fact that we move right along in this wonderful current of scientific discovery, of the invention of machinery, of the literary products of an age that is singularly prolific of good literary work. All these things will be ours and all will contribute to our growth.

But the future history of Riverhead Town depends not nearly so much on what you receive from the outside, as on what you evolve from the inside; not so much on what the world gives you, as on what you give the world; not so much from the contributions you receive from the busy brain workers in the world, as on the character of the work which you produce. Now, society has a perfectly legitimate expectation of you and me, and by so much as we defect that expectation, by so much do we subtract from the possible growth and development of the town or community in which we live. The first thing that society has a right to demand of us is that we should produce something, that we should be producers and not consumers merely.

That don't necessarily mean that we must produce a Paradise Lost, or an Atlantic Cable, or a Corliss engine, or a painting like the Ascension of Christ. These are among the products of genius that stand out solitary and eminent, with a yawning gulf between them and the ordinary product of the average mind. Society don't demand that we be Shakespeares, or Bacons, or Raphaels, or Edisons. It only demands, and it has a perfect right to demand, that we produce the very best of honest work of which we are capable in the sphere in which we live, and that we do that all the time. It is your work, your brain, your arm, highly consecrated and conscientiously directed to the noblest ends, that are going to give to Riverhead Town all of worth that it will develop in the next one hundred years.

Don't make the mistake of setting up a false standard or criterion by which to measure your work. Above all, don't make the mistake of supposing that your sphere of action here in Riverhead Town is necessarily limited or proscribed. It is not always those who have reached distinction in what you feel are wider spheres and by shorter roads that have the most permanently enriched the age in which they lived. And right here and now it is your opportunity to do just as noble and just as lasting work as any the world has ever seen. Do you ask me how you can do this? Now, I can give you no settled or fixed rule by which you may achieve what the world calls success, or by means of which you may be secured against the possibility of what the world calls failure. I can formulate no principles for your guidance which will certainly bring to you fame or distinction.

And possibly the very worst service I could render you would be to tabulate these rules, if any such there were. But I can tell you how your life may become a potential force in the social history of Riverhead Town. It is by setting your ideal of life so high that character rather than reputation, duty rather than distinction, shall be the aim of your living. It is what we aim to do that exalts or belittles us. He who lives out a noble purpose, even in obscurity, so that he lives it out truly, is the benefactor of his race. I confess to you that to me there is no more moving spectacle than to see the noble youth of our town, with a consciousness of the obligation they owe to the age in which they live, girding themselves for the life struggle before them.

It partakes of the highest qualities of heroism. They are going to meet unseen dangers. They know that a thousand foes are lurking in the dark to tempt them from the high standard of life and character which they have set before them. But they are undaunted by all these things. The blood of Revolutionary sires courses in their veins. As they fought for freedom, so these will sternly strive to lay broad and deep the foundation of strong and enduring character. Like Emerson's hero, "they have not omitted the arming of the man. They have learned in season that they are born into the state of war, and that society and their own well-being require that they should not go dancing in the weeds of peace, but, warned, self-collected, and neither defying nor dreading the thunder, they take both reputation and life in their hands, and with perfect urbanity they dare the gibbet and the mob by the absolute truth of their speech, and the absolute rectitude of their behavior."

I am not painting an imaginary struggle. I am not dealing in rhetorical rhapsodies. I am outlining the conditions of the struggle that confronts every strong man and every earnest woman on the threshold of active life—conditions from which we can't escape, but from the right use of which the ripest fruits may be garnered and the proudest distinction gained. It is of the essence of all noble work that it carries with it its own compensation. "Work," says the seer of Concord, "in every hour, paid or unpaid; see only that thou work, and thou canst not escape the reward; whether thy work be fine or coarse, planting corn or writing epics, so only it be honest work, done to thine own approbation, it shall earn a reward to the senses as well as to the thought; no matter how often defeated, you are born to victory. The reward of a thing well done, is to have done it." Can you measure the moral power of the young life before me to-day, if it be so aroused and so directed? What method of calculation will you apply to the gross result of the interplay of such energies and forces in the social life of the next century?

Young man and young woman you live in an age of magnificent opportunities. Those who lived and died a hundred years ago or more, have left you a precious heritage. I don't believe the sun shines upon a land where the rewards to honest toil are so swift and so sure as here. You are barred from no honorable calling by the accident of birth or the limitation of social caste. The only coat of arms that wins genuine homage here is the shield of personal honor and personal worth. And though you be born into a state of war, girded with that shield, the issue of the conflict is never doubtful.

All that the broadest minds and the stoutest hearts have done, you may do. And the one grand lesson of this day and hour is that we live up to the measure of our opportunities. The Divine purpose with regard to man is moving on, and it will be wrought out with us if we stand in the van-guard, over us if we lag behind. The lessons of the past make the prophecy of the future sure. And we can help on the dawning of this brighter day. Will we do it?

"A sacred burden is the life ye bear;
Look on it, lift it, bear it patiently,
Stand up and walk beneath it steadfastly,
Fail not for sorrow, falter not for sin,
But onward, upward, till the goal ye win."

The benediction by Rev. Dr. Whitaker, of Southold, closed the profitable and enjoyable meeting. There were sports of various kinds at the Fair Grounds, and in the evening there was a very creditable display of fireworks set off on the south side of the river, near the water's edge, an excellent place for the purpose. The old lumber yard grounds, and vicinity opposite, were filled with a large crowd of village residents and people who had driven in to witness the show, and the expressions on all sides were that the display was one well worth seeing. At intervals, during the exhibition, the Riverhead Brass Band, from a position near Hallett's Mill, furnished inspiring strains of patriotic music, and altogether a successful and satisfactory celebration was thus, fittingly brought to a brilliant close.

CHAPTER IX

A HISTORY OF RIVERHEAD

Written by William S. Pelletreau, A.M. in 1905

William Pelleatreau was born in Southampton in 1840, a descendant of the earliest settlers of that town. His father and grandfather were famed as silversmiths throughout Long Island and the New England states. He was elected Town Clerk of Southampton at the age of 22 and became interested in old records. Thereafter, he devoted his life to the study and writing of history. He wrote many books regarding the histories of towns and counties in New York State, including the counties of Putnam, Greene, Rockland, and Westchester. He compiled the "Records of Southampton" in three volumes and the "Records of Smithtown". His "History of Long Island" in which he included the history of East Hampton, was in three volumes. He died at the age of 77 after devoting his life to the study and writing of history. In his obituary, it said "He will not be forgotten while the history of Long Island continues to be studied by good Long Islanders."

THE modern annals of Riverhead township, the county town of Suffolk, began with 1792, when it was formed out of Southold. It is fifteen miles in length, with an average width of 5 miles, and contains something like 36,500 acres. Its north shore runs along the Sound, while its south shore is on Peconic Bay, and the Peconic river separates it from Southampton and Brookhaven. Farming is exclusively carried on, but in no part is the land noted for its fertility, and even to the present day large sections of the township can hardly be said to be under cultivation.

Yet within recent years a vast improvement has been effected, and, bit by bit, acres which have been given over for a century or more to wildbrush and weeds have been recovered and are yielding abundant return in the shape of grain or garden truck. Many thriving communities have sprung up, and Riverhead from being, as the Rev. Dr. Dwight described it in 1804, "a miserable hamlet," is now one of the most prosperous and beautiful and progressive towns on Long Island, with a population estimated at about 2,500.

But Riverhead had an interesting story long before it took its place as a political division of Suffolk county. Some of the most interesting aboriginal remains on all Long island were found in the vicinity of Aquebogue, as late as 1879. As related by Mr. R.M. Bayles, the village annalist, Nathan A. Downs, in the year mentioned, found by the frequent appearance of Indian arrows and some specimens of rude pottery that he was on the site of an ancient Indian village. Investigation discovered curiosities that attracted the attention of archaeologists and the public far and near. The ground lay upon the bank of Meeting House creek, on the south side of the Country road and about one-eighth of a mile from it. This creek runs into Peconic Bay, about one and a half miles distant from this point, and its name is suggested by the fact of its head being near the meeting-house or "steeple church." It is supposed that this creek at some time during the remote centuries of the past was the lower section of a river whose source was away to the north, among the hills which range along the sound.

In plowing in this vicinity dark spots were observed in the ground and were at first supposed to have been temporary fire places or ovens that had been filled with ashes, shells, refuse and soil; but on closer examination it was discovered that they contained human bones, and that the oyster shells had been placed where they were while the oyster was intact. A refuse heap some fifty yards long contained hundreds of loads of shells, chips of flint, bones and broken implements, and must have been many years accumulating. Near the shore of the now extinct river the graves of Indian dead were made. The geological changes that have taken place since these graves were made suggest that possibly thousands of years may have passed since that time.

The greater portion of the territory of Riverhead township was purchased from the Indians by inhabitants of Southold; and the first purchase, known as the Aquebogue Purchase, was made in 1649. In

1665 (December 7) a confirmatory deed was procured from the Indi-ans, and this contains the first definite (yet not altogether exact or sat-isfactory) boundaries, and these were substantially the same as contained by Governor Andros' patent, executed in 1676.

According to the second Indian deed mentioned the boundaries were "the River called in the English toung the Weading (Wading) Kreek, in the Indian toung Pauquaconsuk, on the West****and with a River or arme of the sea which runneth upon between Southampton Land and the aforesaid tract of land unto a certain Kreek which fresh water runneth into on ye South, called in English the Red Kreek, in In-dian Toyonge; together with the said Kreek and meadows belonging thereto, and running on a straight line from the head of the afore-named fresh water to the head of ye Small brook that runneth into the Kreek called Pauquaconsuk; as also all neck of lands," etc. The line from the head of Toyonge to the head of Pauquaconsuk was afterward inter-preted as the line from the head of what is now known as Red Creek, in Southampton, to the head of Wading River Creek, and this line, run-ning a northwesterly and southeasterly direction across what is now the southwest part of the town of Riverhead, afterward became the northeastern boundary of Colonel Smith's "St. George's manor," and is still known in real estate descriptions as the "manor line."

The land grants are related in principal part in connection with those of the town of Southold. In 1742 that portion of the township lying southwest of the manor line was divided among William Nicoll, Robert Hempstead, Joseph Wickham, Daniel Wells and Elijah Hutchin-son. Among purchasers were Caleb Horton, David Corey, Thomas Reeve, Richard Terry, Samuel Conklin, John Salmon, William Benjamin, David Horton, James Horton, James Reeve, Elijah Hutchinson, John Goldsmith, Solomon Wells, John Tuthill, John Conklin, Jonathan Horton, David Parshall, Israel Parshall, Joshua Tuthill, Zebulon Hallock, Joseph Wickham, Nathaniel Youngs, Joshua Wells, William Albertson and Noah Hallock.

The controversy between Southold and Southampton, concerning the ownership of certain lands and meadows at Red Creek, in Southampton, is related in the history of Riverhead, and the following Indian deed shows how the claim of Southold first originated. Very few of the original documents which time has spared equal this deed in in-terest.

The name Ucquebaak (which is the earliest form of the word, which in the record appears in various forms as Occabauk, Accobock, Accobog, Agaboke, Aquabauk, and now stereotyped in the form of Aquebogue) was originally applied to lands on both sides of Peconic river, and means "land at the head of the bay," or "the cove place." It is now the name of a village very far removed from the place which the Indians called by that name.

In Southampton, the "Accabog Division" included the lands from Red creek to Riverhead. This deed is of special interest at the present time, as upon it and the patent based thereupon is the foundation of the claim of Southold to a large portion of Peconic Bay. The deed and documents following are recorded in the office of the Secretary of State:

These present witness that Oocomboomaquus, and the wife of Mahakannuck the true Indyan owners of Ocquebouch, for and in consideration of three coats, two fathoms of Wampum, four hatchets, four knives, and four Tobaco Pipes, into their hands at the ensealing thereof. Have granted bargained and sold unto Mr. Theophilus Eaton Governor of New Haven Jurisdiction, and to Mr. Stephen Goodyear, Deputy Governor, for and in the behalf of ye Jurisdiction, the whole tract commonly called Ocquebauk, bounded on the east with the creek Unscawamuck, which is the next creek to the place where ye canoes are drawn over to Mattituck, on the west with the Great fresh river, on the south with the Greate Harbour, and on the north with the Sea. Together with the land and meadows lying on the other side the water southward so farre as the creek Mashmanock, which is the fifth creeke from the fresh river towards Shinnecock. Provided that the aforesaid Indians may enjoy during their lives a small piece of land to plant upon lying between the two creeks Miamegg and Assasquage. And also to take the benefit of the Sassachems. To Have and to Hold all the said tract of land as is before expressed, with the meadows and all their appurtenances (except before excepted) to the said Theophilus Eaton and Stephen Goodyeare Esquires, in the behalfe of the Jurisdiction. To them their heirs and assigns for ever. With Warranty against the said Occomboomaquus and Mahamack their heirs and assigns and all and every other person and persons claiming any title or Interest of from, by or under them, their meanes occasions or Consent in or to all or any the above specifyed, or any part or parcell thereof. In witness whereof the aforesaid Occomboomaquus and Mahamack's wife have set to their hands and seales the 4th day of March, 1648. Sealed and delivered in presence of

JOHN YOUNGS,
HENRY WHITINGS,
JOHN YOUNGS, JR.,
MUCKOMOSH,
SAGGAMOUCH.

Attached to the above is the deposition of certain Indians that "there was an Indian Squaw of the Sachem's blood that was wife of Mahamack who, to their knowledge, was the true Proprietor of a tract of land on ye south side of the Great Harbour, or river called Pea-canuck, from the head of a creek called To Youngs or Mashmamock, and so through the middle of the Island to the creek called Pauqun-consuck on the north side, which creeke by the English is called the Wading creeke, and so along the north sea to Mattituck. And that her right was purchased by Mr. John Youngs, and all the four Sachems then living knew of her sale, and objected nothing against it. And it was constant custom by all other Indians to ask her leave to gather herbage and flaggs for matts." Dated December 27, 1662.

Paucumpt, an Indian, about 80 years old, descended from the house of the Sachems in the end of the Island, before divers English and Indyans, gave testimony "that Occobauke was an ancient seate of Sachem ship and of long standing; that is to say time out of mind; but the first in his time did possess the upland and meadow on the swamp side of the head of the river, lying in the west end of the Bay, five creeks. The first, Massemennuck, the second Nobbs, the third Sugga-muck, the fourth Weekewock-Mamish and the fifth To Youngs, being the out bounds thereof, and lying in opposition to Occabauk, Old Ground, on the north side of the Bay. The name of the last Sachem that possessed the same was called Ockenmungan, who had one son and one daughter, the son dying in his infancy, the daughter is the sole heir and proprietor of Occabauk, which Mr. Youngs purchased of said squaw about eleven years ago, and Munhansett the Sachem did well approve the same. And the bounds of Occabauk go on a straight line from the head of the river to the Wading Creek on the north beach, which is called Pequaockeon because Peaquocks are found there." Dated May, 1660.

The necks mentioned above are all on the south side of the river, in Southampton, and probably begins with what is now "Wells Neck" on the west and extending east to Youngs, or Red Creek.

The very interesting allusion to the meaning of the Indian name for Wading River is here given by the learned antiquarian and student of the Indian language, Mr. William Wallace Tooker, of Sag Harbor:

(Pauquacamsuck or Pauquaconsuk)

"That the bounds of Occabauk aforesaid go on a straight line from ye head of ye river (Peconic) to ye wading creek (now Wading River Creek, see Maps of Long Island), on ye

North Beach which is called *Pequaockeon*, because *Pe-quaoks* are found there." *Pequa-oc-Po-qua-hoc* (Un-kechaug); *Poquan-hock* (Narragansett) abbreviated to *Quohaug*, 'round-claim,' literally, thick or tightly closed shell; the terminal—*oc, hoc,* or *hocki,* 'that which covers' (as a garment); *keon* from *toskeon* (Eliot), 'to wade,' *suck,* 'a brook or outlet of any small stream,' thus making *Pequa-oc-keon-suck,* 'the brook or the outlet where we wade for thick shells' or 'round-claims.'" Book of Deeds, Vol. 2, p. 273, Albany N.Y. The above is quoted from my "The Indian Names of Long Island," pp. 46, 47, 48, Algonquin Series, Vol. 4, Harper, 1901.

From documents in the office of the Town Clerk of Southampton we learn that at one time the lands at Red Creek and vicinity were occupied by a village of Indians who were a part of the tribe which claimed and inhabited the town of Southold.

After this there was a war between the Shinnecocks and Yeanocock Indians, in which the latter were defeated and driven off. After a time they returned and were allowed to settle in their former seats, but the Shinnecocks claimed all the land on the south side of the river, and required acknowledgment of their title according to certain Indian customs. The following document will explain the case more fully:

Richard Howell and Joseph Raynor, aged about forty years, deposed this 15th day of September 1667. Saith as follows. That upon a time about the latter end of May last, Capt. John Youngs of Southold brought over to Southampton, Thomas Stanton with some of the chiefe of Southold Indians, meting at the School house some of chiefe of Southampton Indians with the Sachem, being there. Capt. Youngs being asked the end of his comeing said, To fine out truthe, viz. Whoe had true right to ye land or meadow in controversy betweene the two townes. And the debate thereupon grew on betweene the Indians theire beinge present some of the Southold Inhabitants with divers of ye chiefe of the Inhabitants of Southampton. Thomas Stanton being ye interpreter. These deponents heard the said Thomas ask both parties of ye Indians, whoe had the true right to the said land and meadows. And the said Indians (after long debate) joyntly answered that ye young eagles that were taken in the nests, & the deere that were drowned or killed in the water, it was ye Indians custom to carry ye saide eagles & the skins of the deere to these Sachems or Indians that were the true owners of ye land. Thereupon Thomas Stanton presently replyed, saying, indeed the eagles and the deere were something, but if there was a bear drowned or killed, that would put the matter out of controversie, And the deponent heard Southampton Indians affirme that there was a bear drowned or killed in ye same tract of land now in controversy between ye said townes. Then Thomas Stanton asked to whom the skin was carried, and Southampton Indians answered, To Shinnekuke Indians, And Southold Indians allsoe acknowledged that the said bear skin was carryed to Shinnecock Indians by Southold Indians whoe tooke ye bear.

Taken before me.

THOMAS TOPPING.

For further evidence in the manner, application was made to the Rev. Thomas James, of East Hampton, whose acquaintance with the Indian language rendered his services as an interpreter of great value.

"The Deposition of Mr. Thomas James, taken at Easthampton this 18th Day of October, 1667, Testifieth

"Being earnestly desired by them of Southampton towne to be some meanes in their behalfe to procure ye testimony, or affirmation of ye montaukut Indians concerning ye bounds of Shinnikuke Indians, accordingly, Paqunttown, Counsellor, being here att yt present att Easthampton, I enquired of him whether he knew anything concerning ye aforesd bounds, & he told me he did, as being often employed by ye Sachems in their matters, & wth all told me yt ye bounds of ye Shinnecuke Indians (since ye conquest of those Indians wch formerly many yeares since liued att akkobauk) did reach to a river where they go to catch ye fish we commonly call alewiues, the name of yt Riuer hee said is Pehik; & wth all told me yt there were two old women liueing at Montaukut who formerly were of ye Akkobauk Indians, who could giue further information concerning ye matter.

"So I made a journey with Mr. Rich. Howell and Mr. John Leyton (Laughton) to Montaukut & we mett with ye aforesd women, who affirmed they formerly were of ye Akkobauk

Indians, & they knew the bounds of ye severall plantations
in those parts. One of them an antient woman (called by he
Indians Akkobauk Homo's Squaw), to which the other also
asserted called Wompquaim's Squaw, a middle aged woman,
in they joyntly declared as followeth, that formerly many
years since, there was a small plantation of Indians at
Akkobauk & those Indians being few, were driven off their
land, being conquered by other Indians & that in those
tymes the bounds of those Akkobauk Indians came eastward of the River Pehikkonuk to a creek which she named,
And they gathered flags for mats within that neck of land,
but since those Indians were conquered who lived att
Akkobauk, the Shinnecock bounds went to the river Pehikkonuk, where ye Indians catched Alewives, & the Shin-
nokuk Indians had the drowned deere as theirs, on this side
of the said river, and one beare some years since, & the old
squaw said by ye token shee eat some of it, pointing to her
teeth, and that the skin & flesh was brought to Shinnocut as
acknowledging their right to it, to a Saunk Squaw then living there who was the old Montauket Sachem's sister & first
wife to Awkkonnu. This to the best of my understanding.
This taken upon oath before mee.

JOHN MULFORD."

The foregoing document in the handwriting of Mr. James is in the
Town Clerk's office of East Hampton. Other affidavits showed that the
town of Southampton had claimed and made use of the meadows on
the south side of Peconic river before 1663.

In accordance with their claim, the town of Southampton, as plaintiff, commenced a suit in the Court of Assizes against Southold as a defendant, Captain John Howell and Henry Pierson being attorneys for
the former. The case came to trial in October, 1667, and the jury decided in favor of Southampton. Southold then appealed before the verdict "to be heard in Equity." This was granted, the appeal to be
considered by the Court in October, 1688, "unless they should otherwise agree, which the Court doth recommend unto both parties."

Governor Richard Nicolls sent Hon. Captain Needham and Captain
Matthias Nicolls to act as mediators, and the result was an agreement
made by representatives from both towns, on March 11, 1667-8:

"That ye town of Southampton shall peaceably & quietly
enjoy & possess ye full lattitude of their land bounds they

sometime purchased of Captain Topping, ye west line was &
is to run according to their deed from a place called Seatuck
on the South Side to ye head of a River or Bay called Pea-
conet on ye North Side to be to the said Southampton &
their successors for ever. With this restriction or permission,
that Mr. William Wells of Southold shall have and retain eighteen acres off the above said meadows, which are already
appointed unto him, ye same to be to ye only use & be-
hoove of him and his heirs forever. And all the rest of ye land
or tract of meadow to lye in Common for mowing for all ye
Inhabitants of Both towns, who have interest according to
their property, until ye said towns shall more fully agree to
divide ye same in particular, and when they shall come to be
divided, ye said eighteen acres, belonging to Mr. Wells, shall
be accounted as part of ye quantity which Southold are to
have."

This was a final settlement of the difficulty, and is mentioned in the
patents of Governor Andros and Governor Dongan.

On September 8, 1686, an agreement was made between the two
towns that the Southold people should have the west part of the meadows, "their west bounds to begin at two pine trees that are marked by
the Riverside about half a mile below the going over the Riverhead,
and from the said pine trees, all the meadow eastward to the spring at
the head of the Creek that comes upon on the east side of Fifteen Mile
Island. And Southampton townes part of the said meadows for their
west bounds to begin at said spring at the head of the creek on the east
side of Fifteen Mile Island, and from thence eastward all the meadow
to the creek called the Red Creek. The meadows that Lyes westward of
the aforesaid two pine trees (being by estimation about two Acres of
meadow more or less) is by mutual consent left to lye in common between the two townes until both parties agree to dispose of it."

The part that was given to Southold men was owned by them in
proportion to their individual proprietor rights. Mention is frequently
made in wills and deeds. The jurisdiction was to be to Southampton,
whose claim rested upon the Indian deed to Captain Thomas Topping
which was approved by the Governor. The western part of these meadows is still known as "Wells Neck."

In 1764, Fifteen Mile Island was owned by James Fanning, Jr., who
sold it to Thomas Fanning. He also owned Long Neck and had a
dwelling house on it, and sold the same to Thomas Fanning in 1765.

The map of the "Manor Land" that is given in this history may be thus explained. The eastern boundary of the patent for Brookhaven was at the head of Wading river, and from thence a line running due north to the Sound and south to the middle of the Island. A small stone monument in the northwest corner of the Presbyterian church lot at Wading river marks the place where a peperidge tree formerly stood, which marked the head of Wading river, and the boundary between the two towns. The Second Patent to Colonel William Smith included a large triangular tract bounded on the east by a line running from this point to the crossing of Peconic river at Riverhead. This triangular tract was sold by Colonel Henry Smith to Benjamin Youngs and Samuel Hutchinson of Southold, April 1, 1720, for £50.

They sold the same tract to James Reeve, Joshua Tuthill, Matthias Dickinson, Richard Terry, Charles Booth, Thomas Goldsmith, Caleb Horton, Samuel Conkling, Thomas Reeve, Nathaniel Warner, Josiah Youngs, David Parshall, Joseph Wickham, Joshua Wells, Jr., Joseph Hulse, Jonathan Dimon, Samuel Conkling, John Conkling and Henry Conkling, in sixty shares as partners, reserving shares for themselves. This is dated February 21, 1722.

The map shows the division into lots, with names of owners at that time. The east line of the tract is well known as the "Manor Line."

The population increased very slowly, the settlements were small and widely scattered and the people were poor. The territory added nothing to the wealth of Southold. It had no harbors, no commerce, no excess of crops and was very little heard of even in the town meetings. The county was not particularly adapted for traveling. The distances were great and from Aquebogue westward the territory to the Brookhaven line was in Southold, but not of it. Therefore there was little excitement when it became known that on March 13, 1792, the Legislature had cut off the territory and erected it into a separate township described as follows:

All that part of the said town of Southold, lying to the westward of a line beginning at the sound and running thence southerly to the bay separating the towns of Southampton and Southold, and which is the eastern boundary or side of a farm now in the tenure or occupation of William Albertson and is the reputed line of division between the parishes of Ocquebouge and Mattetuck.

This legislation was enacted on the petition of Peter Reeves and others, but not without opposition. John Wells and others prayed for a postponement until the next session, and Benjamin Horton and others asked for an act providing that town meetings should be held alternately in the old town meeting house in Southold and in the

Aquobogue meeting house. These various petitions were presented January 11, and little more than two months later was passed the law for which Reeves and his associates had asked.

As directed by the organic act, the first town meeting was held on April 3, 1792, when the following officers were elected: Daniel Wells, supervisor; Josiah Reeve, clerk; John C. Terry, Joseph Wills and Benjamin Terry, assessors; Jeremiah Wells and Spencer Dayton, highway commissioners; Daniel Terry, Zachariah Hallock and Daniel Edwards, overseers of the poor; Nathan Youngs, Eleazer Luce, Rufus Youngs, John Corwin, Zophar Mills, Peter Reeve and Merritt Howell, overseers of highways; Sylvanus Brown, collector; and David Brown, Abel Corwin and Benjamin Horton, constables.

The infant township was governed under the laws which were in force in Southold at the time of the separation until 1794, when they appear to have been superseded by others, but the proceedings at the enacting sessions included little of interest to us. One exception to this might be made in the care taken of the poor. When the township was formed it had only six paupers, and these were let out for one year to the bidder who offered to maintain them for the least money, and this method of disposing of such dependents continued to prevail until 1832, when a farm was purchased at Lower Aquebogue and the poor were gathered together and removed there, and that establishment was maintained until the county system came into law and the paupers of Riverhead were transferred, in 1871, to Yaphank, and the old poor farm was sold.

But in spite of its dignity as a township and its position as containing the county town, the township of Riverhead advanced very slowly. In 1800 its population was 1,498; in 1820, 1,857; in 1825, 1,816; in 1835, 2,138; in 1840, 2,373, and twenty years later it had only reached 2,734; two decades still further it had advanced to 3,939, and the census in 1900 showed that it practically stood at these figures, the census returns showing 4,503.

But in the stories of the various villages and settlements deserving of a much more dignified title, we find much deserving of study. Even the story of the village of Riverhead, modern as most of it is, is full of interesting detail, all of which tend to present it before us as a typical country town, and one which at the present day is full of ambition and life and is making full use of its natural beauty of situation and its ready adoption of all that in these modern times is regarded as necessary to municipal success to make it become one of the most attractive and popular of Long Island cities. It is a beautiful place; it combines city and country in its broad and well paved streets, its stately trees lining

the sidewalks everywhere, its business establishments and banks, its ·
many really handsome villas, its steadily increasing popularity among
summer visitors and its loyal, energetic and enterprising body of regular residents, who have an abiding faith in its future at all times to bestir
themselves in every movement likely to aid in its development. It has
its ornaments too, as witness, the beautiful water tower.

Like so many other centers of population on Long Island, Riverhead began with a sawmill, and this was erected on the banks of the
Peconic in 1659 by two pioneers—John Tucker and Joshua Horton.
This is said to have antedated by eighteen years that of Joseph Carpenter, at Maschete Cove, Long Island, for whom the claim was long made
that "he was the first man on Long Island, New York, Connecticut or
New Jersey to set up a sawmill run by water power." The setting forth
of this fact was made by Orville B. Ackerly, of Yonkers, New York, a
member of the Suffolk County Historical Society, in an address delivered upon the occasion of the one hundredth anniversary of the organization of the town of Riverhead, at that place on July 4, 1892. And this
valuable paper the writer acknowledges as the source of much of the
information contained in the following narrative.

This pioneer miller, John Tucker, was a man of importance, known
as deacon, captain and esquire, in a day when these titles commanded
far greater respect than they do now. In 1711 his grandson, also named
John, sold to John Parker one of the original four hundred tracts of
land, and this, with a lot adjoining, constituted the entire business portion of the present village of Riverhead. The Woodhull family was the
bone and sinew of the infant community. Josiah Woodhull, during Revolutionary times, made the roof of his house a watch-tower, and from it
gave notice of the approach of marauding British bands.

In the village was also the home of Major Frederick Hudson, a
prominent citizen and one of Tory proclivities. His son, Oliver Hudson,
sold the estate to Zophar Mills. A peculiar interest attaches to this property in the fact that among Major Hudson's bound servants was Paul
Cuffee, an Indian, whose name subsequently became familiar and honored through his ministrations as a preacher to his rapidly dying out
people. As remarked by Mr. Ackerly, "Strange change of circumstances!
The grave of the Master is somewhere unmarked and unknown, in a
dense thicket of weeds and briars. The grave of the servant, fenced and
guarded with pious care by the roadside at Good Ground, is visited by
hundreds who revere his virtues and honor his name."

The village of Riverhead had enjoyed a certain distinction from a
time long antedating its erection as a shire town. In 1727 an act of the
legislature authorized the justices of the peace to build a "county

house and prison," and the first court in the building which was erected was held March 27, 1729. This was a court of general sessions, and the first court of oyer and terminer in the newly created county of Suffolk began its session on September 4, 1787. To dispose of the judicial side of our subject it may be here said that the old court house was renovated and a new jail built about 1825. In 1854 a new and modern court hose was erected, but it was not until 1881, and after the old building had been repeatedly condemned as unsafe, that a new jail was provided, with all the improvements to which such an edifice could then aspire.

Notwithstanding it was now the shire town, the growth of Riverhead was slow for very many years. In 1812 it contained only four buildings besides the court house, and of these one was a tavern kept by John Griffin, and one was a grist mill operated by Josiah Albertson. In 1828 John Perkins set up a woolen factory. There had been other industries further up the stream long before this, among them an iron forge, built by Jeremiah Petty, about 1797, which was abandoned about twenty-five years later. After the middle of the last century, various modern manufactories were established, and the village entered upon the beginnings of those substantial industrious conditions which characterize it at the present time.

The churches of the village had their origin more or less immediately in the early "Steeple Church" at Upper Aquebogue. The people worshipping were there of various denominations. In 1834 some of these people formed a congregation at Riverhead, holding services in the lower room of the seminary building. In 1833 the Methodists, who had long maintained a class, organized a church, and built a house of worship the next year, and this was replaced by the present elegant edifice in 1870. In 1839 the Swedenborgians built a meeting house, and the Congregationalists builded [sic] in 1841. The Roman Catholic church was built in 1870, and the Free Methodist church in 1872. The Episcopalians, who had formed a society in 1870, erected a church building in 1873.

The seminary referred to was established in 1834, chiefly through the instrumentality of Judge George Miller, and proved a power for good in the advancement of female education.

The excellent tower furnished by the Peconic river began about the middle of the last century to attract many manufacturing enterprises to Riverhead—molding and planing mills, a soap factory, fertilizer works (both fish and wood being the staple of manufacture), organ building and quite a number of other industries added to its wealth and importance. Such establishments rarely add much to the aesthetic beauty of a place and Riverhead in its march of improvement might have lost much of its attractiveness but for the organization, in 1881, of the "Village Improvement Society," which not only accomplished much and lasting good by its own direct work, but exerted a healthy influence on the entire community.

In 1868 the citizens showed their public spirit and their sagacity by purchasing twenty acres of ground in their village and presenting the property to the Suffolk County Agricultural Society as its permanent headquarters. Its history from its organization more than four decades ago was written *in extenso*, in 1881, by Mr. Nat W. Foster, who had long been its efficient secretary, and this excellent paper has been utilized almost *verbatim* in this narrative, which has been continued with supplementary matter furnished the writer by Mr. Sylvester M. Foster, who succeeded his honored father in the secretaryship of the society.

"The Constitution of the Suffolk County Agricultural Society, adopted October 6, 1818," states the object of the society to "be the advancement of agriculture in all its various branches, by collecting and circulating the knowledge of improvements, and by bestowing premiums for the most successful exertions." It provides for two meetings each year at the court house in Riverhead, in May and October; article 10 for an annual fair and cattle show, time and place to be appointed by the managers. The officers were: President, Thomas S. Strong; 1st vice-president, Sylvester Dering; 2nd vice-president, Joshua Smith; 3d vice-president, Nathaniel Potter; 4th vice-president, John P. Osborne; corresponding secretaries, Charles H. Havens and Henry P. Dering; recording secretary, Ebenezer W. Case; treasurer, David Warner. Twelve managers were also elected. We find no mention of any meetings or fairs.

In Volume I of the "Transactions of the New York State Agricultural Society" for 1841 is found the statement that the Suffolk County Agricultural Society was organized in that year. In the "Transactions" for 1842 are several statements by persons receiving premiums for crops from this county society, of which William W. Mills was then president. In the volume for 1843 is a report by William C. Stout, president, stating that the third annual fair was held November 15, and $186.50 paid in premiums. Richard B. Post was secretary, David Brush, treasurer, and there was a manager from each town. "The society is not in so flourishing a condition as I would like to see it, owing almost entirely to the immense length of our county, thereby rendering it difficult to fix upon the proper place at which to hold an annual fair and give general satisfaction. Measures are in progress, however, to correct this evil by organizing two societies."

In the volume of 1846, J. Lawrence Smith, president, writes under date of March 20, 1847, that "the county society was dissolved in 1843, and a new society formed from a smaller and more thickly settled portion of the county." This society was known as the "Western Branch of the Suffolk County Agricultural Society." Its records show that fairs were held each year from 1843 to 1852 (excepting 1844), respectively at Comac, Smithtown, Comac, Islip, Huntington, Greenport, Babylon, Smithtown and Huntington. The officers during this period were as follows, so far as recorded:

Presidents—W.C. Stout, 1843, 1845; J. Lawrence Smith, 1846, 1847; Joshua B. Smith, 1848; Harvey W. Vail, 1849, 1850; Edward Henry Smith, 1851; Dr. John R. Rhinelander, 1852; Edwin A. Johnson, 1853.

Vice-Presidents—W.H. Ludlow, 1845; Lester H. Davis, 1846; Samuel N. Bradhurst, 1847; William Nicoll, 1851; Samuel L. Thompson, 1852, 1853.

Secretaries—Henry G. Scudder, 1845; Nathaniel Smith, 1846, 1847, 1851; Dr. Abraham G. Thompson, 1848-50; Edward K. Briar, 1852; J.H. Carll, 1853.

Treasurers—R.B. Post, 1843; Nathaniel Smith, 1845; Richard Smith, 1846, 1847; Jarvis R. Mowbray, 1848; Elbert Carll, 1849, 1850; William Lawrence, 1851; David C. Brush, 1852; William H. Ludlow, 1853.

At the fair at Comac, October 16, 1843, premiums were awarded amounting to $110. At Smithtown in 1845 the premiums amounted to $95. An address was delivered by Dr. John R. Rhinelander. In 1846 the premiums were $79. An address was given by Samuel A. Smith.

At a meeting (date not given) held between the fairs of 1846 and 1847 it was resolved "that this society be hereafter known and called by the name of "The Suffolk County Agricultural Society." At the fair of 1847 mention is made of "corn planted three feet apart, four stalks in each hill, showing that good corn may be produced on much less ground than is usually required;" and "fine flat turnips grown since oats were taken off." The address was by William H. Ludlow, and the premiums aggregated $94.

At Huntington, October 10, 1848, a new constitution (prepared by the secretary, Dr. A.C. Thompson, as instructed at a previous meeting) was presented and adopted. An address by Dr. Thompson "reviewed the past and present operations of the society, the benefits resulting from the formation of agricultural societies, and urged the importance of system, of industry, and economy in managing agricultural matters."

The first fair was held in the eastern part of the county was held at Greenport, October 2, 1849. The address was by John G. Floyd.

At a meeting of the managers, April 6, 1850, it was resolved, "on condition that the residents of Babylon and vicinity pay or secure to be paid to the treasurer of the society, on or before May 1, 1850, the sum of $100, and that the necessary cattle pens be erected, a suitable building or tent be provided, and that arrangements be made for the conveyance of passengers to and from the railroad free of all charge, that the fair will be held in that village September 24, 1850." Also resolved, "in the case the residents of Babylon and its vicinity do not agree to the above resolution, the exhibition will be held in Islip in case the said conditions are complied with."

In addition to those offered the year before, premiums were offered for crops grown on the "Plain lands." The fair was held at Babylon. "F.M.A. Wicks, of Thompson's Station, exhibited cheese, pumpkins, citron, melons, fine potatoes and Isabella grapes raised on the 'Plain lands,' adjoining the Long Island railroad at Thompson's Station. Ira L'Hommedieu exhibited tomatoes, blood beets and egg plants raised on land of Dr. E.F. Peck at Lake Road station. These productions show conclusively the error of the idea that the lands contiguous to the Long Island Railroad are worthless." "The Society is indebted to Mr. Francis M.A. Wicks and Dr. E.F. Peck for proving beyond objection that these desolate lands can be made productive under a proper course of cultivation. The perseverance shown by these two gentlemen is deserving the highest commendation, and it is hoped that success may attend their efforts." The annual address was delivered by John Fowler, Jr.

At the winter meeting, December 4, 1850, a premium was awarded to Samuel S. Thompson, of Setauket, "for 84-1/2 bushels, 4 quarts and 1 pint of Australian or 'Verplank' wheat, raised on two surveyed acres, the weight being 63-1/2 lbs. per bushel; the standard of 60 lbs. per bushel being allowed, the yield of the crop was 89 bushels 2 pecks on the two acres. * * * Deducting the expenses, the net profit was $341.75."

"William Burling, of Babylon, raised 65 bushels of onions on one-eighth of an acre, being at the rate of 520 bushels per acre." The net profit was $24.65.

At Smithtown, September 25, 1851, the address was delivered by Dr. Franklin Tuthill, of New York City. Mr. Brush, the treasurer, dying before the next fair, John D. Hewlett was appointed treasurer in his stead. At the fair at Huntington, October 21, 1852, the address was by Henry J. Scudder, of New York City. It is reported that another fair was held in 1852, at Islip, but the record shows no further meeting till February 1,

1865, when the Society was reorganized at Thompson's Station, with the title "Suffolk County Agricultural Society." The officers elected for the first year were as follows: President, William Nicoll, Huntington; vice-president, Robert W. Pearsall, Islip; secretary, J.H. Doxsee, Islip; treasurer, William J. Weeks, Brookhaven; directors, H.G. Scudder, Huntington; Caleb Smith, Smithtown; Robert W. Colt, Islip; Thomas S. Mount, Brookhaven; D.H. Osborne, Riverhead; David G. Floyd, Southold.

The first fair after the reorganization was held at Riverhead, September 27 and 28, 1865. "The board of managers are fully satisfied with the results of the fair, both in the interest manifested by the people of the county and the pecuniary result arising therefrom." The receipts were $1,600, and the disbursements $800. From this time the fair has been held each year at Riverhead, excepting 1867, when it was at Greenport.

In 1866 the question of permanent location came up and was discussed and laid over; also "the propriety of uniting with Queens county to form a Long Island Agricultural Society." October 29, 1867, the managers accepted from the citizens of Riverhead a deed donating to the Suffolk County Agricultural Society "lands lying near and westerly of the Riverhead Cemetery, for fair grounds, with this condition—if the Society shall fail for two consecutive years to hold a fair thereon, the grounds shall revert to the donors." The grounds are pleasantly located, conveniently near to the village and to the depot of the Long Island Railroad, and of very ready access from all directions.

The matter of fitting up the grounds was referred to the President, Vice-President and Treasurer, and it was "resolved that the sum of $200 be appropriated to pay the Treasurer for his extra services in behalf of the Society." The first fair on the new grounds was held September 30, and October 1 and 2, 1868. Again $200 was paid to the Treasurer for services.

B.D. Carpenter, Stephen C. Rogers, Joshua L. Wells, John S. Marcy, William Nicoll and Robert W. Pearsall were the building committee that supervised the erection of the Exhibition Hall. The architect was George H. Skidmore, of Riverhead. The contract for building was awarded to Fielder, Skidmore & Company. The building was completed in time for the next annual fair, October 6, 7 and 8, 1869. In the evening of the 6th a public meeting was held in the court house, and papers were read by Robert W. Pearsall, of Brentwood, and Hon. Henry P. Hedges, of Bridgehampton, the latter upon "Fertilizers and Their Application." "Mr. William Nicoll in a few appropriate remarks called attention to the Exhibition Hall, and, with a view of liquidating the debt incurred by its erection, he moved that a committee be appointed for soliciting life members of the Society upon the payment of ten dollars each. The motion having been passed and the committee appointed, Mr. Nicoll manifested his earnestness in the movement by the payment of seventy dollars, making his wife and children life members. Others immediately followed the example till $400 had been contributed."The annual meeting in the evening of the 7th was addressed by Mr. Nicoll.

On June 22 and 23, 1870, occurred the first horticultural exhibition, a festivel and reunion, which was very successful, bringing together a very large and pleasant company. Others were held June 14, 1871, and June 19, 1872. There being few if any professional florists in the county and the strawberry growers being particularly busy marketing their fruit, it was found to be impracticable to attempt at present more than one fair each year.

In 1876, besides the usual annual meeting on Wednesday evening during the fair, meetings were held at the court house on Tuesday and Thursday evenings for discussion of matters of interest to the county and its people; but the attendance was so small that no encouragement was felt to repeat the experiment.

During this year the grounds were improved by planting trees, which were donated to the Society by Isaac Hicks & Sons, of Old Westbury, Queens county; P.H. Foster, of Babylon; E.F. Richardson, of Brentwood, and Israel Peck, of Southold. Adjoining Exhibition Hall was built a cloak or package room, which proved a great convenience to visitors and a source of profit to the society. New features were introduced into the exhibition, viz.: Centennial relics and a display of antiquities. This being the Centennial year this feature seemed to touch every heart, bringing out a warm response throughout the county, and, not stopping with the county limits, was similarly responded to in several other counties as a striking feature in their fairs. The suggestion, coming as it did from this county, at once introduced this society to many sister societies that before hardly knew of it.

A display of plans for farm buildings, etc., by Suffolk county architects (which has been of much service by favorably introducing to visiting strangers such architects as exhibited, and also by elevating the standard of architecture in the county) and a collection of foreign curiosities were very successful in themselves and added much to the exhibit. A new and notable feature of the fair was the gathering of the children of the public schools of the county,—teachers and pupils being admitted free on one specified day,—the effect of which was so gratifying that it has become one of the fixtures of each succeeding fair, thereby cultivating in the rising generation an interest in the Society. This year, too, more largely than ever before, was the power of the county press shown in arousing throughout the county a new and general interest in the Society, and a strong desire to attend the fair.

Altogether, notwithstanding the greater attraction offered by the Centennial Exhibition at Philadelphia, this year seems to have been a turning point in the history of the Society. Partly from the geographical situation of the county, partly from the difficulty experienced in reaching the fair with articles for exhibition, and from various other reasons, a feeling of more than indifference seemed very largely to have possessed the people of both east and west. This now gave place to a desire to promote the success of the local fair.

In 1877 the new features of the preceding year were retained and a new departure, an "exhibit of school work," was introduced, whereby the public schools became interested in the Society; also exhibits of minerals and Indian relics. This fair was made more attractive by a fine display from the Long Island Historical Society of Brooklyn, through the kindness of Elias Lewis, Jr. The attendance was larger, by reason of the improved railroad connections and facilities, whereby people were brought from all parts of the island and returned at reduced rates.

Not only the Society, but many people throughout the county, were much benefited by a donation from J.N. Hallock, formerly of Suffolk county, then publisher of "The Christian at Work," New York City, of subscriptions amounting to $100, which were largely used as premiums. This year $600 was paid on the debt, and in 1878 $400.

In 1879 more new features were introduced—displays of decorated pottery, rare china, native woods, and leaves and nuts of trees growing in the county. Among the cattle exhibited were a pair of immense oxen, weighing over 4,600 pounds, exhibited by Elbert Rose, of Bridgehampton, and some superior Jerseys from the well-known stockyards of William Crozier of Northport. Point judging on cattle and horses was now introduced. The exhibit of school work, first introduced in 1877, showed gratifying progress. The hall was made more cheerful by the exhibit of a large number of the bills and posters of the different county societies of the State. The debt was reduced $250 this year.

A very important feature of the fair of 1880 were the addresses of P.T. Barnum, the renowned showman, at the hall in the afternoon and at the court house in the evening, replete with humor and wisdom. Some very fine Early Rose potatoes, that took the first prize, were grown in beach sand. One man reported a crop of 500 bushels of potatoes raised on an acre of ground. This year the debt was again reduced $250.

At a meeting of the board of managers held at Riverhead, January 27, 1881, Austin Corbin, the newly elected president and receiver of the Long Island Railroad Company, and several of the directors were present; also reporters from the city papers. Mr. Corbin and others explained the condition of the road and the company and their plans and intentions for the future. Mr. Corbin, as a Suffolk county farmer, made a donation to the Society of $250.

Before the fair, the railroad company offered $500 in special premiums for stock, grains, fruit, etc., which greatly stimulated the exhibitors and added much to the interest of the exhibition. H.W. Maxwell, one of the directors of the railroad company, offered five gold medals, of the total value of $100, to be competed for during the fair by the pupils of the public schools of the county, in reading, arithmetic, United States history, geography and English language. Three of these were taken by pupils of the Greenport school, one by a pupil at Yaphank, and one by a member of the school at Patchogue. During this year the grounds were improved by planting more trees. The addresses at the fair were on fish culture, out of the regular course, but of great interest to the whole county. The debt was still further reduced $500.

Again a new departure: The officers of the Society, not content with showing their county's products to those that might come to the county fair, proposed to the farmers and others of the county an exhibit of their good things at the State fair at Elmira, which exhibit, although an experiment, was very encouraging in its results, the first premium ($25) being awarded to R.O. Colt, of Bay Shore, for the best collection of vegetables, besides other premiums to different exhibitors; while a new wagon gear invented and exhibited by C.M. Blydenburgh, of Riverhead, attracted great attention, as did also the wood of which the wagon was built—Suffolk county oak. The exhibit brought the county into very prominent and favorable notice.

For want of space, the narrative of progress from year to year must here be curtailed. Sufficient to say that with the year 1881 the Society had practically reached its present scope. Since that time the improvement has been in the way of erecting additional buildings and beautifying the grounds and increasing the division of classes of exhibited goods, with an accompanying increase of premiums paid. The Society held its fiftieth annual exhibition (dating from the reorganization) on September 16, 17, 18 and 19, 1902. The total disbursements were $10,427.76. Of this amount, $2,597.27 was for permanent premiums, and $2,021.00 was for premiums. The exhibits were classified as follows: Class I, Cattle; Class II, Horses; Class III, Sheep; Class IV, Swine; Class V, Poultry; Class VI, Domestic; Class VII, Grains; Class VIII, Roots and Vegetables; Class IX, Fruit; Class X, Preserves, Honey, etc.; Class XI, Implements and Utensils; Class XII, Carriages and Harness; Class XIII, Flowers; Class XIV, Domestic Manufacture and Enterprise; Class XV, Domestic Manufacture, etc.; Class XVI, Needle and Artistic Work; Class XVII, Paintings, etc.; Class XVIII, Curiosities (including foreign curios, collections of natural objections, of the natural history of the county, of Indian relics, of minerals, of war relics, etc.); Class XIX, Discretionary; Class XX, School Work or Educational, and Class XXI, Children's Department.

In 1902 the Society numbered about 425 life members, of whom a number dated back in membership to 1859. The officers were Henry A. Reeves, of Greenport, president; William B. Dayton, of Port Jefferson, vice-president; George W. Cooper, of Riverhead, treasurer; Sylvester M. Foster, of Riverhead, secretary; and the following named directors: Nathan H. Dayton, Easthampton; Walter L. Jagger, Southampton; David Carll, Huntington; Henry A. Brown, Wyandance; William O. Davids, Peconic; and Edward Thompson, Northport.

At some future day, the historian who is man of intelligence sufficient, and who is possessed of such store of this world's goods that he may give his life time to so pleasant a task, unannoyed by the "diminution grind" of food earning alone, will supplement such a narrative as this out of the excellent material now being accumulated by the Suffolk County Historical Society, composed of resident gentlemen who have entered upon their work with hearty enthusiasm growing out of their pride in the accomplishments of honored ancestors. It may be said here that, rich as is the collection already made, those engaged in the work would seem to have merely made a beginning, so fruitful is the field, and so many are the unsuspected finds of ancient documents and inanimate relics which have a voice of their own after all.

The splendid organization to which our reference has been made, and which has already made for itself a prominent place among the historical organizations of the entire land, owes its founding to a meeting of the board of trustees of the Riverhead Savings Bank, in 1886. The Rev. Dr. Samuel E. Herrick, of Boston, a native of Suffolk county, was a guest at the usual luncheon, which was a feature of the trustees' meetings, and in the course of a most interesting address suggested the formation of an organization which should gather up the records of the past and preserve them. "Too many of these have already been lost," he said, "because such an institution has not existed.

Suffolk county may for all time rejoice in her illustrious citizens. Who would forget Captain Mercator Cooper, of Southampton, who, in the whaleship 'Manhattan,' of Sag Harbor, first carried the United States flag into Japanese waters, at the same time returning to their homes more than a score of shipwrecked sailors he had rescued? Who would be willing to lose record of the illustrious patriotism and devotion of General Nathaniel Woodhull or of the valuable services of Ezra L'Hommedieu and many others? Shall the story of their brave and heroic lives be lost, or shall they be saved to inspire others to good works? Why, then, may not something at once be done?"

Before the close of the year the Suffolk County Historical Society was fully organized, and the material for our account of its progress has been contributed for this work by Mr. Nat W. Foster, now its president.

The early members were: Hon. James H. Tuthill, George F. Stackpole, Nat W. Foster, Daniel W. Reeve, William C. Ostrander, Ahaz Bradley, Professor Charles S. Stone, the Rev. Samuel Whaley, Benjamin K. Payne, Dr. Howard H. Young, William R. Duvall, Holmes W. Swezey, Henry W. Halsey, James L. Millard, John Walsh, Jr., Gilbert H. Conklin and Samuel Tuthill, of Riverhead; Wilmot M. Smith, Hon. John S. Havens, William H. Newins and George M. Ackerly, of Patchogue; Joseph H. Petty, of Amityville; Stuart T. Terry, the Rev. Epher Whitaker, D.D., and N. Hubbard Cleveland, of Southold; Richard M. Bayles, of Middle Island; Salem H. Wales, of New York, with a country residence at Southampton; James Slater, of Central Islip, Henry A. Brown, of West Deer Park; A.M. Salmon, of Peconic; Theodore W. Smith, of Smithtown; Benjamin T. Robbins, of Northport; Charles E. Shepard, of Huntington; Sidney H. Ritch, of Port Jefferson; and W.W. Thompson, of Orient.

The officers for the first year were: President, James H. Tuthill, Riverhead; vice-presidents, the Rev. Dr. Epher Whitaker, Southold, and Joseph H. Petty, Amityville; recording secretary, responding secretary, Richard M. Bayles, Middle Island; treasurer, James H. Pierson, Southampton; custodian, George F. Stackpole, Riverhead.

Mr. Tuthill was re-elected president until his death, in January, 1894. At the next annual meeting after Mr. Tuthill's death, January 20, 1894, Nat W. Foster was elected as his successor, the Rev. Dr. Whitaker declining the position and continuing as vice-president along with Augustus Floyd, of New York, and all those named are yet serving in the positions with which their names respectively appear. At the evening meeting special services, memorial of the life of the late president were held, addressed by the Rev. Dr. Whitaker, the Rev. William I. Chalmers, B.K. Payne and Professor J.M. Belford.

In 1895 Orville B. Ackerly, now of New York City, was made corresponding secretary, and he is yet serving in that capacity.

In 1896 the Rev. Charles A. Stonelake, of Aquebogue, was elected recording secretary, and continued so to act until suddenly called out of the State, when, at the next annual meeting, February 15, 1898, Miss Ruth H. Tuthill, daughter of the late president, was chosen for that position.

At a special meeting of the Society held on July 1, 1893, the Riverhead Savings Bank building at the corner of Main street and Griffing avenue, was purchased for $4,000. One-half was paid and $2,000 remained on bond and mortgage. This mortgage has since been reduced to $1,300. The building thus acquired had historical associations. It had been erected by Suffolk county for the safe keeping of its priceless records, the earliest being far older than the county itself. It was designed also for the use of the county clerk, and was occupied by one officer after another for a series of years. The building was eminently suitable for the uses and purposes of the Historical Society.

Addresses have been delivered at the public meetings of the Society as follows:

June, 1887.—The Rev. Dr. Whitaker, "Union of Church and State, Past and Present."

June, 1888.—Henry P. Hedges, "Priority of Settlement, Southold and Southampton."

October, 1890.—James H. Tuthill, "Proper Work of an Historical Society, and How It Should be Done."

February, 1893.—The Rev. W.I. Chalmers, "Urging Deeper Interest in Historical Work and the Suffolk County Historical Society."

February, 1895.—The Rev. Dr. Whitaker, "The Rise of Woman;" District Attorney W.H. Jaycox, "The Value of Historical Knowledge;" George F. Stackpole, "What May be Done in the Future in the Way of Developing Long Island;" The Rev. R.M. Edwards, "Impressions of Long Island."

February, 1896.—William Wallace Tooker, "Cockinoo de Long Island;" Edward P. Buffett, Jr., "Fort Salonga."

February, 1897.—Augustus Floyd, "Suffolk in Revolutionary Times." The Rev. A.C. Stonelake, "The Collections of the Society."

February, 1898.—R.C. McCormick, "Value of Local Historical Societies." William S. Pelletreau, "Richard Smith, of Smithtown."

February, 1990.—The Rev. Epher Whitaker, "Suffolk County's Last Half-Century."

February, 1901.—St. Clair McKelway, L.L.D., "Makers of Modern America."

The objects of the Society as stated in Article II of its constitution read, "To foster the historical spirit in thought, study and purpose; to encourage historical and antiquarian research; to disseminate historical knowledge; to collect and preserve such autographs and other manuscripts, maps, plans, charts, paintings, engravings and other pictorial representations, books, pamphlets, newspapers, curiosities and antiquities of every kind as may have been or shall be the products of Suffolk county, or of its several towns, some of which are the oldest English settlements and religious and civil organizations within the bounds of the State of New York; and also to discover, procure and preserve whatsoever material of any kind may illustrate the history of its several towns."

Four years ago the Society determined to make special provision to perpetuate the memory and the benign influence of prominent and worthy persons who had passed from sight. For this purpose it instituted the order of "In Memoriam Members." A person is made a member of this order by the gift of $100 to the society. The money has been used so far to reduce the mortgage on the Society's real estate.

The name and date of birth of each Memoriam Member will be annually and perpetually printed in the Year Book of the Society. The Year Book contains also the list of the officers, the honorary and life members of the Society, the acknowledgements of gifts to the Society, and generally the address of the president, or of some other person invited by him, delivered at the Society's annual meeting.

The Year Book is renewed annually. It meets the eyes of intelligent people in all parts of the county and far beyond its bounds. It goes into the homes of men, and into the great libraries of universities, historical institutions and genealogical societies; and it remains there, and is thus seen and consulted in many places.

This memorial is thus perpetually renewed, and, unlike a memorial window or tablet, it is seen in many places. It is both unpretentious and effective for its high and laudable purpose.

The society proposed that its first president and its first recording secretary should have the honor of standing at the head of the roll of the In Memoriam Members. They were forthwith made members by those who best knew their worth and excellencies. Thus the roll begins with the names of James H. Tuthill and Stuart T. Terry. The first was a legislator of the Senate and a Surrogate of the county, as well as prominent for a score of years in the religious and benevolent organizations of the county. The second was known on account of his interest in genealogical affairs, concerns of business having fiduciary qualities, and efficiency and prominence in religious bodies as, for instance, the Synod of New York and the General Assembly of the Presbyterian Church in the United States of America.

The next name on the roll of this memorial order is that of William Sidney Smith of Longwood. He was distinguished by his attractive person and manners; by his prominence among the descendants of Chief

Justice William Smith, the "Tangier" Smith; by the wide extent of his real estate; by his ownership of half of the Great South Bay; by his public services as a legislator of the State and the treasurer of the county; by the manifestation of his public spirit on all fit occasions, and by his winsome courtesy and high moral character.

Another worthy name on the memoriam roll is that of Lewis A. Edwards, whose wise and patriotic service in the Senate of the State of New York was in accord with the excellence of his whole life as a generous citizen and Christian gentleman. He was held in high esteem not only as a ship owner and manufacturer, but as a capable civilian and a generous man in all the relations of life.

The Society, since its organization in 1886, has gathered a large quantity of valuable historical matter, and every year adds greatly to these treasures, which include books, maps, plots of villages, deeds and surveys of land, portraits, genealogical, ethnological, archaeological, antiquarian, biographical, genealogical, and other collections of kindred character. These treasurers already include extremely valuable unique maps and rare and anciently printed books, as well as modern volumes and paintings.

Among the valuable historical works are the following: Records of Boston and New Haven, the former comprising twenty-seven volumes, showing the origin of many Long Island families, presented by Orville B. Ackerly; Mallman's "History of Shelter Island," "Early Long Island Wills," by W.S. Pelletreau; all the town records of the several Long Island towns as published by the town authorities; Thompson's "History of Long Island;" genealogical and biographical record of New York; and a copy of the laws of the Colony of New York from 1691 to 1799, presented by Elbert Carll Livingston, containing in its fly-leaves a family register. (The first death recorded on the fly-leaf in manuscript is that of "Captain Jacob Conklin in December ye 8 1754 on the 1st day of the week at 9 o'clock at night.")

Among the rare documents and publications are: Early Long Island wills of Suffolk county, known as the Lester Will Book; manuscript copy of the roster of soldiers stationed at Sag Harbor under command of Major Benjamin Case in war of 1812; proceedings of the New England Historic Genealogical Society and of the Massachusetts Historical Society, all presented by Orville B. Ackerly; papers in the case of trustees of Southampton against Frederick H. Betts, giving a full history of the early settlement of the town and the partitioning of the lands and meadow rights; unbound journal of New York Assembly Journal, 1796, and Senate, 1806; the origin and meaning of English and Dutch surnames of New York State families; list of ancestors and descendants of John Howell Wells; seventy old almanacs between the years 1811 and 1896; and "Long Island Journal of Philosophy and Cabinet of Varieties," published at Huntington in 1825.

Among the curiosities is a framed commission by the Postmaster General to Elihu S. Miller as postmaster at Wading River, February 1, 1869, to his father, Sylvester Miller, July 30, 1844, and to his grandfather, Zophar Miller, February 26, 1825.

A letter from the Postmaster General to Congress transmitting a statement of the net amount of postage accruing at each postoffice in the country for the year ending March 31, 1826, shows the following to have been the receipts of various Long Island offices: Jamaica, $164.27; Hempstead, $36.57; Huntington, $64.50; Suffolk Court House (now Riverhead), $29.40; Wading River, $2.74; Bridgehampton, $50.22; Cold Spring, $18.63; Cutchogue, $10.20; Deer Park, $7.37; Easthampton, $59.33; Islip, $20.40; Jericho, $18.07; Jerusalem, $1.27; Mattituck, $18.86; Oyster Bay, $23; Oyster Bay South, $7.39; Oyster Pond (Orient), $25.32; Patchogue, $24.31; Sag Harbor, $117.06; Setauket, $28.46; Smithtown, $56.16; Southampton, $47.62; Southold, $35.35; and Westhampton, $9.61.

Among the other interesting documents are the records of the First Strict Congregational convention, held at the house of the Rev. Daniel Young, Riverhead, August 26, 1791: The Rev. Daniel Young, pastor of the First Congregational Church of Riverhead, organized March 26, 1758; the Rev. Jacob Corwin, the Rev. Noah Hallock, Bridgehampton, and Deacons Daniel Terry and Richard Robinson, delegates from the churches at Riverhead and Wading River; the Rev. Jacob Corwin, pastor of the Second Congregational Church, founded at Aquebogue, or East Riverhead, in 1787, and the Rev. Paul Cuffee, a native Indian of the Shinnecock tribe, located at Canoe Place, "a man of great influence and reputation." His grave is prominent to-day in the cemetery east of Good Ground Station.

The appointment of Calvin Cook as ensign of "the regiment of militia in Suffolk County," signed by Daniel D. Tompkins, is prominently displayed. There is an interesting exhibit of flax seed, a sheaf of the flax raised in Suffolk county, unbetchelled and betchelled flax, thread and linen cloth. There are also shown the various old-fashioned flax machines, including flax hackler, flax wheel and swift reel.

A relic of historical interest is a piece of cedar from the British sloop of war "Sylph," built in Bermuda in 1811 and wrecked on Southampton Bar on January 17, 1811, when, out of a crew of 121, 115 were lost, including Captain George Dickens, commanding officer; Lieutenants George Butt and H.S. Marsham, Surgeon James Still and

Thomas Atwell, master. This piece of cedar was part of a fence post underground on a farm at Quogue for seventy-five years, and is still as fragrant as ever.

Among the Indian relics are arrow heads, stone axes, hoes, tomahawks, mortars, found mainly in Southold and Southampton. Some of these were taken from a well twenty feet underground, and the stone was of a character such as is found only in the outcropping ledges of Massachusetts. It puzzles scientists to know how four of the pre-glacial stone arrow and spear heads came to be found on Long Island and at such a depth below the surface, where they have evidently been buried for ages past.

Wampum and other Montauk Indians relics are also displayed here. An old plow with a wooden mould board, used in the town of Southold a hundred years ago, and several British cannon balls fired over to Long Island from British men-of-war of 1812-15 and picked up by the farmers in their fields are shown.

Among other curiosities are: Curious fish found in the waters of Suffolk county; "shin-plasters" issued by local merchants in the war of the Rebellion; old merchandise bills and receipts; old State bank and Continental bills; piece of first flat rail used on the Long Island Railroad in 1836, size of rail two and one-half by three-fourths, ordinary tire iron, also the chain used for holding the ends of the rails; ivory paper-cutter used by Daniel Webster and presented to him by Charles Taylor, of Peconic; photographs of the exhibits at the Suffolk County Agricultural Society's fair, by H.B. Fullerton; a bear's skull, found at Great Pond many years ago; a ten-pound piece of meteor that came down on the farm of R.M. Browne at Glen Cove in 1794 (the original piece weighing fifty pounds); a Latin Vulgate and Greek text Bible, printed in 1544 in Venice; assessment roll of Riverhead in 1839, in an ordinary writing book; a picture of tombstone of John Gardiner, proprietor of Gardiner's Island, who was born in 1752 and died in 1823, and of David Gardiner, second proprietor of Gardiner's Island, in the Hartford Cemetery, Connecticut.

Among the engraved portraits are those of Thomas George Hodgkins, who was born in England in 1703, and died in Setauket in 1792; the Rev. Charles J. Knowles, former pastor of the Congregational Church at Riverhead, who died in 1880; Ezra L'Hommedieu, member of Continental Congress in 1779-83, member of the Senate of New York, clerk of Suffolk county, 1784-1810, and regent of the university, 1787-1811.

Another institution which has proved a great service to the upward progress of Riverhead is the Savings Bank, which was established in 1872, mainly through the efforts of Mr. Nat W. Foster and Orville B. Ackerly. The latter, who was for many years a resident of Riverhead, has been engaged in business in New York for a considerable time past. He was county clerk of Suffolk for six years and had previously been deputy clerk for twelve years, and not only proved a most capable official but was one of the most popular men in the county, and that popularity he still retains, although the prosecution of his business necessarily removes him from his associations—at least to the same extent as formerly.

The bank opened with the following trustees: James F. Tuthill, John Downs, N. W. Foster, Jeremiah M. Edwards, Gilbert H. Ketcham, Daniel A. Griffing, J. Henry Perkins, Moses F. Benjamin, Edwin F. Squiers, John R. Corwin, Orville B. Ackerly, Richard T. Osborn, Isaac C. Halsey, Simeon S. Hawkins, Richard H. Benjamin, John F. Foster, Thomas Coles, J. Halsey Young, John S. Marcy, Abraham B. Luce, Jonas Fishel and John P. Mills. It was a success from the first, and during all the years that have passed, in spite of periods of panic, depression and financial restlessness, it has maintained a clean and honorable record, and by its wise management has done much to develop the prosperity of the town. According to a late report its resources amounted to $3,189,770, and its deposits to $2,859,829, giving it a clear surplus of $329,941. But that report showed another detail which ought to be a matter of local pride, showing as it does the thrifty character of the people, and that was the average of each account in 1900 was $457.93, an amount exceeded by only two others of the savings banks on Long Island.

But the Savings Bank rendered a most valuable service to Riverhead and to the county in a widely different direction from its finances, for it was at a meeting of its board of trustees in 1886 that the organization of the Suffolk County Historical Society was first broached.

Mr. Nathaniel W. Foster, conspicuously identified with various important institutions—the Historical Society, the Agricultural Society, the Bible Society and the Savings Bank, is one of the best known men as he is one of the most useful in Suffolk county, and he is a native of the village which has been the scene of his life work.

Aquebogue has more to boast of in the way of antiquity than Riverhead. It seems to have been the site of an Indian village of considerable size, so it is possible that the early settlers in the district from Southold simply took up the red man's improvements in the way of clearances and trails, and the strange temple and graves discovered in 1879 demonstrate the affection and reverence which a primitive race must have had for the territory—possibly an older race than that which sold the ground to the white pioneers from Southold.

A Presbyterian Church seems to have been organized at Upper Aquebogue, beside the now ancient cemetery, but little concerning it has been learned beyond the names of two of its early pastors, a Mr. Lee and the Rev. Timothy Symmes, and as the latter became a minister in New Jersey in 1746 the period of the beginning of the Aquebogue congregation must have preceded that date by several years.

At Lower Aquebogue a Presbyterian church was erected in 1731, and at Baiting Hollow in 1803. None of these early churches survive. A Congregational Church was organized at Upper Aquebogue in 1758. In 1785 a congregation of the body known as the Strict Congregational Convention of Connecticut was organized at Wading River, and in 1791 a similar congregation was formed at Baiting Hollow, and these three bodies continue to the present time. In 1815, a Swedenborgian Church was established at Baiting Hollow and existed up to a few years ago.

From Lower Aquebogue, which some suppose to have been settled before any other part of the district, the comparatively modern village of Jamesport was formed about 1830, seemingly one of those paper cities which for a time was so common in the story of American life, and was ridiculed so mercilessly in Dickens' novel, "Martin Chuzzlewit."

Dr. Prime tells us that in 1833 there was not a single house in the place and that it owed "its origin to the speculation fever of a single individual who ruined himself by the operation." The site was nicely mapped out, streets were surveyed, a wharf was built and a rather imposing hotel was erected. For a year or two it seemed as if the hopes which centered in it would be realized; one or two whaling ships made use of the wharf. But there was no earthly reason why ocean boats should seek a harbor at such a place, at the very extremity of Peconic Bay, that was open to vessels larger than coasters, and that was at all times difficult of access.

So the mariners, after a trial or two, sought other and more convenient headquarters, and Jamesport's commerce fell away and its hopes were blighted. A few years ago its beautiful situation began to attract "the summer people," and it has become quite popular with that class, so much so that at the height of the season it is rather difficult for all who desire accommodations to secure them. But that is a matter that can be remedied and there is little doubt it will be. Under these circumstances Jamesport can look forward to a brighter future than was ever anticipated for it as its inception or that seemed possible in 1843, when the early glamour had passed and it boasted some forty houses.

At the other extremity of the township, on the boundary line dividing it from Brookhaven, is the village of Wading River, the terminus, for the present at least, of what is known as the Port Jefferson branch of the Long Island Railroad. It is supposed that a settlement was effected about 1670, and in 1708 a mill was established by John Roe. Some four miles eastward is the settlement of Baiting Hollow, which is said to date from 1719. Like Wading River, it did a considerable business in the first half of the nineteenth century in cutting and marketing firewood, but the source of supply did not prove inexhaustible, and, when it passed, farming remained the only industry, for even to the present day the summer boarder has not discovered this region to any great extent.

During the war of 1812 an exciting skirmish is said to have been fought on the shore between Fresh Pond Landing and Jericho Landing. Several sloops belonging to Baiting Hollow and engaged in carrying firewood, were espied on the beach by a British squadron cruising in the Sound, and two boats' crews were dispatched to seize them. The local militia, was, however, on the lookout, and under Captain John Wells opened fire on the invaders with such effect that although they had landed and had boarded one of the sloops, they were glad to effect a retreat. It is said that the British had a cannon in each of their boats and used them, but this part of the story may well be doubted.

Manorville (380) population, Calverton (350) Northville (412), Roanoke (200), Buchananville (200), Laurel (197), are all farming centers, and there are a number of other still more slenderly populated, of which nothing more interesting can be said. In fact, outside of Riverhead village, the township is almost wholly given over to farming.

Notes

[i] Hull Osborne, Esq., attorney and counsellor at law, although a native of Southold, spent the most of his professional life here. He was the son of Daniel Osborn, a lawyer of Southold, a representative in assembly in 1787, '88, and a man of respectability and talents, whose death took place July 11, 1801, leaving seven sons (of whom the subject of this notice was one) and three daughters. His wife was the daughter of Dr. Hull, a physician of Southold.

Hull Osborne was born in 1771, studied law with his father, and was admitted to the bar in 1796. His talents as a pleader were quite limited, being unable to conquer his natural timidity, or gain sufficient confidence in himself to allow of his frequent appearance at the bar; yet he was well grounded in the principles of jurisprudence, and his counsel and advice were much sought after and relied upon.

His candor and integrity were proverbial, and, by his industry and economy, he accumulated considerable property. A few years before his death, he retired from practice, to a small farm, situated on the south side of the island, where he died at the age of 63, Dec. 25, 1834.

[ii] John Cleves Symmes, was born here July 10, 1742, and married Anna, daughter of Henry Tuthill of Southold. His early life was employed in teaching a country school in this part of the island, and the surveying of lands. He was at one time owner of the farm, now belonging to Hezekiah Scidmore at Mattetuck, which he sold on his removal from Long Island to Flat-brook, New Jersey.

In Feb. 1777, he was appointed associate judge of the supreme court of that state. Here he lost his wife, and married a widow Halsey, who lived but a few years thereafter, when he married Susannah, daughter of the Hon. William Livingston, a sister to the late Hon. Brockholt Livingston, and to the wife of Governor Jay.

In 1787, he purchased an extensive tract of land north of the Ohio, and was appointed United States district judge for the north western territory. The tract purchased by him, included the site of the city of Cincinnati, which he was instrumental in founding. He died at the house of his son-in-law, General William Henry Harrison in Feb. 1814, and was buried at North Bend.

His daughter Anna, lived with her grandfather Tuthill in Southold, till grown up, and was educated at Clinton academy in Easthampton. She then went to reside with her father, where in 1795, she married General Harrison. She is still living and the mother of eight children. One of her sons married Clarisa, only child of Gen. Zebulan Montgomery Pike.

A writer well acquainted with Mrs. Harrison, says, "I cannot let the opportunity slip, without offering a passing tribute to the virtues of this estimable woman. She is distinguished for her benevolence and piety; all who know her, view her with esteem and affection; and her whole course of life, in all its relations, has been characterized by those qualifications that complete the character of an accomplished matron."

[iii] John Cleanes Symmes, jun., son of Timothy and nephew of the judge, was a native of this town, and was a man of capacity and genius. He was adopted by his uncle, and accompanied him to the west. During the last war, he was appointed a captain in the army, and distinguished himself by his bravery on the Niagara frontier.

He was the projector of a novel theory, upon which he delivered lectures in various places, and gained some disciples among scientific men. He supposed the earth to be a hollow sphere, open at the poles, and that within it were other concentric hollow spheres, open also at their poles; that it was possible to pass from one pole to the other through the center of the earth.

This strange hypothesis met with little success, and a morbid melancholy took possession of the author's mind, which brought him to the grave, at Butler county, Ohio, where he died June 19, 1829.

[iv] Called by the Indians "*Pan-qua-cum-suck.*"

[v] Established in 1835.

[vi] Upon the river at this place is a fall of 6 ft.; and a hydraulic canal, connecting two small ponds with the river, has been constructed, in which is a fall of 8-1/2 ft.

[vii] Called by the natives *"Mi-a-mog,"* or *"Mi-an-rogue."*

[viii] 6 Cong., 2 M.E., 2 Swedenborgian.

Sources

Ackerly, Orville B. *Celebration of the 10th Anniversary of the Organization of the Town of Riverhead, Suffolk County, N.Y., at Riverhead, July 4, 1892.* New York: The Republic Press, 1894.

Barber, John W. *Historical Collection of the State of New York; A General Collection of the most Interesting Facts, Traditions, Biographical Sketches, Anecdotes, &c. Relating to its History and Antiquities, with Geographical Descriptions of Every Township in the State.* New York: S. Tuttle, 1841.

Bayles, R.M. *History of Suffolk County, New York with Illustrations, Portraits and Sketches of Prominent Families and Individuals.* New York: W.W. Munsell & Co., 1882.

French, J.H. *Gazetteer of the State of New York: Embracing A Comprehensive View of the Geography, Geology, and General History of the State, and a Complete History and Description of Every County, City, Town, Village and Locality.* Syracuse: R.P. Smith, 1860.

Hedges, Henry P. *Development of Agriculture in Suffolk County; Bicentennial, History of Suffolk County Comprising the Addresses Delivered at the Celebration of the Bicentennial of Suffolk County, New York, in Riverhead; November 15, 1883.* Babylon, New York, 1885.

Miller, George. *History of the Town of Riverhead, Suffolk County, N.Y. Written by Hon. George Miller, and read by T.M. Griffing, Esq., at the Centennial Celebration, July 4, 1876.*

Pelletreau, William S. *History of Suffolk County, New York, with Illustrations, Portraits and Sketches of Prominent Families and Individuals.* New York: W.W. Munsell & Company, 1882.

Prime, Nathaniel S. *A History of Long Island, From its First Settlement by Europeans to the Year 1845, with Special Reference to its Ecclesiastical Concerns.* New York: Robert Carter, 1845.

Thompson, Benjamin F. Excerpt from *The History of Long Island; From Its Discovery and Settlement to the Present Time.* Vol. I. Gould, Banks & Co., New York, 1843.

Selected Bibliography

Abbott, Wilbur C. *Colonel John Scott of Long Island, 1634(?)-1696.* New Haven, Connecticut: Yale University Press, 1918.

Adams, James Truslow. *History of the Town of Southampton.* Bridgehampton, New York: Hampton Press, 1918.

————*Memorials of Old Bridgehampton.* Bridgehampton, New York, by the author, 1916.

Andrews, Charles M. *The Colonial Period of American History.* 4 vols. New Haven, Connecticut: Yale University Press, 1934-1938.

Atwater, Edward. History of the Colony of New Haven to its Absorption into Connecticut. 2 vols. Connecticut: Journal Publishing Company, 1902.

Bailyn, Bernard. *The New England Merchants in the Seventeenth Century.* Cambridge, Massachusetts: Harvard University Press, 1955.

Bayles, Richard. *Historical and Descriptive Sketches of Suffolk County, and Its Towns, Villages, Hamlets, Scenery, Institutions and Important Enterprises; with a Historical Outline of Long Island, from Its First Settlement.* Port Jefferson, New York: Richard M. Bayles, 1874, 1873.

Becker, Lloyd. "Two Local Studies by Jeannette Edwards Rattray." *Street Magazine* II, no. 2 (1976): 39-42.

Beecher, Lyman. *Autobiography.* 2 vols. Edited by Barbara M. Cross. Cambridge, Massachusetts: Belknap Press of Harvard University Press, 1864, [c1961].

————*.A Sermon, Containing a General History of the Town of East*

171

Hampton. Sag Harbor, New York: Alden Spooner, 1806.

Berbrich, Joan D. *Three Voices from Paumanok*. Port Washington, New York: Ira J. Friedman, Inc., 1969.

Black, Robert C. *The Younger John Winthrop*. New York: Columbia University Press, 1966.

Boughton, E. S., ed. *Historic East Hampton, Long Island; the Celebration of Its Two Hundred and Fiftieth Anniversary.* East Hampton, New York: E. S. Boughton, 1899.

Boxer, C. R. *The Dutch Seaborne Empire, 1600-1800*. New York: Knopf, 1965.

Breen, T. H. *Imagining the Past: East Hampton Histories*. Reading, Massachusetts: Addison-Wesley, 1989.

————. *Puritans and Adventurers: Change and Persistence in Early America*. New York: Oxford University Press, 1980.

Bridenbaugh, Carl. *The Colonial Craftsman*. Chicago: University of Chicago Press, 1950.

Brodhead, John Romeyn. *History of the State of New York*. 2 vols. New York: Harper & Bros., 1853-1871.

Cave, Alfred A. *The Pequot War*. Amherst, Massachusetts: University of Massachusetts Press, 1996.

Ceci, Lynn. "The Effect of European Contact and Trade on the Settlement Pattern of Indians in Coastal New York, 1524-1665: The Archaeological and Documentary Evidence." Ph.D. diss., University of New York, 1977.

Clemente, Vince, ed. "John Hall Wheelock." *Paumanok Rising*. Port Jefferson, New York: Street Press, 1981, 81-113.

————. "John Hall Wheelock: Poet of Death and Honeysuckle." *Long Pond Review* (Jan. 1976). 10-18.

————. "Walt Whitmen in the Hamptons." *Street Magazine* II, no. 1 (1975).

Clowes, Ernest S. *The Hurricane of 1938 on Eastern Long Island*. Bridgehampton, New York: Hampton Press, 1939.

Cole, John N. *Away All Boats*. New York: Henry Holt and Company, 1994.

————. *Fishing Came First*. New York: Lyons & Burford, Pub., 1989.

————. *Striper*. Boston: Little, Brown and Company, 1978.

Daniels, Bruce Colin. *The Connecticut Town: Growth and Development, 1635-1790*. Middletown, Connecticut: Wesleyan University Press, 1979.

deKay, Charles. "East Hampton the Restful." *The New York Times Illustrated Magazine*. 30 October 1898: 40-43.

————. "Summer Homes at East Hampton, L.I." *The Architectural Record*, XII. no. 1 (Jan. 1903). 21-29.

Demos, John. *Entertaining Satan: Witchcraft and the Culture of Early New England*. New York: Oxford University Press, 1982.

Dunn, Richard S. *Puritans and Yankees: the Winthrop Dynasty of New England, 1630-1717.* New York: Norton, 1962.

Duvall, Ralph G. and Jean L. Schladermundt. *History of Shelter Island, 1652-1932; with a Supplement 1932-1952.* Second Edition. Shelter Island Heights, New York, n.p., 1952.

East Hampton, New York (Town). *Journal of the Trustees of the Freeholders and Commonalty of the Town of East Hampton, 1725-1960.* 10 vols. [East Hampton:Town of East Hampton, 1926-1976].

East Hampton, New York (Town). *Records of the Town of East Hampton, Long Island, Suffolk Co., New York, with Other Historic Documents of Ancient Value.* vols. 1 and 3. Sag Harbor, New York: J. H. Hunt, Printer, 1887-1905.

Edwards, Everett Joshua and Jeannette Edwards Rattray. *"Whale Off!": The Story of American Shore Whaling.* New York: Frederick A. Stokes Company, 1932.

En Plein Air: the Art Colonies at East Hampton and Old Lyme, 1880-1930. East Hampton, New York: Guild Hall Museum, 1989.

Fernow, Berthold, (ed.). *The Records of New Amsterdam from 1653 to 1674 Anno Domini.* 7 vols. New York: Knickerbocker Press, 1897.

Flint, Martha. *Early Long Island: A Colonial Study.* New York: G. P. Putnam's Sons, 1896.

Fiske, John. *The Dutch and Quaker Colonies in America.* 2 vols. Boston: Houghton, Mifflin, 1902.

Force, Peter. *American Archives, Fourth Series: Containing a Documentary History of the English Colonies in North America, from the King's Message to Parliament, of March 7, 1774, to the Declaration of Independence by the United States.* 11 vols. Washington, D.C.: M. St. Clair Clarke and Peter Force, 1837-1853.

Foster, Stephen. *Their Solitary Way, the Puritan Social Ethic in the First Century of Settlement in New England.* New Haven, Connecticut: Yale University Press, 1971.

Fryxell, Fritiof. *Thomas Moran, Explorer in Search of Beauty.* East Hampton, N.Y.: East Hampton Free Library, 1958.

Furman, Gabriel. *Antiquities of Long Island.* New York: J.W. Bouton, 1874.

Gabriel, Ralph Henry. *The Evolution of Long Island: a Story of Land and Sea.* Port Washington, New York: I. J. Friedman, 1960, 1921.

Gardiner, Curtiss Crane. *Lion Gardiner and His Descendants.* St. Louis:A. Whipple, 1890.

Gardiner, David. *Chronicles of the Town of East Hampton, County of Suffolk, New York.* New York: [Bowne Printers], [1840, 1871].

Gardiner, John Lyon. *Gardiners of Gardiner's Island.* East Hampton, New York: Star Press, 1927.

Gardiner, Lion. "Leift Lion Gardiner, His Relation of the Pequot Warres". Chap. in *Collections of the Massachusetts Historical Society*, Vol. 3, 3rd, Series, 131–160. Cambridge, 1833.

Gardiner, Sara Diodati. *Early Memories of Gardiner's Island; (The Isle of Wight, New York)*. East Hampton, New York: East Hampton Star, 1947.

Gaynor, James M. and Nancy L. Hagedorn. *Tools: Working Wood in Eighteenth-century America*. Williamsburg, Va.: Colonial Williamsburg Foundation, 1993.

Godbeer, Richard. *The Devil's Dominion: Magic and Religion in Early New England*. New York: Cambridge University Press, 1992.

Goodman, Charlotte Margolis. *The Savage Heart*. Austin: University of Texas Press, 1990.

Hauptman, Laurence M. and James D. Wherry, eds. *The Pequots in Southern New England: The Fall and Rise of an American Indian Nation*. Norman: University of Oklahoma Press, 1990.

Heatley, Jeff, ed. *Bully!: Colonel Theodore Roosevelt, The Rough Riders & Camp Wikoff, Montauk Point, New York 1898, a Newspaper Chronicle with Roosevelt's Letters*. Montauk, New York: Montauk Historical Society; Pushcart Press, 1998.

Hedges, Henry Parsons. *A History of the Town of East-Hampton, New York: Including an Address Delivered at the Celebration of the Bi-Centennial Anniversary of Its Settlement in 1849, Introductions to the Four Printed Volumes of Its Records, with Other Historic Material, an Appendix and Genealogical Notes*. Sag Harbor, New York: John H. Hunt, Printer, 1897.

Heyman, Christine Leigh. *Commerce and Culture: The Maritime Communities of Colonial Massachusetts, 1690–1750*. New York: Norton, 1984.

Howell, George Rogers. *The Early History of Southampton, L.I., New York*. Albany: Weed, Parsons & Company, 1987.

Hummel, Charles F. "The Business of Woodworking, 1700–1840." Chap. in *Tools and Technologies: America's Wooden Age*. eds. Paul Kebabian and William Lipke, 1979.

————. *With Hammer in Hand: The Dominy Craftsmen of East Hampton, New York*. Charlottesville, Virginia: University Press of Virginia, 1968.

Huntington, Cornelia. *Odes and Poems and Fragmentary Verses*. New York: A. Huntington, 1891.

————. *Sea-Spray: A Long Island Village*. New York: Derby & Jackson, 1857.

Innes, John H. *New Amsterdam and Its People; Studies, Social and Topographical, of the Town under Dutch and Early English Rule*. 2 vols. 1909. Reprint, Port Washington, New York, I. J. Friedman, [1969].

Innes, Stephen. *Creating the Commonwealth: The Economic Culture of*

Puritan New England. New York: W. W. Norton, 1995.

Jameson, J. Franklin, ed. *Narratives of New Netherland, 1609–1664*. 1909. Reprint, n.p., Barnes & Noble, [1959].

Jennings, Francis. *The Invasion of America: Indians, Colonialism, and the Cant of Conquest*. New York: Norton, 1976, 1975.

Jones, Mary Jeanne Anderson. *Congregational Commonwealth Connecticut, 1636–1662*. Middletown, Connecticut: Wesleyan University Press, 1968.

Karlsen, Carol F. *The Devil in the Shape of a Woman: Witchcraft in Colonial New England*. New York: Norton, 1987.

Kelsey, Carleton. *Amagansett, a Pictorial History, 1680–1940*. Amagansett, New York: Amagansett Historical Association, 1986.

Kennedy, John Harold. *Thomas Dongan, Governor of New York (1682–1688)*. New York: AMS Press, 1974.

Kupperman, Karen Ordahl. *Providence Island, 1630–1641: The Other Puritan Colony*. Cambridge, Massachusetts: Cambridge University Press, 1993.

Lancaster, Clay, Robert A. M. Stern. *East Hampton's Heritage*. Second Edition. East Hampton, New York: Ladies Village Improvement Society, 1996.

Lockridge, Kenneth A. *A New England Town: The First Hundred Years: Dedham, Massachusetts, 1636–1737*. New York: Norton, 1985.

Long, Robert, ed. *Long Island Poets*. Sag Harbor, New York: The Permanent Press, 1986.

Love, William DeLoss. *The Colonial History of Hartford; Gathered from Original Sources*. [Chester, Connecticut]: Centinel Hill Press, [1974].

———. *Samson Occom and the Christian Indians of New England*. Boston: Pilgrim Press, 1899. Syracuse, New York: Syracuse University Press, 1998.

Marhoefer, Barbara. *Witches, Whales, Petticoats & Sails: Adventures and Misadventures from Three Centuries of Long Island History*. Port Washington, New York: Associated Faculty Press, 1983.

Martin, John Frederick. *Profits in the Wilderness: Entrepreneurship and the Founding of New England Towns in the Seventeenth Century*. Chapel Hill, N.C.: North Carolina Press for the Institute of Early American History and Culture, Williamsburgh, Virginia, 1991.

Mather, Frederick G. *The Refugees of 1776 from Long Island to Connecticut*. Albany: J. B. Lyon Company, 1913.

Matthiessen, Peter. *Men's Lives*. New York: Vintage Books, 1988, 1986.

Mayo, Lucinda A. "'One of Ours': The World of Jeannette Edwards Rattray." In *Long Island Women: Activists and Innovators*. ed. Natalie A. Naylor and Maureen O. Murphy. New York: Empire State Books, 1998.

McGrath, Franklin, ed. *The History of the 127th New York Volunteers,*

"Monitors," in the War for the Preservation of the Union—September 8th, 1862, June 30th, 1865. n.p.: ca. 1898.

McIntyre, Ruth A. *William Pynchon; Merchant and Colonizer, 1590-1662.* n.p.: Connecticut.Valley Historical Museum, 1961.

Miller, Mary Esther Mulford. *An East Hampton Childhood.* East Hampton: Star Press, 1938.

Miller, Perry. *Errand into the Wilderness.* Cambridge, Massachusetts: Belknap Press of Harvard University Press, 1956.

————.*Nature's Nation.* Cambridge, Massachusetts: Belknap Press of Harvard University Press, 1967.

————. *The New England Mind: from Colony to Province.* Cambridge, Massachusetts: Harvard University Press, 1953.

Miller, Perry and Thomas H. Johnson, eds. *The Puritans: A Source book of Writings.* 2 vols. New York: Harper & Row, 1963.

Mowrer, Lilian T. *The Indomitable John Scott: Citizen of Long Island, 162?-1704.* New York: Farrar, 1960.

Munsell, W.W., ed. *History of Suffolk County, New York, with Illustrations, Portraits and Sketches of Prominent Families and Individuals.* New York: W.W. Munsell & Company, 1882.

New York Historical Society. *Collections of the New-York Historical Society for the Year 1809.* New York: I. Riley, 1811.

Niles, Nath. *Samson Occum. The Mohegan Indian Teacher, Preacher and Poet, with a Short Sketch of His Life.* Madison, New Jersey: [Privately printed anonymously], 1888.

Nylander, Jane C. *Our Own Snug Fireside: Images of the New England Home, 1760-1860.* New York: Knopf, 1993.

O'Callaghan, E.B., ed. *Documents Relative to the Colonial History of the State of New York.* 11 vols. Albany: Weed, Parsons and Company, 1853-1861.

————*History of New Netherland; or, New York under the Dutch.* New York: D.Appleton, 1848.

Occum, Samson. "Account of the Montauks." In *Collections of the Massachusetts Historical Society.* 106-111. Boston: The Massachusetts Historical Society, vol. X, 1809.

Onderdonk, Henry. *Revolutionary Incidents of Suffolk and Kings Counties: With an Account of the Battle of Long Island, and the British Prisons and Prison Ships of New York.* New York: Leavitt, 1849.

Osgood, Herbert L. *The American Colonies in the Seventeenth Century.* 3 vols. Glouchester, Massachusetts: P. Smith, [1904], 1957.

Palfrey, John Gorman. *History of New England.* 5 vols. Boston: Little, Brown & Company, 1858-1890.

Pena, Elizabeth S. *Wampum Production in New Netherland and Colonial*

New York: The Historical and Archaeological Context. Boston: Boston University, 1990.

Pennypacker, Morton. *General Washington's Spies on Long Island and in New York*. 2 vols. Brooklyn: The Long Island Historical Society. East Hampton, New York: East Hampton Free Library, 1939, 1948.

Phelan, Thomas Patrick. *Thomas Dongan, Colonial Governor of New York, 1683–1688*. n.p, 1933.

Pisano, Ronald G. *Long Island Landscape Painting*. 2 vols. Boston: Little, Brown, 1985, 1990.

Prince, Henry W. *Civil War Letters & Diary of Henry W. Prince, 1862–1865*, compiled by Helen Wright Prince. Riverhead, New York: Suffolk County Historical Society, 1979.

Quick, Dorothy. "Long Island Poet." *The Long Island Forum* 3, no. 8 (Aug. 1949): 165–66 and 168.

Rattray, Everett T. *The Adventures of Jeremiah Dimon*. Wainscott, New York: Pushcart Press, 1985.

———. *The South Fork, the Land and the People of Eastern Long Island*. New York: Random House, 1979.

Rattray, Jeannette Edwards. *East Hampton History, Including Genealogies of Early Families*. Garden City: Country Life Press, 1953.

———. *Montauk: Three Centuries of Romance, Sport and Adventure*. East Hampton: The Star Press, 1938.

———. *Ship Ashore!: A Record of Maritime Disasters Off Montauk and Eastern Long Island*. New York: Coward-McCann, 1955, 1962.

———. *Up and Down Main Street: An Informal History of East Hampton and Its Old Houses*. East Hampton: East Hampton Star, 1968.

Ritchie, Robert. *Captain Kidd and the War Against the Pirates*. Cambridge, Massachusetts, 1986

———. *The Duke's Province: A Study of New York Politics and Society, 1664–1691*. Chapel Hill: University of North Carolina Press, 1977.

Roosevelt, Theodore. *The Rough Riders*. New York: Scribner, 1902; reprint, Da Capo Press, 1990.

Seabury, Samuel. *Two Hundred and Seventy-five Years of East Hampton, Long Island, New York: A Historical Sketch*. East Hampton, New York: privately printed, 1926.

Seyfried, Vincent F. *The Long Island Rail Road: a Comprehensive History*. 7 vol. Garden City, N.Y.: Seyfried., 1961.

Shammas, Carole. *The Pre-industrial Consumer in England and America*. New York: Oxford University Press, 1990.

Sleight, Harry D. *Sag Harbor in Earlier Days*. Bridgehampton, New York: Hampton Press, 1930.

Stone, Gaynell. "Long Island As America: A New Look at the First Inhabitants." *Long Island Historical Journal* 1, no. 2 (Spring 1988): 159-169.

————. "Long Island Before the Europeans." In *Between Ocean and Empire: An Illustrated History of Long Island*. ed. Robert MacKay, Geoffrey L. Rossano, and Carol A. Traynor, 10-29. Northridge, Calif.: Windsor Publications, 1985.

————. *The History & Archaeology of the Montauk*. 2d ed., rev. Stony Brook, New York: Suffolk County Archaeological Association, 1993.

————. ed. *The Montauk Native Americans of Eastern Long Island*. East Hampton, New York: Guild Hall, 1991.

————. ed. *The Shinnecock Indians: A Culture History*. Stony Brook, New York: Suffolk County Archaeological Association, 1983.

Stone, Gaynell and Nancy Bonvillain, eds. *Languages and Lore of the Long Island Indians*. Stony Brook, New York: Suffolk County Archaeological Association, 1980.

Strong, John A. *The Algonquian Peoples of Long Island from Earliest Times to 1700*. Interlaken, New York: Empire State Books, 1997.

Taylor, Robert Joseph. *Colonial Connecticut: A History*. Millwood, New York: KTO Press, 1979.

Thompson, Benjamin F. *History of Long Island from Its Discovery and Settlement to the Present Time*. Third Edition. New York: Robert H. Dodd, 1918.

Tooker, William Wallace. *Early Sag-Harbor Printers and Their Imprints*. Evanston, Ill., 1943.

Trelease, Allen W. *Indian Affairs in Colonial New York: The Seventeenth Century*. Ithaca, New York: Cornell University Press, 1960. Reprint, Lincoln, Nebr.: University of Nebraska Press, 1997.

Underhill, Lois Beachy. *The Woman Who Ran for President: The Many Lives of Victoria Woodhull*. Bridgehampton, New York: Bridge Works Pub.; distributed by, Lanham, Md.: National Book Network, 1995.

Van der Zee, Henri and Barbara van der Zee. *A Sweet and Alien Land: The Story of Dutch New York*. New York: Viking Press, 1978.

Van Rensselaer, Schuyler, Mrs. *History of the City of New York in the Seventeenth Century*. N.Y.: Macmillan, 1909.

Van Wyck, Frederick. *Select Patents of New York Towns*. Boston: A.A. Beauchamp, 1938.

Waard, C. de, jr., ed. *De Zeeuwsche Expeditie Naar de West onder Cornelis Evertsen den Jonge, 1672-1674, Nieuw Nederland een jaar onder Nederlandsch Bestuur*. ës-Gravenhage, M. Nijhoff, 1928.

Weeden, William B. *Economic and Social History of New England, 1620-1789*: 2 vols. n.p.: Houghton, Mifflin & Company, 1890. Reprint. N. Y.

Hillary House Publishers, 1963.

Wheelock, John Hall. *Afternoon:Amagansett* Beach. New York: Dandelion Press, 1978.

————. *The Gardener and Other Poems*. New York: Charles Scribner's Sons, 1961.

————.*Poems Old and New.* New York: Charles Scribner's Sons, 1956.

————.*This Blessed Earth*. New York: Charles Scribner's Sons, 1978.

————.*What Is Poetry?* New York: Charles Scribner's Sons, 1963.

————.ed. *Editor to Author:The Letters of Maxwell E. Perkins*. New York: Charles Scribner's Sons, 1950.

Wheelock, John Hall, New York, letter to Mrs. [N. Sherrill] Foster, East Hampton, 6 Feb. 1976. [X FG 86], Long Island Collection, East Hampton Library, East Hampton, New York.

Whitaker, Epher. *History of Southold, Long Island, Its First Century*. Southold, New York: by the author, 1881.

Whitman, Walt. "From Montauk Point." *Complete Poetry and Selected Prose*, ed. James E. Miller, Jr. Boston: Houghton Mifflin Company, 1959.

————.*Leaves of Grass*. New York: W. W. Norton & Company, Inc., 1973.

Winthrop, John. *The Journal of John Winthrop, 1630–1649*. ed. Richard S. Dunn and Laetitia Yeandle. Abridged ed. Cambridge, Mass: Belknap Press of Harvard University Press, 1996.

Wood, Silas. *A Sketch of the First Settlement of the Several Towns on Long Island with Their Political Condition to the End of the American Revolution*. Brooklyn: Alden Spooner, 1828.

Woodward, Nancy Hyden. *East Hampton: A Town and Its People 1648–1992*. East Hampton, New York: Fireplace Press 1995

Zaykowski, Dorothy. *Sag Harbor: The Story of an American Beauty*. Sag Harbor, New York: Sag Harbor Historical Society, 1991.

Ziel, Ron and George H. Foster. *Steel Rails to the Sunrise*. New York: Hawthorn Books, 1965.

INDEX

181